DIVIDED MEMORY

DIVIDED MEMORY

*French Recollections of World War II
from the Liberation to the Present*

Olivier Wieviorka
Translated by George Holoch

STANFORD UNIVERSITY PRESS

STANFORD, CALIFORNIA

Stanford University Press
Stanford, California

Divided Memory was originally published in French under the title *La mémoire
désunie: Le souvenir politique des années sombres, de la Libération à nos jours*
© Editions du Seuil, 2010.

This book has been published with the assistance of the French Department of
Memory, Heritage, and Records.

Library of Congress Cataloging-in-Publication Data

Wieviorka, Olivier, 1960– author.
    [Mémoire désunie. English]
    Divided memory : French recollections of World War II from the Liberation to
the present / Olivier Wieviorka ; translated by George Holoch.
        pages cm
    "Originally published in French under the title La Mémoire désunie."
    Includes bibliographical references.
    ISBN 978-0-8047-7444-4 (cloth : alk. paper)
    1. France—History—German occupation, 1940–1945.   2. World War,
1939–1945—France.   3. Holocaust, Jewish (1939–1945)—France.   4. Collective
memory—Political aspects—France.   5. Historiography—Political aspects—
France.   6. France—Politics and government—1945–   I. Title.
DC397.W484613   2012
940.53'44—dc23

                                                    2011032772

Those who piously died for the fatherland
Deserve that the crowd pray at their graves.
Among beautiful names theirs are the most beautiful.
All glory passes by them and falls, ephemeral;
And as a mother would,
The voice of an entire people soothes them in their graves.

—VICTOR HUGO, "HYMNE," *Les Chants du crépuscule*, 1835

Contents

Preface

The history of memory has become a particularly dynamic field of research. Marked by pioneering works dealing with World War II, it has become established and is constantly growing both in France and elsewhere. I am thinking here primarily of works by Sylvie Lindeperg on representations of World War II in film, by Henry Rousso on the memory of Vichy, and by Annette Wieviorka on the memory of the Shoah. But although individual studies are abundant, works of synthesis are rare, and general readers seeking to inform themselves may experience great difficulty in tracing a path through the dense thicket of available works. This book is intended to fill this gap by presenting a political history of the French memory of the dark years.

The book began as a commission from the Direction de la mémoire, du patrimoine et des archives (DMPA) of the Ministry of Defense. Anxious to go beyond the borders of France, the ministry, perhaps seeking inspiration, wished to analyze foreign examples, which led it to issue a call for proposals; a group of fifteen researchers, headed by Antoine Prost and me, presented the winning proposal. Having taken on particularly the memory of World War II, I mentioned the project to Thierry Pech, then managing editor of Le Seuil, who jumped at the chance to suggest that I go into greater detail, a suggestion that I accepted with pleasure.

This book focuses on the study of public policy since the Liberation. It examines the debates, controversies, and disputes these policies provoked, as well as presenting a somewhat briefer consideration of the social and cultural history of that memory. This is not to suggest that those concerns are illegitimate or of secondary interest. Literary and artistic works have helped shape the contours of memory; imaginative representations play a major role in giving form to memory; and it is obvious that a good deal of memory comes through individual and family channels, creating a circulation that may be hidden but that plays a decisive role. But that is not the subject of this book, which is intended primarily to define the influence of the dark years on political debate by considering the respective positions the state, political parties, and associations adopted in giving an account of them.

Acknowledgments

The Ministry of Defense supported this project and generously opened its archives to me. On the rue de Bellechasse, Inspector General of the Armed Forces Éric Lucas, Christian Léourier, Richard Schneider, Joseph Zimet, Bernard Koelsch, Sylvie Leroy, and Mariam Babaud de Monvallier helped me disentangle the complicated web of sources and organization charts, assistance that was most welcome. In Caen, Daniel Arnaud and Christian Lemarchand, assisted by Catherine Hiéblot, did everything to make my visits profitable, and their invaluable help largely contributed to making those visits as fruitful as they were pleasant. At the Service Historique de la Défense, General Gilles Robert, Nathalie Genet-Rouffiac, Cyril Canet, and Stéphane Longuet helped me select relevant documents and, with a good deal of kindness, facilitated their consultation.

Several kind souls agreed to read all or part of the manuscript, and I would like to thank François Besse, Patrice Higonnet, Julie Le Gac, Pieter Lagrou, Fabrice Virgili, and Annette Wieviorka for their wise advice. This book owes a great deal to their comments and criticisms.

At Le Seuil, Thierry Pech was a stimulating and attentive reader, and the manuscript owes a good deal to the attentive reading of Patricia Duez.

For the English version I have had the pleasure of counting on the translation skills of George Holoch. This book also owes a great deal to Eric Jennings, a colleague whose scholarship is matched only by his generosity. The cost of translation has been generously supported by the French Ministry of Defense. Finally, I am deeply honored by the American edition of this book. I would simply like to thank Norris Pope for accepting it on behalf of such a prestigious publisher.

I am immensely grateful to all of them for their help.

Abbreviations

ADIR	Association nationale des anciennes déportées et internées de la Résistance
AFL	Association des Français libres
ANACR	Association nationale des anciens combattants de la Résistance
ANCVR	Association nationale des combattants volontaires de la Résistance
AWM	Australian War Memorial (or Australian War Museum, depending on the period)
BCRA	Bureau central de renseignements et d'action
CDJC	Centre de documentation juive contemporaine
CDR	Conseil de la République
CECA	Communauté européenne du Charbon et de l'Acier
CED	Communauté européenne de défense
CEF	Corps expéditionnaire français
CFLN	Comité français de libération nationale
CNCVR	Confédération nationale des combattants volontaires de la Résistance
CNDIR	Commission nationale des déportés et internés résistants
CNL	Comité national de libération
CNPG	Comité national des prisonniers de guerre
CNR	Conseil national de la Résistance
CVR	Combattant volontaire de la Résistance
DIP	Déporté-interné politique
DIR	Déporté-interné résistant
DMPA	Direction de la mémoire, du patrimoine et des archives
DPMAT	Direction du personnel militaire de l'armée de terre
FFC	Forces françaises combattantes

FFI	Forces françaises de l'intérieur
FFL	Forces françaises libres
FN	Front national
FNDIR	Fédération nationale des déportés et internés de la Résistance
FNDIRP	Fédération nationale des déportés et internés résistants et patriotes
FNDT	Fédération nationale des déportés du travail
FNPGD	Fédération nationale des combattants prisonniers de guerre et déportés
FTPF	Francs-tireurs et partisans français
GPRF	Gouvernement provisoire de la République française
IWM	Imperial War Museum
JO	*Journal officiel*
MAC	Ministère des Anciens Combattants (Caen or Paris offices)
MNPGD	Mouvement national des prisonniers de guerre et déportés
MRP	Mouvement républicain populaire
ONAC	Office national des anciens combattants et victimes de guerre
ORA	Organisation de résistance de l'armée
PCF	Parti communiste français
PDR	Prisonniers, déportés et réfugiés
PG	Prisonniers de guerre
RIF	Résistance intérieure française
RNPG	Rassemblement national des prisonniers de guerre
RPF	Rassemblement du peuple français
SFIO	Section française de l'internationale ouvrière
SHD	Service historique de la défense (Vincennes)
STO	Service du travail obligatoire
UFAC	Union française des anciens combattants
UNADF	Union nationale des associations de déportés, internés et familles de disparus

Introduction

"It is good that a nation have a tradition and a sense of honor strong enough to find the courage to denounce its own mistakes. But it should not forget the reasons it might still have to value itself." Formulated at the time of the Algerian War, this observation by the French writer Albert Camus applies with particular pertinence to the memory of World War II. Revisiting the tragedies France experienced during the dark years, an honest observer cannot help but be distressed by and condemnatory of the unscrupulous Vichy government. Imposing an authoritarian regime; collaborating with the Third Reich; handing over German political refugees, Jews, Resistance fighters, and opponents of the occupying power; and greeting the Allies who had come to liberate North Africa with cannon fire, the French state under Marshal Pétain—an aggravating circumstance—found the necessary cooperation in both French society and the French administration to carry out its dirty work. At the same time, however, a fraction of the country refused the choices dictated by so-called realism. Continuing the battle by responding to Charles de Gaulle's appeal launched on June 18, 1940, developing a resistance in France that gained depth over time, the sounder part of the population, in the shadows, helped to save 75 percent of the Jews of France, refused en masse the Compulsory Labor Service (Service du travail obligatoire, or STO), and often opposed the arrogance of the occupying forces by the "silence of the sea," to adopt the title of the celebrated book by Vercors.

The memory of World War II bears the stamp of that ambivalence, an ambivalence that was able simultaneously to commune in the masochistic denunciation of past aberrations and celebrate with pomp the grandeur of heroes, humble or famous, who against all odds saved the national honor and contributed to victory.

This observation suggests the magnitude of the problems connected to the definition of the French memory of World War II. Boundary disputes raise a first question at the outset: how should the term be defined. For the "memory of the war" in fact covers three distinct phenomena. It refers in the first place to the experience of the war, a war, it hardly needs saying, that only briefly affected metropolitan France: aside from Allied bombing and military confrontations between Resistance fighters and the repressive forces (for example, in le maquis du Vercors), France was exposed to the violence of arms only in May and June 1940, and then from the summer of 1944 on, when Allied troops landed in Normandy and later in Provence. At the risk of exaggerating, the experience of forty million French people between 1940 and 1945 was anything but an experience of war. But the French did suffer—this is the second aspect of this memory—under the yoke of an occupation, first of northern France (occupied zone and forbidden zone—the Nord-Pas-de-Calais was attached to the German administration in Brussels and Alsace-Lorraine was de facto annexed to Germany), and then after November 11, 1942, to all of metropolitan France. Although the German yoke was characterized by its brutality, it appears to have more closely resembled—all things being equal—occupations suffered over the centuries by territories ruled by a merciless conqueror than a "brutalization" following battle. The French, finally, bore for four years the iron rule of the Vichy state. For the first time in the history of the nation the extreme right came to power and, under cover of the National Revolution, was intent on applying its program, seconded by some men from the traditional right and even some from the left. Born of defeat and a product of the war, the regime of Philippe Pétain, through the conditions of its birth and in order to perpetuate itself, tied its fate to that of the Third Reich, which it accompanied in retreat to Sigmaringen. It did not, however, intend to slavishly copy the Nazi model. Drawing its inspiration from the legacy of the reactionary and revolutionary right, adopting the men and ideas of the interwar period, its roots lay deep in French soil that made it more or less explicitly impossible to imitate Il Duce or Der Führer.

Historians have not always distinguished among these three aspects, bringing together under the vague terms *dark years, black years,* and sometimes *shady years* (the list could go on indefinitely) the period from 1940 to 1944. But everything encourages us to dissociate them—except in terms of memory. For although scholarship can allow itself to separate these different levels of analysis, the French, subjected to roundups, bombing, shortages, and authoritarianism, don't bother with these subtleties, blending the memory of their days into a single whole.

The memory experienced by the mass of the population, that is, all the representations forged after the fact by the state, political parties, associations, and individuals, linked these three aspects together from the outset. And memorial policies carried out by institutions—the state, municipalities, associations—put them together just as much. At the top of the pyramid the government simultaneously had to eliminate the aftereffects of the war, the Occupation, and the Vichy regime—the "four years to erase from our history," in the words of the prosecutor André Mornet at the trial of Philippe Pétain. First it had to eliminate the supporters of the old regime, black sheep whose disloyalty to the Republic had worsened the condition of millions of the French and betrayed the humanist principles of the country. It also had to try to remedy the harm the war had caused both to civilians and to soldiers. It had to restore the rights of the recently proscribed, victims of the Occupation and Nazi barbarism. Finally, and perhaps most important, it had to shed light on the meaning of this tragic period by integrating it into a national narrative. These were, in outline, the purposes of a memorial policy carried out beginning with the Liberation, aimed at both healing wounds and offering a sensible and acceptable interpretation of the dark years.

The government, then, set to this titanic task. It had simultaneously to bury the dead, exalt the heroes, punish the traitors and hurl them into an ocean of opprobrium—or oblivion—compensate the victims, and provide them with a status. This policy turned out to be particularly arduous because it mixed together different phenomena. Unlike World War I, the memory of World War II could not be limited to the impressions and scars of battle. The unity of time could not cover the disparity of places and actions. Hence, the memory of battle soon occupied a relatively minor portion of the space of memory, in competition with noncombat memories, STO conscripts yesterday, or so-called political deportees (a category that covered primarily Jews but included hostages and Communists not in the Resistance) today. Aside from the fact that it helped blur the meaning attributed to World War II, this juxtaposition turned out to be just as rash in that it provoked—as it still does—competition among victims, with groups experiencing their relation to the past in the form of rivalry rather than complementarity.

The vagueness of the borders separating the camps—and their possible fluctuation—also posed formidable problems. Of course, those who joined the Resistance in 1940, Jews sent to their death, and the collaborationist members of the Milice in 1944 unquestionably belonged to clearly marked groups. It was different for men who, committed to Vichy for a time, later joined the Resistance—like a number of soldiers who came together in the Army Resistance Organization (Organisation de résistance de l'armée, or ORA). Likewise, what place should be given to the men who had fought on the wrong side, whether they had obeyed the orders of the French state or been forced to put on a German uniform? These men had certainly been combatants, whether at Dakar, in Syria, in North Africa, or the Russian steppe. But should they be granted the rights that went with that status?

In the immediate aftermath of the victory in 1918, governments had striven to eliminate the aftereffects of the war, but the questions posed by that painful conflict had received an unequivocal answer. The sides were clearly identified. France, attacked by Imperial Germany, after defending its soil and its values, recovered "its place in the world to pursue its magnificent journey in the infinity of human progress, once the soldier of God, today the soldier of humanity, always the soldier of the ideal,"[1] in the famous formulation of Georges Clemenceau announcing the Armistice to the French parliament in 1918. If the victims of the first German occupation deserved compensation, the glory unquestionably went to the poilus. This identification was notably easy because nearly eight million Frenchmen in all had been mobilized. Generous France opened its arms finally to its lost children. Considering that the inhabitants of Alsace and Lorraine, as German citizens,[2] had merely done their duty, it gave them ad hoc pensions without hesitation.

The situation after World War II appeared in a very different light. If one were to draw up the macabre list of victims, one would find that combatants made up only a minority alongside many other categories—Jewish, political, and Resistance deportees; civilians who had been bombed; and members of the Resistance and the FFI who had died in battle. The very category of military victims of the war was confused. Should it include Resistance fighters who died with their weapons in hand although they were not wearing uniforms? Should it incorporate men of Alsace and Lorraine who had fought against their will in the Wehrmacht or even the Waffen SS? What should be done with conscripts who had enlisted, for example, in the *Das Reich* division, notorious for having massacred the population of the village of Oradour-sur-Glane and committing other war crimes? But the ambiguity of the status of combatant concealed even more pitfalls. How, for example, was one to consider prisoners of war, most of whom, caught in roundups, had never engaged in armed struggle? Similarly, how should one consider the internal Resistance fighters whose struggle had often been conducted in the framework of civilian resistance, which gave pride of place to the distribution of the underground press, the fabrication of false documents, and the sheltering of draft dodgers or outlaws and had sometimes deliberately rejected the military dimension in favor of unarmed combat?[3] Should these men and women in the end benefit from both a right to compensation and a right to recognition? The answer, as one might imagine, was not obvious. It can even be asserted that the memory of World War II and, as a result, its handling by government authorities raised painful questions: the state experienced great difficulty in imposing unequivocal and therefore consensual criteria.

The variety of lived experiences further complicated the situation. Between 1940 and 1945 the French experienced varying fates. Whereas the image of the poilu, stoically buried in his trench, summed up the Great War, no model by itself made it possible to subsume the diversity of paths traveled during World War II. Deportation, resistance, forced labor in Germany, rationing, bombing, fighting in the Forces françaises combattantes of General de Gaulle were all different and, strictly speaking, incomparable situations. "All those who 'took up arms' between 1939 and 1945 did not bear the dominant collective experience, in France as in the whole of Western Europe, where the figures of the deportee and indeed the captive in general competed from the outset with the figure of the Resistance fighter."⁴ If one agrees that memory is in part the reflection—or the mimesis—of an experience lived through collectively, one must recognize that the heterogeneity of conditions thwarted the emergence of a common memory. No discourse, no place, no symbol can, by itself, account for the plurality of ordeals undergone by the forty million contemporaries who lived through the dark years. This diversity unquestionably led to the fragmentation of French memory of World War II. It also helped politicize it, because every group, if not every individual, tended to interpret the past in accordance with its itinerary and ideological preferences, mobilizing the memory of the war in the service of its contemporary battles and interests. Some, for instance, opposed the Algerian War and torture by invoking the memory of the Resistance, like the Resistance fighter Claude Bourdet, who denounced "your Gestapo in Algeria."⁵ Others, such as the Christian-Democrat Georges Bidault, defended the imperial cause and even established an ephemeral Conseil National de la Résistance to preserve the rights of France in North Africa. The multiple meanings of the Algerian War, as these examples suggest, provided everyone active on the French political scene a set of references whose mobilization, they hoped, would make it possible to legitimate their combat and discredit their adversaries, suspected of having betrayed "the true France."

The desire to defend one's material and moral rights, finally, largely helped amplify the fragmentation of memory. Every group tried to acquire and preserve its own rights. Resistance members, for example, fought to obtain the status of combatant. But beyond material issues— which were significant—they also sought to obtain symbolic recognition from the nation. This struggle amplified the balkanization of memory and fanned the flames of conflict, because the individual construction of identity threatened other communities that feared the devaluation of their past combat, that it would be identified with causes considered, rightly or wrongly, less noble. Political and racial deportees, for example, were disturbed by the claims of former STO conscripts who demanded to be given the title "labor deportee," thereby fostering conflict among veterans. The proliferation of statuses above all impeded the emergence of a shared language able to integrate the variety of experiences into a common narrative.

In other words, the memory of World War II, then as now, seems to be a fragmented memory, conflicted and politicized, that divides rather than brings together.

This sense of conflict also posed genuine political problems by inflaming passions and dividing public opinion, whereas the memory of the Great War had had rather unifying and integrating qualities. The prosecution brought against the criminals of the *Das Reich* division in 1953, for instance, created conflict between the population of Alsace, which called for clemency for those drafted against their will into the SS, and the population of the Limousin, which was outraged at seeing the French responsible for the massacre of Oradour-sur-Glane escape punishment. Georges Pompidou's pardon of the *milicien* Paul Touvier troubled French society throughout 1971 and 1972. The obstacles the government placed in the way of prosecuting two former high officials of the Vichy regime, René Bousquet and Maurice Papon, also provoked vigorous debate and darkened François Mitterrand's second term as president. All this amounts to saying that the memory of World War II, far from being a neutral or secondary issue, has sometimes influenced the political agenda, forcing the state to intervene in a potentially explosive field. It has also evolved in a remarkable way from the Liberation to the present, pursuing goals and adopting forms that have deeply changed in the course of time.

Confronted with this reality, in the sixty-plus years that separate us from the capitulation of the Third Reich, the state has played a role that has been both huge and limited. First it tried to deal with the most pressing issues, burial for the dead and compensation and recognition for the living. It also conducted a memorial diplomacy, subjecting the memory of conflict to reconciliation with yesterday's enemies. It put similar effort into conferring an overall meaning on World War II, by trying to attenuate conflicts in order, over time, to bring all participants together into the national narrative—with the exception of thoroughgoing collaborators. But this peaceful interpretation was not accepted without conflict. By recognizing the most varied rights, the government tended to shatter the coherence of the national narrative and to amplify the balkanization of memory. As a further perverse effect, "We moved from a modest memory, that asked only finally to be recognized, respected, integrated into the great record of collective and national history, to an essentially accusatory memory that destroyed that history," in the words of the historian Pierre Nora.[6]

Most important, the government did not always play the game of truth and, rather than confronting unpleasant facts—the politics of the Vichy regime, for example—it chose to favor denial:

What is specific in the French reaction to the worldwide surge of memory and what makes it so virulent is probably the contrast between the power of the immaculate image that France learned to adopt for itself and the painful, belated, and thwarted confrontation with historical realities that contradict that image, shatter it, and seem themselves darker than they were. On Algeria, the Occupation, the Resistance, the 1914 war, colonization . . . there have been legends, lies, falsifications, blockages, denials. These obstacles, fortified by all the means at the state's disposal to prevent knowledge of the truth (beginning with archives kept secret) laid the groundwork for all the grievances and belated prosecutions. They fostered the unhealthy idea of a skeleton still hidden in the closet. They made us into virtual penitents, ready to believe that the caricatures were true and reparations legitimate.[7]

In other words, by giving in, for good or bad reasons, to pressure groups, by preferring legend over history, the government did not perhaps conduct a coherent politics of memory—even if its action had a pacifying effect by including the previously banished, except for a few black sheep, in the national community.

That said, not everything depended on the state, and that is still true. The government, of course, had enormous resources at its disposal to impose its views. Definitions of status, the choice of dates to commemorate, the organization of ceremonies, the establishment of school curricula, and the support provided for building monuments or museums were all its prerogatives. But other participants played essential roles in shaping the contours of memory: associations, local communities, historians, journalists, and artists (particularly writers and filmmakers). In cinema Louis Malle's *Lacombe Lucien* and Claude Lanzmann's *Shoah* unquestionably helped shift the frontiers of memory by changing the issues. The same thing was true of Robert Paxton's book *Vichy France* (1972). Consequently, the state often had to negotiate with various forces and intervened more as a regulator, or even an arbitrator striving to respond to the sometimes conflicting appeals of diverse groups or lobbies, rather than as an initiating force defining in majesty its politics of memory.

These observations confirm the complexity associated with the memory of World War II, a memory, as I have said, that is atomized, conflicted, and politicized, that divides more than it brings together, and whose definition is not under the solitary control of government authorities. With this groundwork laid out, I turn to an assessment of the policies carried out from 1945 to the present.

CHAPTER I

The Work of the Provisional
Government of the French Republic
(1944–1946)

The period that began with the Liberation and ended with the departure of General de Gaulle on January 20, 1946, was a heroic age, in the
full sense of the word. France had finally recovered its freedom and independence after four years of occupation, thanks to the Allied armies and
the Resistance forces. Deportees, conscripts, and prisoners took the road
home, often happily returning to their families and friends. But the Liberation balls and the jubilation that greeted the GIs could not mask the
sorrow of a country that had been pillaged by the Germans, ruined by the
fighting, and bled dry by the repression suffered by Jews and Resistance
and opposition figures. Above all, France had not forgotten the defeat
and continued to mull over the incomprehensible collapse of 1940. Finally,
there was a threat of civil war: the army of shadows and the Communist
Party intended to settle accounts with the supporters of the Vichy regime.
As head of the Provisional Government of the French Republic (Gou-
vernement provisoire de la République française, or GPRF), from June
3, 1944, to January 20, 1946, de Gaulle recognized the magnitude of the
trauma. He avoided dwelling on the inglorious episodes of the dark years
and devised a memorial policy intended to heal the wounds and restore
the confidence of a divided nation.

The Gaullist Policy

Charles de Gaulle defined the meaning that should be given to World War II as early as 1941.[1] To his mind it represented the final phase of the "Thirty Years' War" that had begun in Sarajevo in 1914 and was to come to an end in the ruins of Berlin. On the eve of the German surrender he declared: "A proud and glorious nation, once again identified with the victory of law and the triumph of justice, is witnessing the end of a struggle of more than thirty years in which, by turns, the power, the weakness, and the restoration of France have played an essential role."[2]

This vision had three important aspects. It emptied the conflict of ideological content, reducing it to an eternal Franco-German (not to say Prussian) rivalry, which, by keeping the debate off the political plane, fostered the coming together that de Gaulle intended to promote. It built a bridge between the veterans of 1940 and their glorious forebears of the Great War, which avoided stirring up the rift between the veterans of the two wars, a rift that had surfaced when the Legion of Veterans (Légion des combattants) was created in 1940, from which the heroes of World War I for a time sought to exclude the architects of the defeat of 1940. And it made it possible to identify France as a victorious nation, a claim that perhaps did not seem obvious to contemporaries marked by the terrible debacle of 1940, but one that the head of the provisional government would constantly reiterate. For example, he said to his secretary on October 12, 1944: "Don't you find it odd, Mauriac, that people have their eye [on] one thing: a change in their situation or in that of France? And you too; you speak of liberty, honor, and purification. And what about victory? What I have my eye on, first and foremost, is a victorious France."[3]

This global vision, which no evidence suggests was shared by contemporaries at the time, was accompanied by a twofold negation. For one thing, Charles de Gaulle minimized the role played by the Allies, a principle asserted in the famous speech of August 25, 1944, exalting "liberated Paris" without really mentioning the decisive action of Anglo-American troops. "[Paris] liberated by itself, liberated by its people, with the help of the armies of France, with the support and assistance of all of France, with the France that is fighting, the only France, the true France, eternal France!" And for another, he denied the French State, considering the abdication of the National Assembly on July 10, 1940, as "null and void." "As for me," he explains, "I have never considered any of the acts carried out by the so-called Vichy Government to be legitimate."[4] This twofold denial produced conversely a celebration of the Resistance, of which he took an expansive view, considering that the French had massively participated in it. "Resistance, in its multiple forms, has become the basic reaction of the mass of the French. . . . It is everywhere, determined and effective. It is in the organization created in France itself, synthesized in our National Resistance Council (Conseil national de la Résistance, or CNR), to which we address fraternal greetings. It is in factories and fields, in offices and schools, in streets and houses, in hearts and minds."[5] Consequently, collaboration and betrayal concerned only a "handful of scoundrels"; the people had at bottom remained sound.

A reduction of World War II to a military conflict, a negation of the Allies and of the French State, an expansive view of the Resistance encompassing virtually the entire French population: these are the pillars of the Gaullist vision of the dark years. The primary goal was to legitimate the new authority by attenuating the break represented by the founding act of the Appeal. "The Gaullist government that came out of a break with the defeat of France on June 18, 1940, sought to take root in a memory of national continuity."[6] It also intended to bring the French together to prevent the accumulated tensions from degenerating into a civil war or from favoring the designs, real or imagined, of the French Communist Party (Parti communiste français, or PCF). It is hardly necessary to specify that these assumptions established the contours of the politics of memory General de Gaulle followed from 1944 to 1946.

Celebrating and Decorating Heroes

This political approach was designed first of all to celebrate heroes by fostering—at least in appearance—genuine syncretism. "The cult of these exemplary figures, able to bring together all of French society around the rather abstract symbolism of Resistance commitment, was much better suited to the style and the political objectives of General de Gaulle than a politics embodied by the mobilization of memorial groups through mass organizations, along the lines of the movements of veterans of the Great War."[7] So, for example, in 1945 a number of metro stations were renamed in honor of major figures belonging to the French Resistance or identified as such (Jacques Bonsergent, Charles Michels, Guy Môquet). This effort was taken up by municipalities that did not hesitate to name streets after humble or celebrated Resistance figures. A habit developed of using the names of famous (Pierre Brossolette) or anonymous (avenue de la Résistance, rue des Martyrs) Resistance figures; Communist municipalities, particularly in the "red belt" around Paris, paid homage to their heroes (Gabriel Péri, Danielle Casanova, Pierre Semard, Fabien).[8] De Gaulle received some of this tribute. As early as 1940, towns in the empire, such as Douala in Cameroon and Papeete in Polynesia, had named public roads after him. The movement swelled as time went by, with 418 towns taking this step between 1940 and 1946.[9] On November 19, 1944, the town council of Brou, Eure-et-Loir, "addresse[d] its warm congratulations to that great patriot General de Gaulle for the energy he has displayed since 1940; the energy to pursue the struggle against the hated Boche with the same tenacity until he was totally crushed; expresse[d] its trust in him to successfully carry out the political, economic, and financial restoration of the Government," and unanimously voted to give his name to the rue de la Gare.[10]

The government that came out of the Liberation also took care to reward acts of courage with medals. In this connection two honors—the Croix de la Libération and the Médaille de la Résistance—were explicitly dedicated to volunteers who had joined the army of shadows or the Forces françaises libres (FFL). Between the date the first decoration was created, on January 29, 1941, and the date after which it was no longer awarded, January 23, 1946, only 1,036 individuals were made Compagnons de la Libération, a group joined by five towns and eighteen combat units. This honor was thus from the outset reserved for a small elite; the order thought of itself as "chivalric, closer to the Knights Templar than to the poilus: a corps of bodyguards for great men who would be distinguished [together with General de Gaulle] for their courage and foresight."[11] Conversely, the Médaille de la Résistance, established by the decree of February 9, 1943, was awarded less parsimoniously. Until its awarding was ended on March 31, 1947, it was given to forty-four thousand Resistance fighters (10 percent of whom were women), and twenty thousand underground fighters were decorated posthumously. Eighteen communities, twenty-one military units of the three services, and fifteen institutions (lycées, hospitals, convents) also received it.

Commemorating

The Provisional Government also began to shape a commemorative policy blending the old with the new, using traditional sites of parades or demonstrations to honor combatants, whether civilian or military, French or Allied. General de Gaulle, for example, took the head of the Liberation march on the Champs-Élysées on August 26, 1944, with elements of the American Fourth Infantry Division following suit the next day. The head of the GPRF even frequently laid flowers at the foot of the statue of Clemenceau on that world famous avenue. Les Invalides was likewise a setting for parades: on April 2, 1945, General de Gaulle restored to French regiments the flags that had been hidden or destroyed during the Occupation. And he strove to associate the tradition embodied by the army with the renewal symbolized by the Forces françaises de l'intérieur (FFI) and the Forces françaises libres, called on to participate in the many parades that filled 1945, notably for the celebration of the Appeal on June 17 and 18.

The head of the GPRF thereby intended to establish a national military memory "in which symbols (Invalides, Arc de Triomphe, flags) had as much importance as individuals (Foch, Clemenceau)."[12] He implicitly identified the memory of the Great War with the celebrations of World War II—a way of incorporating the 1939–1945 episode into the totality of the "Thirty Years' War." More generally, he strove to forge anew the links in the chain of events by presenting the latest conflict as an episode that, although out of the ordinary, nonetheless fit into a history that had been going on for centuries. On May 16, 1945, for instance, he celebrated the festival of Joan of Arc with some display by organizing a march in the Place des Pyramides. The cult of the young shepherdess had, to be sure, always represented "a stake in the partisan warfare between French ideologues, particularly since the late nineteenth century."[13] Her memory had been widely exploited by the French State. Embodying a form of nationalism to which Philippe Pétain adhered, the deeply Catholic Maid of Orleans also had the inestimable virtue of having been burned at the stake by perfidious Albion, which had enabled Vichy propaganda to draw a bold parallel between the stake erected in Rouen and British bombing, a parallel that the repeated raids on the capital of Normandy in April and late May through early June 1944 could not fail to reinforce. By paying homage to Joan, de Gaulle recovered a heroine whose vibrant patriotism, deep faith, and humble origin could at bottom sum up the Gaullism of the war, while playing on two symbols, "the birth in Lorraine of one and the Croix de Lorraine of the other."[14]

But the government did not hesitate to innovate by transforming Mont Valérien, the primary site for executions under the occupation, into a site of memory. The idea, initially broached by the former Resistance fighter Henri Frenay, was to commemorate November 11, 1945, by transferring the remains of fifteen of the dead to Suresnes hill, near Paris: "Despite the different places and circumstances in which they gave their lives, all or almost all of them were volunteers and all of them died with the same determination and the same hope in their hearts. It was essential that the forthcoming November 11 ceremonies strengthen national unity by emphasizing, despite the diversity of their battles, the deep unity of our dead and therefore of the nation."[15] By this measure,

that November 11 marked the victory of the dramaturgy of Gaullist memory that called to the Croix de Lorraine on Mont Valérien all the dead of the 1939–45 war, linked by the ceremony to the military memory of the 1914–18 war, to the private memory experienced by companions in battle, to family memory, to the memory of the Parisian crowd, to the historical memory of the Arc de Triomphe and the Invalides, to religious memory through masses and tolling bells, to the memory of eternal France, evoked in his speech at the Arc de Triomphe as it had been in his April 3 speech at City Hall.[16]

But two major differences separated the memory of the two conflicts. Whereas a single tomb of the unknown soldier sufficed to symbolize World War I, it took no fewer than fifteen coffins to attempt to sum up World War II. And if the flame watching over the warrior of 1914 was set in the heart of Paris, burning at the foot of the prestigious Arc de Triomphe, the Croix de Lorraine was planted on the outskirts of the city on a site untouched by any memory.

In any event Mont Valérien had taken its place by 1945 as an essential memorial site that was soon identified with the Gaullist epic. It seemed to be the natural setting to celebrate the act of foundation represented by the Appeal; the organization of ceremonies commemorating General de Gaulle's action was incidentally not the province of the administration but of the Order of the Liberation, which made them private rather than public in nature.

The policies adopted by Charles de Gaulle thus exalted a memory of combat that focused first and foremost on the army. They explicitly tied World War II to World War I by paying homage simultaneously to the leaders of the Great War and the generals of the new army. In form and in execution, the marches on June 17 and 18, 1945, recalled the triumphant procession of July 14, 1919.[17] The government was inserting the tragic experiences of 1939 to 1945 into the long duration of the history of France.

This memorial strategy, however, excluded civilians—Jews, deportees, STO conscripts, bombed populations—that the government disregarded, choosing to celebrate the recovered glory of victorious France, which also led it to mask the fate of prisoners of war. This approach did not mean, of course, that the authorities took no interest in the fate of the "absent," a category devised by the former leader of the Combat movement. Appointed to head the Ministry of Prisoners, Deportees, and Refugees (PDR), the "ministry of suffering," as he called it, Henri Frenay strove to facilitate the return of deportees, prisoners, and workers sent to Germany—groups representing an impressive total of 2,250,000 men and women sent across the Rhine.[18] He had considerable success. "In less than ninety days, two thirds of those freed were repatriated. In the course of the year 1945, in a completely disorganized country, more than 1.5 million men, women, and children, were repatriated in under one hundred days."[19]

Frenay, incidentally, officially refused to make distinctions among the respective merits of the returnees, refraining, for instance, from stigmatizing voluntary workers. He sent these directions to prefects in November 1944:

Although it is well established in particular that, in several cases, voluntary labor for the victory of Germany was performed by a few fanatics whose cases come under the category of treason, it is nonetheless certain that the "Relève" ["relief" scheme, whereby three French specialized workers were sent to Germany for each French prisoner freed] was a gigantic deportation that was voluntary in name only, and that no distinction is possible between those who were constrained by the material force of conscription and those who were driven by the moral force of an entire politics of deception. Aside from the cases pointed out above that are generally notorious, any distinction between "conscript" and "volunteer" is contrary to the interests of the country and would moreover be a betrayal of French citizens who are now absent and whose struggles over the coming months that they will carry on until their liberation side by side with their comrades—prisoners and political deportees—against the German oppressor will unite ever more firmly. When Germany falls and all the absent return, France cannot allow itself to make a distinction in its welcome that has not been made in the struggle.[20]

But this order was not always followed. "Indeed, throughout the months of May, June, and July, incidents were reported throughout France. Whereas extra-judicial violence had often taken place in the symbolic heart of communities—prefecture, town hall, church, or market—the volunteers returning from Germany were assaulted on railway platforms"—especially women.[21] The regional commissioner of Nancy noted: "In the Vosges . . . there are reports of incidents at the arrival of voluntary laborers returning with the repatriated. Women are especially singled out. The police had to call for reinforcements to avoid violent incidents."[22]

A gulf thus separated the help the state actually provided to the victims from the symbolic recognition that it refused to grant them. Deep disgrace weighed on the prisoners. "The average Frenchman identified all captives with those captured without a fight."[23] STO conscripts were suspected of having exerted little effort to escape their fate. Women who had gone voluntarily to work in Germany stirred suspicion. A Catholic source noted:

Some of them left on a whim . . . others hoped to join a prisoner. But these women workers, placed in indescribably overcrowded and miserable conditions, were practically condemned to become concubines or prostitutes. The *Lager* of the women were often true "hells" of immorality and poverty: one could find corpses of newborns thrown in the garbage and, in the rooms, neglected babies in wooden boxes next to the bunk beds. The conduct of French women in Germany deeply humiliates most French prisoners and workers, and Christian activists in Berlin will have some difficulty acknowledging as their "sisters" those whom [their chaplain] will try to raise from the mud.[24]

The war had decidedly not eroded stereotypes identifying women with the figure of Eve the temptress.

Hence, while asserting in words that it made no distinctions among returnees, the Ministry of Prisoners, Deportees, and Refugees took no steps to foster any unity. Aside from the fact that it maintained, always symbolically and sometimes materially, a distinction between deportees on one side and prisoners and conscripts on the other, it avoided encouraging the establishment of a single organization bringing together all the victims of Nazism—an idea that some leaders entertained. As Jean d'Arcy, director of social affairs in the "ministry of suffering," explained,

the makeup of such a vast body: fighters from 14–18, prisoners, workers, deportees, Resistance members, the devastated, and so on, is characterized precisely by the absence of any *common bond* connecting these men who share only the fact of having suffered. It will therefore be a lifeless body, or an organization with an artificial life because it is *provoked* to make demands.

It is not good to unite victims who feel they have claims on the state and will therefore always stand up against it. . . .

For the moment, we think the categories which we should favor are those of the captivity in Germany, with a few others: the devastated, Resistance members, veterans. We may *later* unite: first combatants and captives, but at no cost put victims of the war in the same bloc, on the pretext, and that is the only motive, that there is a government department for veterans and war victims which is the result of a twenty-year evolution. One cannot manhandle time as one will.[25]

On an entirely different level the government refrained from organizing tributes or festivities to celebrate the victory of May 8, 1945. "The enthusiasm expressed on the Champs-Élysées into the wee hours of the morning was not echoed by any government initiative for a ball or fireworks display."[26] It is understandable, of course, that the authorities favored an austere approach: at a time when deportees, prisoners, and conscripts were returning to the country, it would no doubt have been out of place for the government to organize festivities. In the region of Champagne, "on May 9, 1945, despite the celebration of victory, no ball was organized at the request of the Maison du Prisonnier in Reims. It was again a matter of indicating official solidarity with a population of returnees who were still on the road home."[27]

Although these motives unquestionably played a role, other reasons probably lie behind this lack of enthusiasm. The Gaullist government was not particularly eager to celebrate a victory in which France had played only a modest part, regardless of official statements to the contrary. Excluded from the Yalta Conference (February 4–11, 1945), the country would have found it difficult to appear as an ally carrying the same diplomatic weight as the three Great Powers. In General de Gaulle's eyes May 8 could therefore have only a secondary significance, which led him to minimize the event. The fact that as president of the republic he always refused to grant that date the prestige of an authentic commemoration strengthens this interpretation.

It should also be pointed out that the GPRF did little to create museums devoted to World War II, a step that would not at all have been premature. Even before the guns had fallen silent, museum organizations had been established in France, Great Britain, and Australia to recall the ordeals experienced during the Great War. As early as 1917, a pair of industrialists named Leblanc hastened to collect all documents related to the conflict and its causes. Those documents, after being donated to the state the same year, gave birth to the Library and Museum of the War—the future Library of Contemporary International Documentation (Bibliothèque de Documentation Internationale Contemporaine, or BDIC). Also in 1917, an Australian war correspondent, Charles Bean, decided to collect relics of the conflict so that veterans' families, the public, and researchers could have access to primary materials. In his view there was no contradiction between the sanctification of memory and the preservation of these relics, because the relics were themselves sacred. Besides, they would not be used to glorify war—they were not trophies—but to understand it. Exhibited in a museum, they would help both analyze and commemorate the fighting of the Diggers. Collection began in May 1917, and the director of the future museum was appointed in 1920. The cornerstone of the Australian War Memorial (AWM) was laid in 1929, and the building opened its doors on November 11, 1941. That year the Australian authorities decided to include World War II within the memorial mission of the AWM.[28]

Similarly, in 1917 Sir Alfred Mond, first commissioner of works in the British government, suggested that a museum dedicated to the war be established. Christened the Imperial War Museum (IWM) in 1918, it was inaugurated in June 1920. In the words of its first director general, Martin Conway, it was to be a place "the veterans can visit with their comrades, their friends, or their children, and there revive the past and behold again the great guns and other weapons with which they fought, the uniforms they wore, pictures and models of the ships and trenches and dug-outs in which weary hours were spent."[29] And as soon as World War II broke out, the IWM, following the model of the AWM, declared its intent to include the new conflict in its memorial mission.

The wish to make a current conflict a matter for a museum was thus neither an aberration nor an original idea, since Australia and Great Britain had earlier taken the same step. But the GPRF refused to adopt it, a sign that World War II as it had been experienced in France did not lend itself to an enterprise that would have led to giving the conflict a single unambiguous meaning. This difficulty resurfaced in the succeeding decades; the authorities were unable—assuming they had the desire—to create a powerful museum institution encompassing the entirety of the years 1939–1945.

In any event the memorial policy of Charles de Gaulle had the virtue of coherence. For that very reason, perhaps, the French Communist Party fought against it vigorously.

Communist Counterattacks

History has always occupied an important place in the French Communist Party. Marxism-Leninism attributed a decisive role to history because it believed that the "laws of history" governed the course of events. The lessons of the past also provided certain guides to action. Dedicated to the admiration of the masses, its heroes, and its great deeds—from the fall of the Bastille to the October Revolution—also offered theoretical and practical models able to cast light on the path to power. At the time of Liberation they had lost none of their relevance. That said, less lofty considerations inspired Communist leaders. The tortuous line they followed between the signature of the Nazi-Soviet pact on August 23, 1939, and the launching of Operation Barbarossa on June 22, 1941, was a poor match with the image that the "Party of 75,000 martyrs" claimed for itself. Unstinting support for the Soviet Union, the desertion of its secretary general, Maurice Thorez, and ignorance as to his place of refuge, and the request the Communist official Maurice Tréand had made to the German occupying authorities in June 1940 to allow *L'Humanité* to again be published undermined the myth of a party fully committed by 1940 to the struggle against the Third Reich and the French State. Other unfortunate episodes helped tarnish the legend. From July 4 to July 27, 1940, the then underground Communist newspaper *L'Humanité* expressed pleasure at the fraternization between French workers and German soldiers, carefully explaining that the soldiers were merely workers in uniform.[30] From their prison cells, several Communist deputies, most prominently François Billoux, elegantly claimed the right to testify against Léon Blum at the Riom trial. On June 11, 1942, Jacques Doriot's collaborationist newspaper *Le Cri du Peuple* delighted in publishing a statement by Marcel Cachin, a founding member of the PCF, explicitly condemning immediate action. This historic figure in the party declared: "I have been asked if I approve [of] individual attacks on the lives of German soldiers. My answer is that individual attacks produce a result contrary to that aimed at by their perpetrators. I have neither advocated nor encouraged them, and always advised my comrades against them."[31] Coming from a group that had constantly condemned the wait-and-see attitude of Gaullists and socialists, the reminder of this ill-considered statement could not fail to upset the careful memorial organization of the party led by Maurice Thorez.

At the same time, the PCF and its satellites, the Front national (FN) and the Francs-tireurs et partisans français (FTPF) had courageously plunged into resistance, playing an essential role in the miners' strikes in Nord in May and June 1941, multiplying attacks against the occupying forces and collaborators, and setting up underground networks. They had endured fierce repression carried out with grim determination by both Vichy organs and German services. The "Party of 75,000 martyrs" had, in other words, excellent claims to recognition, although the record of repression revealed more modest numbers. The most recent statistics estimate that approximately three thousand Communists were judicially sentenced to be executed, to which should be added fifteen thousand victims of the "war on gangs"—a number far from Communist estimates.[32] In any event the duality of a party that was both compromised and heroic during the dark years produced a troubling ambivalence: the Resistance was an "obvious source of strength but also of potential fragility."[33] Hence, the PCF tried to lift the burden. "Its tactic was to make its role in the Resistance and the Paris insurrection unforgettable; it had to make people forget the Nazi-Soviet pact, the party's support of it, and its pacifist line from 1939 to 1941."[34]

The memorial strategy the party deployed from the Liberation forward was built around four major elements. First, the PCF paid homage to its martyrs, whose diverse fates symbolized the heavy tribute paid to the war. In 1944 it reserved plots in Père-Lachaise cemetery, not far from the Mur des fédérés (Communards' Wall), where many party figures were already buried, so it would be able to inter its dignitaries with imposing ceremonies, as in the funeral of Colonel Fabien and two of his companions on January 2, 1945, and the funeral of fourteen Communist patriots (seven of whom had been executed at Châteaubriant) on July 22, 1945.[35]

Then it strove to connect the struggle conducted under the Occupation to glorious memories of revolutionary episodes. The choice of the Mur des fédérés was a first link between the memory of the Commune and the memory of the war. The Paris insurrection was sanctified, and the barricades of August 1944 recalled the revolutionary past of a capital that had revolted three times, in 1789, 1848, and 1871. From this perspective July 14, 1945, took on exceptional proportions; the PCF tried to take control of a segment of the celebrations. To the official morning demonstrations orchestrated by the government, the Paris Liberation Committee, headed by the very orthodox André Tollet, responded with a march in the afternoon. Proceeding from the Concorde to the Bastille, it took on the "sense of a parallel and an equivalence: what it proclaimed was that the army of the internal Resistance led by the PC had been as important as the Forces françaises libres led by de Gaulle."[36] Calling upon the shades of the French Revolution, the days of July 13, 14, and 15 attempted to revive the memory of mass mobilization.

In the third place the Party developed a strategy designed to mask its false steps with clever rhetoric. With this in mind it celebrated the great antifascist strike of February 12, 1934, which had come in response to the far right demonstration on February 6 of that year. By suggesting that the traitors of 1940 had already committed their misdeeds in the shadows in 1934 by attacking the radicals, the party instituted the memory "of a continuous time running from 1934 to 1945."[37] "The argument amounted to asserting the persistence of the political conduct of allies and adversaries (temporizing and treason) the better to implicitly lay the groundwork for the idea of the constancy of the Party's farsighted antifascism and patriotism. On February 12, they did not commemorate what had existed—a collective feeling of solidarity among antifascists—but what had not existed, day-to-day political perspicacity."[38] The speeches also referred to the Munich accords, recalling that Communist parliamentarians had voted against their ratification—a tangible sign that they had challenged the shameful surrenders of the French leaders as early as 1938.

Similarly the Communists fought to have Romain Rolland's remains interred in the Panthéon. The author of *Jean-Christophe* had died on December 30, 1944. From January 4 to 19, 1945, the Communist daily *Ce Soir* sought to have his remains transferred to the Panthéon, adopting a rather transparent argument. To begin with, this act would amount to "legitimating the sequence pacifism-antifascism which was at the same time the pattern of the PC's line in 1933–34 and in 1940–41."[39] But far from creating unanimity, the proposal provoked a counterattack from *Le Figaro*, which suggested on January 7 that Charles Péguy should also be given that honor. It was a clever maneuver: by promoting Péguy, who may have been a Dreyfusard but who had died on the field of honor, the right was challenging the patriotic status of Romain Rolland, the spirited herald of pacifism. The PCF therefore shifted its argument and presented the writer as a symbol of a "memory of national reconciliation in the antifascist struggle."[40] It had just as little success. In the meantime, to be sure, the Popular Republican Movement (Mouvement républicain populaire, or MRP) had complicated the discussion by putting forth the name of Henri Bergson. Francisque Gay, Maurice Schumann, and Pierre Corval, leaders of the party, explained in an appeal published in *L'Aube*: "His entry into the Panthéon would be a resounding reparation owed and given to the Jews, and in them to all the hostages, all the deportees, all those whom a monstrous regime had tried to separate from the human community."[41] This proposal was quickly buried, and the Panthéon received none of the three. That said, the antifascist theme had a substantial advantage: "All opponents of fascism and all its victims could recognize themselves in it and join a large antifascist family that fraternally united combatants and victims, heroism and martyrdom. And the Communist Party was the good head of the family, both through its historic commitment and its unfailing support for their cause in postwar society."[42] Communist memory politics, finally, strove to minimize the role of General de Gaulle and that of the Anglo-American Allies. The party tried, for example, to assume a leading role in the organization of celebrations. On November 11, 1944, it announced that "the representatives of veterans' associations ask the Paris Liberation Committee, the supreme organ of the Resistance in Seine, to organize on November 11, in cooperation with the government, a patriotic march to the tomb of the unknown soldier," a way of sidestepping government prerogatives.[43] Similarly, *L'Humanité* more frequently lauded the heroic deeds of the Red Army than the exploits of Anglo-American troops. In the same vein the Communists tried to impose a geography of memory from which the high points emerged. Containing as it did the Mur des fédérés, Père-Lachaise was a key element in this arrangement. Ivry and Châteaubriant, because of the Communists executed there, also belonged to this archipelago. In contrast Mont Valérien, site of a fierce competition between Gaullists and Communists, belonged to the camp of the Croix de Lorraine by 1945, not that of the hammer and sickle, even though the cemetery of Ivry was indirectly connected to this memorial site because the prisoners executed on the hill of Suresnes had been buried there.

The memorial battle thus began early between Gaullists and Communists, although they both participated in a government of national unity.[44] It is true that other forces carried little weight. Having failed to establish a resistance organization of their own, the Socialists had trouble exploiting the sacrifice of their numerous martyrs—assuming they wanted to. The secretary general of the underground Socialist Party, Daniel Mayer, always refused to "beat a drum roll on the coffins" of the Socialist heroes who had died in the upheaval. Gathered under the banner of the Popular Republican Movement, the Christian Democrats struggled to distinguish themselves from Gaullist orthodoxy; their group claimed to embody the "party of loyalty." The men of the Resistance movements, finally, could muster only battalions that were too small to impose their vision of the dark years, especially because their relations with both Gaullism and Communism were the source of deep divisions. The conflict therefore came down to a face-to-face confrontation between the Croix de Lorraine and the red flag, which did not prevent the government from working to resolve through law the situation of the war's victims.

First Statutes

The Provisional Government drafted statutes for the purpose of regulating the rights to reparation and recognition of the combatants of World War II. On March 3, 1945, a decree dealt with the situation of veterans and defined the categories of resisters who could claim that status. Another decree on May 11, 1945, considered the case of deportees and granted a "welcoming grant" to all the repatriated, whatever their military or administrative situation.[45] Considered political deportees at the time were "the French transferred by the enemy outside the national territory, then incarcerated and interned for any reason other than a common-law infraction." From the outset, however, a hierarchy was imposed: only political deportees (meaning members of the Resistance) "having willingly sacrificed their freedom in the struggle against the invader, whose families have lived painfully without wages or help during the occupation, and who often return to France completely destitute" were given a supplementary grant of five thousand francs and a free suit. A scale of merit with deportees from the Resistance at the summit was taking shape, although Jewish deportees and STO conscripts benefited in part from these measures, which provided, in addition to a grant and payment in kind (civilian clothing and shoes), for vacations.

In this way, by putting together various measures, such as exchanging marks brought back from Germany, a prisoner of war received wages of between 9,150 and 12,864 francs, a deportee between 10,150 and 13,854 francs. These sums officially represented between twelve and fifteen weeks of a laborer's wages, but considering the prices on the black market, they were the equivalent of three, four, or five weeks of actual wages.[46] A decree of November 2, 1945, granted the recognition "Died for France" to civilians killed as a result of Allied violence—primarily bombing. This was a violation of tradition, because legislation developed after World War I had reserved this title for victims of enemy operations alone, a qualification that it would be hard to attribute to the bombardiers of the RAF or the US Air Force. Conscripts who had died in Germany also fell into this category, which gave families the possibility, in fact seldom used, of having the names of the dead engraved on memorial monuments. All of these measures, it should be emphasized, differed by their speed from the situation that had prevailed after the 1918 armistice. For if the disabled had received a pension by March 31, 1919, the combatants had to wait until June 28, 1927, to obtain similar status.[47]

The arrangement devised under the aegis of General de Gaulle was therefore coherent: the state defined the meaning of the recent conflict, rewarded individual and collective merit with decorations, and determined the right to reparations and recognition, while also establishing new sites of memory. This policy was accompanied by organizational rationalization. The government merged the National Office of War Orphans (established in 1917), the Office of Disabled and Invalid Veterans (founded in 1918), and the Office of Combatants (established in 1918) to form the National Veterans Office (Office national des anciens combattants et victimes de guerre, or ONAC), which was to take care in all circumstances of the material and moral interests of its members. This institution was charged with delivering combatants' certificates and awarding retirement and disability pensions. Although the arrangement appeared logical, it nonetheless concealed pernicious elements.

A Narrow Approach to the Resistance

In giving pride of place to military aspects and striving not to magnify the gulf between the two world wars, the Gaullist vision did not reflect but rather interpreted the facts of the conflict. In doing so, despite its declared ecumenicalism, it tended to exclude the versions that differed from its doctrine and bequeathed to its successors some thorny mnemonic problems. For the negation of the facts of Vichy and, putting it mildly, the expansive attribution of membership in the Resistance to all of the French were so many time bombs. This view, of course, had the virtue of bringing the population together and removing the risk—which was in fact limited—of a civil war between heroes and "collabos." But this peacemaking vision, removed from reality, heralded the harsh awakening that would take place at the dawn of the 1970s, fostering a crisis in the national identity whose effects are still being felt today.

The first among the French intended to impose his vision of the Resistance, considered as a military phenomenon above all. As a result, he excluded, without compunction, heterodox sensibilities, whether of the

French who had worked in the British networks of the Special Operations Executive (SOE) or of the men and women involved in movements that, for a variety of reasons, had favored civilian action. The texts of 1945 and 1946 defining the status of members of the Resistance, for example, considered them soldiers by default because *"although* not belonging to the land, sea, or air forces . . . [they] have contributed to ensuring the salvation of the country."[48] Similarly, the greater part of the Croix de Libération were awarded to the Forces françaises libres (nearly three-fourths of the recipients), with only a modest one-fourth going to the internal Resistance. Soldiers—career, reservists, or enlistees—were particularly well served, since 750 Compagnons were in uniform at the time they were awarded the Croix. Finally, only six women were honored with this high distinction, a proportion that takes no cognizance of the role women played in both movements and networks.[49] It is also worth noting the small proportion of colonial soldiers in the Order, although seventy foreigners were honored. In the same vein the SOE networks of Maurice Buckmaster were rarely honored by the French authorities. Right after the Liberation, the Sylvestre-Farmer network, which claimed to have 150 P2 agents,[50] received no French decoration for its members.[51] The Adolphe network, with 58 P2 agents and 350 P1 agents, asked for 6 Légions d'honneur, 106 Resistance medals, and 18 citations of regimental order; as of June 11, 1946, no honors were awarded its agents, even though the group had suffered four killed by the enemy, twenty-one deportees who had not returned, and thirty returned deportees or prisoners held for more than three months.[52]

It is noteworthy that the government did not undertake a politics of monuments—museums, commemorative plaques, or monuments—a lack that, as we will see, was amply compensated for by associations. But this failure to act resulted from the same logic that had prevailed after the Great War: the state had allowed associations and local authorities to take action.

The Question of the Purge

The desire to bring together the entire French population and to strengthen national unity also led to a cautious policy in carrying out the purge. For the Gaullist government, contrary to what is often claimed, did not settle old accounts in a bloody purge. But this dark legend had a persistent life. For many years it marked the memory of former Vichyites and to some degree fostered memorial disputes about the dark years.

The purge was, to be sure, rigorous in many respects. Opening 350,000 dossiers, the government scrutinized the conduct of nearly one French citizen out of a hundred, obviously a substantial proportion. Also, fifteen hundred collaborators were executed after a trial by civilian authorities (high court, criminal courts) or military tribunals—which, in relation to the population, placed France at the head of the list of capital sentences imposed in Europe against traitors. A total of 13,339 people were sentenced to hard labor; 2,044 to life in prison; 22,883 to shorter jail terms.[53] Other punishments openly or surreptitiously doubled these sanctions. For example, civic courts (*Chambres civiques*) imposed another penalty on 46,645 people, national disgrace.[54] A law of honor directed against "those who were able to betray their country while continuing to obey the law,"[55] this symbolic measure was not without concrete consequences because it deprived the guilty of many rights, notably the right to vote.

The government likewise used and abused administrative internment, a method that, by protecting the presumably guilty from popular assault, avoided lynching and score-settling; but the procedure also made it possible to punish individuals against whom evidence was lacking, although they had behaved shockingly during the dark years—at least in appearance. A study of Maine-et-Loire confirms this ambivalence.[56] For example, the wife of a doctor from Beaufort-en-Vallée begged the commissioner of the Republic, Michel Debré, to put her husband under house arrest in the capital when he was released from prison because "the return of my husband to Beaufort has become completely impossible. There is some dreadful hatred that might put his life in danger."[57] Debré, in fact, pointed out that "the sanctions of administrative internment or house arrest, without prosecution, should be reserved . . . for persons whose moral or intellectual attitude has been deplorable and whose continued freedom in their normal places of residence or employment would provoke a public scandal when no fact or precise act can be held against them."[58] Last but not least, a professional purge came on top of the judicial purge, even in bodies that have sometimes been thought to have been spared from the upheaval. Of the 40,000 agents of the national police (excluding the Seine department), 5,603 were sanctioned, 1,312 of them dismissed.[59] Most important, and contrary to a stubborn legend, the authorities were harsher to higher officers (37 percent of directors, assistant directors, and chief inspectors were dismissed) or even midlevel officers (14.7 percent of captains had to resign) than to the 37,890 patrolmen and sergeants (only 2.66 percent of whom were forced to leave uniform).[60] After four frightful years of occupation the French hungered for justice, and the purge satisfied that hunger.

But the state refused to unleash blind vengeance—which did not mean that populations refrained from all violence. Some twenty thousand women were forced to have their heads shaved at Liberation for having collaborated or allegedly slept with the enemy.[61] But the upper levels of the government had no intention of declaring a civil war between the traitors and the pure. According to former Minister of Justice Pierre-Henri Teitgen: "I estimated that tens of thousands of prosecutions were still in progress against accused persons who were really only imbeciles, frightened men, or victims of the myth of the "victor of Verdun," and besides that 40,000 Resistance fighters could not claim to judge by their measure forty million French citizens. I therefore favored a system of justice that, while retaining its integrity, would be as indulgent as possible."[62] Charles de Gaulle, president of the Provisional Government, stuck to his line and also wished to promote the coming together of all French citizens, without weighing their respective merits. Less lofty constraints, finally, dictated their law. At a time when the country was pursuing the war against Nazi Germany, was initiating its reconstruction, modernizing its organization, and attempting to preserve its empire—at the risk of launching the Indochina War—the cooperation of all its sons was necessary, which sometimes involved turning a blind eye to past compromises. In the army the purge was thus relatively indulgent until May 8, 1945, in order to maintain the bulk of the troops in the campaign against the Third Reich; but the process was relaunched in 1946 and 1947, until it was reversed in 1948: the disturbances in Madagascar and the Indochina War required the recall of experienced officers. "Overall, the French army experienced only four years of obscurity, from 1946 to 1949, during which the purge measures were very harshly applied."[63]

Conducted under difficult circumstances, the purge and its imperfections could not fail to foster disputes. Those who were nostalgic for the

French State or the former Nazi sycophants denounced a victor's justice that, far from restoring harmony and civil peace, fanned the flames of civil war. Glorifying the sacrifice of the fascist writer Robert Brasillach, who had, they said, been unjustly executed, depicting—like Marcel Aymé in *Uranus* (1948)—peaceable villages suddenly plunged into sordid score-settling and subjected to Communist arbitrariness, they contrasted the harshness of the present to the magnanimity of the Bourbon Restoration. Indeed, far from sanctioning the men who had served the Revolution and the empire, hadn't Louis XVIII left them in peace or even taken them into his service, as the example of Archbishop Talleyrand suggested? "In other words, one would have to be as blind and intolerant as the French of 1945 to refuse to understand that history is made up of those 'successive loyalties' that today are called 'treason.'"[64] The Communists, in contrast, constantly protested against the indulgence the powerful, particularly company heads, had enjoyed at the Liberation. Only the Gaullists, Christian Democrats, and Socialists considered that the purge had in the end been a success and that it would have been difficult, given human nature, to achieve perfection.

In any event, far from forging a consensus, the purge provoked two black legends whose effects fostered memorial disputes for long years thereafter. Some, arguing on the basis of the excessive harshness displayed by the judges and relying on erroneous numbers, propagated the image of a wicked and bloody purge and consequently called for a review of the sentences. This view led both to the amnesty laws of 1951 and 1953 and to constant demands that Pétain's remains be laid to rest among his companions in arms in Douaumont, the memorial site dedicated to the battle of Verdun. Conversely, the idea that the purge had failed, allowing important dignitaries to slip through the net, fostered suspicion, driving some groups to call for new prosecutions aimed primarily at Vichy officials, who had in fact been little punished, such as Jean Leguay, René Bousquet, and Maurice Papon. This demand was supported in particular by Jewish groups who expressed surprise in the 1970s at the clemency that their oppressors had enjoyed.

The government adopted a measured policy with regard to the purge, and it was just as cautious about the inhabitants of Alsace and Lorraine, perpetuating the accepted if inaccurate image of populations that had remained loyal to the ravaged nation. But this view omitted more troubling facts: some fringes of the society of Alsace and Moselle had not looked unfavorably on annexation by a Third Reich that was piling victory on victory, particularly because the first annexation, after the Franco-Prussian War, coinciding with a major economic expansion and significant social measures, was not remembered in purely negative terms. The Provisional Government disregarded these nuances. Although it punished collaborators, it refrained from launching a witch hunt. A decree of April 21, 1944, had barred from elective office members of parliament who had voted yes on July 10, 1940, along with those who had served the Vichy regime. Their rights could, however, be restored on the basis of actions in the Resistance, first by a prefect and later by a *jury d'honneur* established by the decree of April 6, 1945. Prefects, followed by the *jury d'honneur,* were more than indulgent toward parliamentarians from Alsace and Moselle—deputies from these regions who belonged to Action Populaire enjoyed a record exoneration of 90 percent, despite rather thin Resistance records.[65] Along the same lines, men from the lost provinces who had served in the Wehrmacht and the German armed forces were granted "the advantages provided in the May 11 decree for political deportees. They were not, of course, granted to those who joined German forces of their own free will. The measure did not grant its beneficiaries the status of political deportees."[66] Likewise, soldiers wearing German uniforms who had fallen in battle received the right of permanent burial in national cemeteries.[67]

In the same vein, workers who had voluntarily gone to work in Germany were seldom sanctioned, even though they had directly or indirectly helped to support the economic efforts of a Reich engaged in total war. Their numbers were substantial: 260,000 individuals (including 42,654 women) had not waited to be conscripted into the STO. But the authorities made no attempt to punish them, judging that in the majority of cases, these pseudo-volunteers had made a choice "imposed by unemployment, food shortages, and German propaganda, that is, events that had forced their choice and appeared to be extenuating circumstances."[68] In contrast, workers who had combined their voluntary labor and a political or propaganda involvement in favor of Nazi Germany—activity in a collaborationist group, for example—were punished because their volunteering revealed their guilty intention.

The measured purge and the unconditional reincorporation of the lost provinces into the nation together confirmed the will toward unity given impetus by Charles de Gaulle, sometimes at the cost of some distortion of historical truth.

The Gaullist government presented its own interpretation of the conflict, sanctifying the Resistance—emphasizing its military and external components—ignoring the Allies, denying Vichy, and forgetting the Jewish deportees. This policy had the advantage of restoring confidence to the French who had legitimate doubts about national prestige after the terrible defeat of 1940, a harsh occupation, and four years spent under the rod of Pétain. It also made it possible to bind up the wounds resulting from the conflict by not stirring up disputes and not provoking a possible civil war. But it was not welcomed with unanimity, because the Communists, as noted above, proposed a different reading of the conflict.

Battle over Memory, or Consensus?

By 1945 the two political forces in contention had begun a battle for memory whose winner is hard to determine. General de Gaulle unquestionably scored many points because of his great prestige and the acknowledged services he had rendered to the country but also because he was able to stage his return brilliantly. Going beyond the magic of his speeches, he imposed his symbols: the Croix de Lorraine; his calendar: June 18; his rites: a militarization of the memory of the war; and his places: Mont Valérien. Above all, he avoided symbolic ruptures by tying the memory of World War II to that of the Great War, by inserting the conflict into the long chronicle of the history of France, and by occupying the entire space of Paris with no distinction between the bourgeois west and the popular east. For example, the marches of June 17 and 18 took place on the Champs-Élysées but also on the boulevard Saint-Germain and the place de la République. His vision of a resisting and victorious France was at the time subject to little challenge. It no doubt was in harmony with the aspirations of a population proud that France, through de Gaulle's rhetorical magic, had recovered its "rank" and was undertaking its reconstruction without delay.

The Communists also registered some successes. They appeared to be an authentic force of the Resistance, succeeding for a time in smoothing over their false steps in the period from 1939 to 1941. Their praise of the Red Army met agreement among the French, 61 percent of whom, remembering Stalingrad, thought that the USSR had played the largest role in the defeat of the Third Reich. It is less certain, however, that the Communists succeeded in imposing their sites—Père-Lachaise or Châteaubriant—and their rites on the mass of the population. Their commemorations remained partisan, valued only by the militants who attended and failing to attain a form of universality; their sites of memory—places, monuments—scattered through hundreds of communities, never attained national prominence, with very few exceptions, such as Châteaubriant. But this analysis requires modification. The PCF won one-fourth of the vote at Liberation, and though it cultivated primarily its own ranks, it carried some weight. It brought together a substantial portion of the population, and its memorial policy marked millions of the French, thereby exercising some authority over the shapes of memory. But we should not overestimate the divergences between the two camps. For

in this battle to root the memory of combat in a respectable past and point it toward a future worthy of history, the protagonists joined together to organize the forgetting of the majority of the daily experiences of the French. Not only did they organize the shameful memory of collaborationist enemies, but they reduced to almost nothing the memory of the great majority of the French as a conquered people that had merely survived.[69]

By putting the emphasis on the memory of battle, commemorations also preserved "the omission of the millions of prisoners and labor deportees who had haunted Vichy's official speeches and the bad conscience of the French."[70]

In many ways *La bataille du rail* illustrates this convergence. This quasi-official film directed by René Clément, destined to engender many imitations, was the product of a compromise between the Communist sensibility represented by the Committee for the Liberation of French Cinema (Comité de libération du cinéma français, or CLCF) and the General Cooperative of French Cinema (Coopérative générale du cinéma français, or CGCF), and the Résistance-Fer movement, backed by the management of the SNCF (Société nationale des chemins de fer français, the French national rail service), more Gaullist in tone. Initially, the project was intended "to conform to a class argument and to glorify the internal Resistance." But the enlargement of the production group to include the SNCF and Résistance-Fer required a "'unanimist' vision" of the railroad company.[71] "The addition of new characters such as the engineer and the two retirees helped to impose an idyllic image of a railroad family feeling solidarity from top to bottom, to which rail workers of every age and rank are attached by indestructible bonds."[72]

Overall, films shot in the period immediately after the war did not contradict the Gaullist-Communist vision, "the myth of a heroic community"[73] largely dominating film production, but at the same time refrained from openly embracing the arguments of one side or the other.[74] Despite the rivalry between Gaullist and Communist producers, most of these narratives "fit into the framework of a mystified, peaceable, Manichaean, and sanctifying history that exalted the armed exploits of the crusaders of the Resistance (to the detriment of the diverse forms of 'civilian Resistance') while agreeing to suppress events likely to cause dissension."[75]

In reality both forces were primarily interested in having done with the war, a desire that resorted to "two heroic models: the model of Communist memory, heir to the French Revolution, and the model of Gaullist memory, heir to the entire history of France."[76] Besides, they had no qualms about proposing festive commemorations that contrasted with the gravity surrounding them today, with rare exceptions. The population of Paris, for example, was invited on July 14, 1945, to take advantage of free matinees given by some theaters (the Châtelet, for example) and to attend nautical performances on the Seine. The celebration of the insurrection of Paris produced ten days of parties, managed by the PCF, which organized torch races and sporting events in the "populist style analogous to the traditional prewar July 14 celebrations."[77] Above all, as I have already noted, the two forces exploited their memorial policies to conceal troubling truths—the dark facts of Vichy and the Occupation in one case, the tortuous line followed between 1939 and 1941 in the other.

It is a commonplace that commemoration exists on two levels. On one level it pays homage to victims, indicating the debt and respect the living owe the dead. In that sense it functions as a mimesis: the celebration reflects the ordeals endured by a population. On a more voluntaristic level it aims to impose a meaning on lived experience, at the risk of presenting a travesty of the facts or even the essence of that experience. This was the choice made by the major political forces in the aftermath of the war.

That said, did the institutions and parties have any choice? All things considered, it may be agreed that the French had no desire to hear unpleasant truths whose import they were familiar with. Settling of scores, moreover, might have degenerated into civil war. At a time when the country was facing the dual challenge of reconstruction and modernization, it was doubtless more opportune to present positive models for the adulation of the masses than to adopt a morose posture of repentance. These strategic calculations no doubt guided the course of action the leaders followed, Charles de Gaulle most of all. But through its biases this memorial policy bequeathed thorny problems to the general's political successors, as an examination of the policies followed under the Fourth Republic suggests.

CHAPTER 2

Conciliation and Tension

THE WORK OF THE FOURTH REPUBLIC
(1946–1958)

The period that opened with the departure of General de Gaulle from government and closed with the collapse of the Fourth Republic presents an uneven picture. Although the state strove to carry out a policy of reconciliation, it saw mixed results: the memory of World War II was a site of sometimes very violent though never fatal conflict.

Although the new regime did not signal the advent of the New Jerusalem that the army of shadows had expected, it was dominated, in its first legislative session at least, by figures largely from the ranks of the underground forces, who took an interest in memorial issues and intended to preserve the spirit of the Resistance.

Statutory Definitions

The Fourth Republic embarked on a vast legislative effort by creating or supplementing the statutes designed to grant victims a right to recognition and a right to reparations. For instance, the parliament passed two statutes for deportees, one targeting "deportees and internees of the resistance" (August 8, 1948), the other "political internees and deportees" (September 9, 1948). The gap between members of the Resistance and "politicals" (primarily Jews) was thereby officially sanctioned, which Resistance spokesmen had called for. Sitting in the National Assembly, Émile

Lambert, Roger Devémy, and Edmond Michelet, admittedly members of the National Federation of Deportees and Internees of the Resistance (Fédération des déportés et internés de la Résistance, or FNDIR), were intent on perpetuating that distinction: "Without underestimating, of course, even to the slightest extent, the merit of the unfortunates who suffered, for whatever reason, from the terrible scourge that afflicted our country, so cruelly tested, everyone will nonetheless acknowledge all the difference there is between an ordeal imposed by fate and risk freely chosen. Clearly, volunteers of the Resistance, deliberately and in a spirit of abnegation, accepted in advance all the consequences of their acts."[1] Further, the law of March 25, 1949, specified both the nature of the title of member of the Resistance and the means henceforth defined for gaining recognition of that status.[2] These texts were intended primarily to relieve the real distress of the victims. Members of the Resistance were facing sometimes tragic circumstances. Having interrupted their education or the normal course of their professional lives, they struggled to reintegrate into postwar French society, a delicate undertaking, often made worse by internment or deportation. The fate of Jewish victims was even more worrying. The few deportees who had come back from the extermination camps—they amounted to a mere twenty-five hundred—encountered terrible material and psychological hardships; the same thing was true for families decimated by Nazi barbarity. From this perspective the statutes adopted in the wake of the Liberation provided the right to welcome assistance.

But the development of legal standards also outlined the contours of memory for the future, even for posterity. By imposing their conception of what the war, the Resistance, and the deportation had been, the state in general and the legislature in particular determined the public image of the dark years for many years to come. The Resistance, for example, was considered primarily from the military angle, as junior Veterans Affairs Minister Robert Bétolaud pointed out. In parliamentary debate on December 14, 1948, he explained:

The only definition, in my opinion, that can be accepted is participation in the fighting activity of the resistance. . . . All those who participated in the military side of the Resistance during the requisite period should be considered voluntary Resistance combatants but . . . conversely, those who participated in the political action of the Resistance do not have the right to that definition.[3]

The junior armed forces minister shared this view:

The characterization acts of resistance against the enemy should be applied only to acts involving direct or indirect participation in operations conducted against the enemy [that is] the pursuit of intelligence of any kind likely to provide the allies with indications enabling them either to piece together the enemy's plans and organizations or to pinpoint the situation of the Forces Françaises de l'Intérieur; the transmission of this intelligence by whatever means to the allied forces; providing refuge for persons sought by the enemy; hiding materiel; the contribution of resources to the organs of the Resistance; assistance to escapees.[4]

Similarly, the laws adopted provided that the ninety days required to obtain the volunteer combatant card had to have been completed before June 6, 1944. This elitist approach kept out the "September resisters," who, in the eyes of some, had joined up when the battle had already been won. It may also have made it possible to exclude the men and women who, having participated in the insurrections of the Liberation, might be suspected of harboring Communist sympathies.

Foreign Parallels

This approach, far from a French monopoly, also characterized many European countries. In Belgium the "statute of armed resistance" (September 19, 1945) excluded civil resistance from its field of application.[5] A decree establishing the status of civil resistance was finally promulgated on December 24, 1946, but its application was distorted by the representatives of the Flemish Catholic camp. Robert de Man, the minister in charge of the question, determined that "acts of sabotage carried out in the exercise of one's profession" also covered administrative sabotage conducted by agents who had stayed on the job during the Occupation, and not just workers who had slowed down war production in factories. Similarly, "works of patriotic solidarity," which, in the eyes of the drafters, was meant for the patriotic agitation displayed by the Communist Independence Front (FI), ended up designating any charitable work—assistance to bombing victims, for example. The spokesmen of the Front were disturbed by this distortion. "The maneuver is obvious. They want to drown civil resistance, submerge it beneath a wave of heterogeneous bodies the better to devalue it. Moreover, the unstated purpose is to introduce by stealth through the back door an entire collection of figures who are supposed to have conducted 'administrative resistance,' whereas in fact they were collaborating with the enemy."[6] The application of the statute, however, belied this pessimistic prediction—Belgian officials turned out to be particularly vigilant. As a result, "the title of 'civil resister' remained limited to an elite able to provide evidence of its involvement and, against all expectations, the administration remained remarkably impervious to political interference."[7]

In Italy the government granted the right to reparation to partisans, on condition that they had borne arms, participated in sabotage, or supplied intelligence to the Allies—a view that consequently excluded civil combatants and those who had provided logistical support to the underground fighters, notably women. The latter were granted the recognition due "those who deserve well of the war of liberation," given to those who, although not having taken up arms, had made possible the struggle of the partisans. Another title was also attributed to any man or woman who was "killed in the war, mutilated, or disabled for the liberation struggle," that is, combatants or political prisoners, hostages or victims of reprisals, assassinated by the Nazis or the fascists. Veterans' pensions, however, were denied to partisans except when they held high rank.

These first rigid statutes were, however, modified by the Parri government (June–December 1945), which, in a decree on August 21, 1945, specified the conditions for acceding to the title "partisan combatant." It was reserved for men and women decorated or wounded in combat, to resisters who, north of the Gothic Line, had served for at least three months in a recognized unit and participated in three military operations. The Gothic Line, which in 1944 separated the northern zone controlled by the Germans from the southern zone liberated by the Allies, established a clear demarcation. Individuals who engaged south of this line in a unit recognized by the National Liberation Committee (CNL) could also be recognized. In contrast, traitors or partisans who had gone over to fascist units were excluded from the scheme. The title of *patriot* was given to "those who had collaborated in or contributed to the war of liberation, by fighting in partisan units, even for a brief period, or had provided irregular troops constant and substantial assistance." A final status defined those who "died for the war of liberation." This category covered a variety of disparate cases. It was intended for those killed because of their actions, those who died as a result of wounds contracted on the field of battle, and political prisoners, hostages, or deportees to concentration camps assassinated by the fascists or the Nazis. The decree of August 4, 1945, identified the dead, the mutilated, widows, and orphans who belonged to the partisan camp with the victims of regular warfare. It also extended some rights to the victims of political or racial persecution. For example, the right to a pension was open to deportees, internees, and victims of roundups who, under certain conditions, could enjoy preferential hiring in the civil service. That said, these statutes, as in France, established a hierarchy of merit. Simple participants in the war of liberation received an allowance of one thousand lire; partisans who had fought more than three months, five thousand; wounded or mutilated resisters, ten thousand. Civilian victims of the war, finally, were also recognized. Fitting into this category were the displaced, refugees, evacuees, civilians repatriated from abroad, civilians who had survived internment or deportation, and the spouses of civilians who had died or disappeared because of the war.[8]

In France, as elsewhere, the authorities in fact tended to offer a primarily military reading of the resistance, a position that excluded civilian resistance from its purview.

In an entirely different register, laws defining the status of deportees and internees in France made no distinctions among sites of internment. The specificity of the extermination camps was thus not acknowledged. The few Jewish survivors were admittedly not serving in a military capacity at the time to have the unique nature of their fate recognized. Moreover, racial deportees were identified with civilian victims, which deprived them of the decorations reserved for fighters, because the authorities established a hierarchy, with the Resistance deportees at the top and playing down political deportees (in reality Jews). A jurist observed: "The intent was to grant to those who had anticipated their fate by fighting against the enemy and their accomplices fuller reparation than to those, singled out, for example, because of their origin or designated as hostages, who had simply endured it."[9] It should be emphasized that this distinction was particular to France. Belgium, for example, recognized only one status, that of "political prisoner," accorded to all individuals who had been detained for at least thirty days for any reason other than a criminal offense (law of February 26, 1947). Similarly, the FRG (Federal Republic of Germany) included in a single category all the victims of the Nazi regime with no distinction between "resisters" and "politicals" (laws of September 18, 1953, and June 26, 1956),[10] even though, in the Hague agreements with Israel and at the Jewish Claims Conference in 1952, it granted specific indemnification to Jews. Finally, "the designation 'political' applied to all deportees and internees, except for those of the Resistance and common law criminals, stripped the word of any meaning. Was a passerby seized in a roundup political? What about Jewish children and old men? The term made it possible to sidestep the question of the deportation of the Jews, completely absent from the discussion."[11]

The statutes adopted under the Fourth Republic thus had the virtue of materially improving the situation of resisters and deportees. Symbolically, they also fostered national cohesion by focusing the memory of the war on the figure of the Resistance fighter, sometimes a hero, sometimes a martyr, in the Nazi camps and jails. This primacy should not come as a surprise. "The Resistance was proof of the moral health of the Nation, the symbol of renaissance. It played that role in postwar political discourse and in many memoirs and historical writings, formulated either in the moral vocabulary of 'restoration and renewal,' or in the more academic vocabulary of 'continuity and discontinuity.'"[12]

The authorities, however, were rather generous with regard to prisoners of war, interpreting membership in a combat unit rather liberally. Indeed, for the period as a whole, "ninety percent of former prisoners were able to claim a combatant's card."[13] But the statutes also had perverse effects by denying the specificity of the genocide of the Jews and by excluding civilian resistance, considered as a form of secondary, if not negligible, combat—to the fury of participants who thought they had not been unworthy in the clandestine struggle.

The Shadow of the Great War

There were several reasons for this blindness. To begin with, the authorities remained prisoners of the Gaullist view that favored the military epic over a more ideological reading of the conflict. By identifying World War II with the Great War, this view had the virtue of not deepening the divide between the veterans of 1914—still numerous and active—and their less glorious successors of 1940—a concern that haunted the leaders of the time. In 1948 the MAC estimated the number of veterans of the Great War receiving military pensions through its services at 844,991, obviously a significant figure.[14] In 1973, seven hundred thousand veterans of the Great War were still alive, a group it would have been difficult to treat with contempt.[15] The authorities consequently insisted that the period of three months in a combat unit—a criterion established in the aftermath of World War I—be applied to combatants in World War II, resisters included. The rapporteur of the law bringing the status of deportees and internees of the Resistance before the Conseil de la République, Émile Fournier, refused to give importance to time spent in the camps, "in order not to violate the principle of equality with the situation of combatants at the front in the wars of 1914–1918 and 1939–1945. They often spent hard years in the trenches and under fire. They fought at Verdun, the Somme, the Chemin des Dames; sometimes they spent days between the lines with no food. Besides, we will avoid having them make demands that might be justified."[16] Examining the proposed law establishing the status of Resistance deportee-internee, the jurist Pierre Nicolaÿ observed that article 10, which contemplated attributing to deportees twice the time actually served, as well as a bonus of six months, was not justified because of the cost and because there was "really no valid reason to favor deportees over front-line soldiers in the 1914–1918 and 1939–1945 wars. We should therefore limit ourselves at most to aligning the situation of deportees with that of front-line soldiers, and the situation of internees with that of prisoners of war."[17] Minister of the Interior Édouard Depreux, for his part, was worried about the fate in store for the disabled of the Great War. He instructed prefects:

I have been informed that disabled men of the 1914–1918 war have been excluded in some departments from distributions of American supplies in favor of disabled veterans of the 1939–1945 war, deportees, prisoners, and refugees. As a consequence, and in agreement with my colleague from the Ministry of Veterans Affairs, I ask you to make certain that any inequality of treatment between the different categories of victims of the two wars be avoided.[18]

Minister of prisoners, deportees, and refugees in de Gaulle's first cabinet (September 9, 1944–November 21, 1945), Henri Frenay had taken care to unite the memory of the two wars on November 10 and 11, 1945, for "if we were to celebrate the victories of 1918 and 1945 at two different dates, I would be afraid that the memory of the victory of 1918 would soon fade in the mind of future generations."[19]

This obsession even invaded memorial spaces. The Resistance commitment of the hero of *Le père tranquille*, a film released in October 1946, was clearly placed in the framework of "the Thirty Years' War." Played by Noël-Noël, this hero, a veteran of the Great War, "resumes combat against the hereditary enemy in the name of a patriotism that he expresses in the form of a visceral attachment to territorial integrity."[20]

From 1951 on, the government was less enthusiastic in celebrating the great deeds of the Resistance. "The closer one got to the end of the Fourth Republic, the larger the commemorations of the 1914–1918 war, while commemorations of the 1939–1945 war decreased."[21] The return of the right to public affairs fostered by its 1951 electoral success explains this policy in part. With the notable exception of the Gaullists, the right had often rubbed shoulders with Pétainists and, because of this association, had some difficulty celebrating the glory of the French Resistance. But more immediate political concerns also inspired governments of every stripe. To the determination not to forget the heroes of 1914–1918 was obviously added the desire not to displease the still powerful lobby that they represented, both in numerical terms and because of the strength of their associations. In addition, the feelings, if not Vichyite, then at least Pétainist, that many poilus still held for the victor of Verdun no doubt encouraged the authorities to act cautiously in memorial matters. Likewise, the associations of Great War veterans were not inclined to welcome the veterans of World War II into their ranks, "afraid to devalue their own claims to honor."[22]

The Communists, it should be noted, shared this unifying vision, assembling all deportees and internees into a single large family. "We consider," said Deputy Roucaute, "the great family born of the resistance, internment, and deportation as a whole and we make it our honor and our duty to take in hand, with the same feeling of mutual aid and solidarity, the defense of the widows and orphans of French internees or deportees, fine and honest, who died in deportation or were shot as hostages because of their religion by the enemy against whom we fight."[23] In conformity with the nationalist ideology of Thorez that exalted the nation, this approach had the merit of making the "Party of 75,000 martyrs" the best defender of the French Resistance, both materially and morally.

The political view put forward by various participants masked clientelist approaches that it would be futile to deny. For instance, elected officials frequently turned into spokesmen for special interests supported by a multiplicity of associations born after the war.

The World of Associations

World War I had created a precedent by fostering the emergence of powerful veterans' associations. This example, carefully considered, encouraged some men to form organizations able to defend the moral and material interests of their comrades, while simultaneously sometimes serving their political aims.

Given confidence by the unity formed in the shadows around the National Movement of Prisoners of War and Deportees (MNPGD), prisoners of war, at the congress held from April 5 to 8, 1945, were quick to establish the National Federation of Combatant Prisoners of War and Deportees (FNPGD), which soon brought together the veterans of the Stalags and Oflags. Out of some 1.6 million prisoners, the FNPGD soon gathered a million, or two-thirds (there were still 811,216 dues-paying members in 1952 and 564,000 in 1960).[24] A powerful mass movement, the Federation reached second place in the world of associations, behind the General Confederation of Labor.[25] Considering itself complementary to, not in competition with, the FNPGD, the National Union of Associations of the Camps, created in April 1945, brought together according to geographical criteria the associations that captives had established at their sites of misfortune. The National Union of Draft Dodgers, for its part, claimed to bring together the men who had succeeded in avoiding conscription.[26]

Several associations wished to speak in the name of the Resistance. The National Association of Veterans of the Resistance (ANACR),

Communist-leaning, presented itself as the heir of the FTPF. As early as October 28, 1944, veterans of the movement led by Charles Tillon announced in the newspaper *France d'Abord* the launch of the Friends of Veterans of the FTPF, which soon changed into the National Association of FTPF Veterans. On July 2, 1952, this association became the ANACR, which probably had more than thirty thousand members.[27] Two groups aimed to compete against it. Established in February 1953, the National Association of Volunteer Resistance Combatants (ANCVR) supported an elitist view of resistance involvement and brought together only around fifteen hundred commissioned and noncommissioned officers of the army of shadows. The National Confederation of Volunteer Resistance Combatants (CNCVR), launched in October 1953, saw itself in not such strict terms—it took in some ten thousand veterans—while being just as Gaullist as the ANCVR.[28] The Free French, finally, created their own association, but in December 1947, it had only six thousand dues-paying members.

Split into diverse if not rival associations, the Resistance was therefore unable in the aftermath of the war to form itself into a unitary and powerful structure able to carry its voice into the public square. The small size of the army of shadows explains in part this lack of vitality. Unlike for the Great War, veterans were few in number. The modesty of their forces prevented the establishment of powerful organizations. In addition, political splits undermined from the outset the unity of a world that had embraced contrasting ideological choices. The veterans of 1939 to 1945, above all, were not always inclined to meet, put off by the example of veterans of the Great War. Many refused to consider themselves "veterans" and had trouble imagining themselves communing at ritual banquets. This prospect even made them shudder, especially because the incantations of the veterans of 1914 to 1918, quick to intone the hymn of "never again" or "the war to end all wars," had wearied them in their youth. "I hate associations," said a member of Défense de la France after the war. "We were so bored by those assholes with their decorations and their dead, that we rejected all that," said another.[29] Many associations, as a result, soon experienced a membership crisis. In April 1948 General de Larminat, chairman of the Association of the Free French (AFL), thought that the number of dues-paying members had to triple as soon as possible:

Obviously, if our efforts in this area fail in 1948, I believe that we can draw one conclusion: the Free French are not interested in themselves and what they were, and in that case you cannot bring a corpse to life. Then we'll close the organization in its current form and change it into a club of old gentlemen who will distribute bread ration tickets and will play a modest and trembling role in official ceremonies.[30]

For lack of authentically representative organizations, the voice of the Resistance could not be heard.

Several other organizations also claimed to be speaking in the name of deportees. Founded on October 7, 1945, the National Federation of Deportees, Internees, and Patriots—renamed the National Federation of Resistance and Patriot Deportees and Internees (FNDIRP) on January 11, 1946—which was close to the Communist Party, tried to bring together all deportees, Resistance or racial, with the exception of common criminals. With between five thousand and ten thousand members, it quite logically sought to have the distinction between those two categories abolished, demanding at its April 1949 congress that "the established categorization be erased." Defending the principle "for equal harm, equal reparation," it also demanded that indemnification be granted to deportees or internees of foreign origin. In contrast, it consistently denied the right of STO conscripts to claim the title of deportee. "The title of deportee should be reserved for detainees in concentration camps. The Congress again asks the workers who were victims of Nazism and forced to work in Germany to understand this."[31] Conversely, the FNDIR, established in 1945 and close to the Third Force (the coalition of parties opposed to both Gaullists and Communists), reserved membership for members of the Resistance alone. Aside from associations of veterans of the camps, other associations also spoke in the name of deportees. The Association of (Female) Deportees and Internees of the Resistance (ADIR), whose charter was filed on July 22, 1945, brought together members of the Resistance who had been the victims of repression and was long headed by Geneviève Anthonioz-de Gaulle.[32]

The conscripts, finally, came together in the National Federation of Labor Deportees (FNDT), established in March 1945 from the fusion of two parallel associations and given its name on November 14, 1945.[33] In

1946 it had between 400,000 and 560,000 members—an impressive figure by any measure.[34]

All these associations were more or less pursuing the same goals. They intended in the first place to defend the material and moral rights of their constituents. They also conducted medical and social programs, leading them to help their members in health, legal, professional, and financial matters. At the Liberation, for example, the FNPGD took charge of twelve thousand children who had been separated from their families by circumstances, a figure that fell to ninety-one in 1947.[35] In 1972 it was still running a medical center, four health and social institutes, eight rest homes, eight vacation colonies, a campground, three retirement homes, and three leisure centers.[36] These associations, following the example of the FNDIRP, wished to stimulate commemoration and historical research in order to "perpetuate the memory, deepen knowledge of World War II and the deportation."

Sometimes assembling tens of thousands of members, the associations did not hesitate to lobby both the executive and legislative branches; elected officials were often receptive to requests coming from a potentially powerful electoral clientele. For instance, several members of parliament fought to have the bar prohibiting Resistance veterans from filing their demands removed. This perseverance was rewarded. Six laws from 1952 to 1957 extended the deadlines until Charles de Gaulle finally closed the filing of claims on January 1, 1959.

As a result, the authorities seem to have chosen to show consideration to the associations rather than conducting an unsparing examination of the past.

Integrate to Unify?

This logic of integration was at first directed toward all the soldiers in the 1939–1940 campaign, all of whom the legislature wanted to consider as combatants. After long discussion, on January 29, 1948, the government issued a decree whose implementing provisions, promulgated on May 3, 1948, were highly favorable to former captives. A combatant's card was given "for operations begun on September 3, 1939—to forces mobilized or

enlisted in the armies of land, sea, or air, having fought in France or outside of France, having undergone captivity, or having been wounded."[37]
From this perspective prisoners earned the qualification of combatant not
because of their participation in the battle of France (entirely theoretical
for many of them) but because of their detention. The text fully met the
expectations of the National Federation of Prisoners of War and Deportees. Indeed,

the men, returning from the camps after the hard years of captivity, refused to
accept responsibility for the defeat or the nickname "knights of the white flag,"
exasperated by the disdain of other groups of combatants and the scorn of the
veterans of 14–18. The fight for the card thus took on for the former captives first
and foremost a moral dimension. It signified a categorical rejection of what were
considered to be calumnies as well as a challenge to the men who had dared to
cast doubt on the honor of the P[risoners of] W[ar].[38]

The French Veterans Union (UFAC), however, contested this decision and
brought the matter before the Conseil d'État. On May 13, 1948, the council
invalidated these provisions, explaining that the legislature had intended
to indemnify "those who had participated actively in the fight against the
enemy." From then on two arguments were in confrontation. The administration ratified the position of the Conseil d'État, considering it

wrongful to confer the status of combatant on soldiers at bases or in any other
body that had not taken part in combat and who fell into enemy hands without
resistance. . . . For the attribution of the title "combatant," only the fact of having participated in combat can be taken into account. The suffering endured by
the Prisoners confers on them certain rights, but cannot replace the material fact
of fighting, which must be the only criterion considered. Otherwise, the civilian victims of the War (STO Deportees, for example) could also claim a combatant's card.[39]

Similarly, the Personnel Department of the Army (Direction du personnel militaire de l'armée de terre, or DPMAT) pointed out that "belonging for a definite period of time to a Combat Unit should be the only
relevant criterion with regard to the attribution of a combatant's card."[40]
Conversely, many members of parliament called for giving all captives the
title of combatant because of the resistance they had (or would have) displayed in the camps, since "prisoners were able . . . to really make their activity into a new combat. Sabotage, rebellion, and acts of demoralization

were countless."[41] The decree of December 23, 1949, settled the issue, deciding that the quality of combatant was recognized as a matter of law:

First, for all prisoners of war who belonged to a combat unit at the time of their capture and who had either been detained for six months in territory occupied by the enemy, or registered in a camp in enemy territory; second, for all prisoners of war who, either before their capture or after their detention had belonged to a combat unit, on condition of having been detained for six months in territory occupied by the enemy or for ninety days in a camp situated in enemy territory.[42]

In other words, membership in a combat unit—a juridical legacy of World War I—remained a decisive criterion. A prisoner could not be considered a combatant. But this clause did not correspond with the wishes of the authorities, who wanted to indemnify all captives, which led the state to be rather generous in the list defining combat units. In the end the government had hedged, striving to reach an acceptable compromise between two contrary arguments. The FNPGD asserted that "a prisoner of war is a combatant in the absence of evidence to the contrary"; the UFAC retorted that "a prisoner is not a combatant in the absence of evidence to the contrary."[43]

The authorities also validated, with some hesitation, the services performed by the involuntary conscripts in the German army. At first the arrangement was limited to providing pensions based on death or disability (ordinance of March 10, 1945) and to deducting from military obligations "the length of service carried out in the German army by Frenchmen . . . drafted by force" (decree of October 16, 1945). In addition, the ordinance of November 2, 1945, granted the notice "died for France" to "any soldier who died . . . after having been drafted by force or after having joined, under constraint or because of the threat of reprisals, the enemy armies." A favorable judgment, however, could not be rendered "for individuals who died combating freely in the service of the enemy or fighting against the French liberation forces in the course of voluntary service in a foreign country on behalf of the enemy."[44]

Even so, was it necessary, in defiance of tradition, to take into account military service accomplished in foreign armies to offer the beneficiaries the full rights granted to combatants in the French army? Minister of Finance Robert Schuman, with roots in Moselle, it's true, leaned in that direction, asserting that "military service accomplished in the Wehrmacht

by inhabitants of Alsace and Lorraine conscripted by force could be identified with service accomplished in the French army, on condition, of
course, that those concerned had not been subject to prosecution by the
Civic Courts after the liberation."[45] The decree of August 22, 1952, was a
sign of relative progress in that it attributed by right the combatant's card
to wounded or disabled soldiers and to soldiers who had escaped or refused to follow the orders of their superiors. But as Colonel Orliac noted:

> It seems that the legislature was harsher toward those conscripted by force in
> the course of the 1939–1945 war than toward their compatriots who had become
> French by virtue of the Versailles Treaty, because it must be acknowledged that
> given the suspicion that often surrounded them, it must have been very hard for
> them either to escape or to refuse to submit to the orders given, and no less dif-
> ficult to provide evidence of having done so.[46]

The debate was concluded only toward the end of the Fourth Republic.
In a decree of May 10, 1955, the executive considered first "refusal to obey
a collective or individual summons in German military [or paramilitary]
units" as well as desertion by forced conscripts as "acts characterized as resistance to the enemy."[47] The law of August 7, 1957, moreover, identified
time served in the German police or army as "military service,"[48] thereby
opening to the inhabitants of Alsace and Lorraine the right to the combatant's card, which they were granted as a group on March 4, 1958. We know
that the emotion provoked by the trial in Bordeaux, in which involuntary
conscripts from Alsace serving in the SS *Das Reich* division had been sentenced for participating in the massacre of Oradour-sur-Glane (February
13, 1953), led, on the initiative of Premier René Mayer, to the swift passage
of an amnesty law (February 18, 1953) that produced the immediate release
of the guilty men.

Similarly, the fact of having obeyed the orders of the French State,
even in the operations of Dakar, Syria, or North Africa, was not materially sanctioned by the authorities, despite a few attempts along those lines.
For example, in a decree on January 22, 1947, the Socialist minister André Le Trocquer abolished double counting of time served for "soldiers in
the armistice army [the Vichy forces] who participated in war operations
between June 26, 1940, and November 7, 1942."[49] But this measure gave
rise to some agitation: active and reserve officers were "offended by some
partisan provisions regarding the way in which campaigns or wounds

should be deducted depending on which camp one belonged to at the time of hostilities."[50] The junior minister of the navy confirmed this for his service: "They cannot accept that the fact of soldiers having shed their blood has become grounds for unjust reprobation, whereas the same victims were almost all decorated for their courage at the time of the events in question."[51] The reform instituted by Le Trocquer was consequently revoked by decree on March 11, 1952.[52]

STO Conscripts: A Special Case?

The status of those conscripted for forced labor in Germany was established by a law passed on May 15, 1951, a rather late date. An earlier proposal had been offered by the Communists, supported by their Socialist colleagues, in June 1948. It had not passed; parliament chose to consider first the situation of Resistance and political deportees. In late 1948 the parliamentary commission adopted a unitary text, but the Gaullists maneuvered to delay its consideration. On May 23, 1950, the National Assembly voted unanimously in favor of the law, but the Council of the Republic vetoed it, demanding that the term *conscript* replace the formulation "labor deportee."[53]

In the end the law granted to "individuals forced to work in enemy territory" the benefits applicable to political deportees and internees. The French Republic, "in consideration of the suffering [they] have endured,"[54] awarded them a lump-sum payment and the right to a pension, with the time spent in Germany deducted from the amount. They could not claim the title "labor deportees," which indicated the subaltern rank the conscripts occupied in the hierarchy of virtues as in the circles of hell. They were far from being heroes; they might even be seen as traitors. Indeed, propaganda, both during and after the war, had insisted that refusing the orders of the French State represented the sacred duty of every patriot. It had claimed that the *réfractaires* (STO draft dodgers) would easily find the necessary help among the French or in Resistance organizations. At the Liberation the line was that the STO in France had failed: the slavedriver Sauckel had never succeeded in filling his quotas. In these circumstances the approximately six hundred thousand French citizens exiled to Germany could appear, at best, only as unlucky or unfortunate, at worst as cowards or even traitors. The ordeals undergone in German factories, moreover, could not decently be compared to the hell lived through by deportees in the concentration and extermination camps. The government agreed to compensate in material terms the very real suffering endured by the conscripts. Nonetheless, in symbolic terms, it had no intention of transforming them into heroes or martyrs, which explains why the May 14, 1951, statute, while granting the STO conscripts a title, merely—to their great chagrin—christened them "individuals forced to work in enemy territory" and refused to provide them with a card (although the laws had provided for that), a lack that was not remedied until 2008.

It is therefore easy to understand that the FNDT did everything to preserve for its members the title of deportee, a qualification that some associations of deportees denied them. They had in fact been seen in that light in the darkness of the occupation: between 1942 and 1944 the term designated primarily, if not exclusively, the STO conscripts. In 1974, five representatives of deportee organizations sued the Federation and won a judgment in the Paris court of appeal on February 13, 1978, a judgment confirmed by a decision of the Cour de Cassation on May 23, 1979. The association then had to change into the National Federation of Victims and Survivors of the Nazi Forced Labor Camps.[55] But this episode was not the end of its difficulties. The courts required the association to change the title of its periodical. Established in 1945, *Le Déporté du Travail* was renamed *Le Proscrit*. On January 31, 1992, the Cour de Cassation definitively prohibited the use of the term *deportee*.[56] The government had at bottom adopted a twofold strategy on the subject. In symbolic terms it did not intend to sanctify the STO conscripts, men who, neither heroes nor martyrs, had just been victims of the misfortunes of the time. At the same time, however, it offered them material compensation, thereby facilitating their reentry into society and hence strengthening national cohesion.

To a great extent the same logic imbued policy toward former Pétainists. The Fourth Republic was hardly sparing in tributes and celebrations glorifying the Resistance and its heroes. But, behind the scenes, government figures worked in relative discretion to heal the wounds by reintegrating the outlaws into the national community.

The Amnesty Laws

Amnesty did not have a good press in the aftermath of the war. Marked by a cruel occupation, France chose to celebrate the heroes of the Resistance rather than to pardon its prodigal children: only extreme right circles campaigned for absolution.[57] The government was, however, aware of the political and social risks posed by the purge. Yet rather than proposing that parliament pass an amnesty law, it chose to use the pardoning power the Constitution had granted to the president of the republic. Pardons would, to be sure, keep resentment from calcifying. "Pardon kills hatred. Death creates martyrs," said President of the Republic Vincent Auriol. By rectifying the sometimes disproportionate penalties imposed by the courts, pardons were also a form of regulation after the fact. According to Auriol, "The pardoning power must adjust disproportionate penalties by equalizing them according to the standards of justice, equity, and reason."[58] Exercising his sovereign power, the president therefore distinguished between intellectual errors and passive participation in organizations on one side—calling for indulgence—and political acts resembling in form common law crimes on the other—for which severity was in order. "Generally speaking, those who carried out the dirty work of collaboration were much more easily hauled before firing squads than those who inspired them."[59] But from 1948 on, the government was inclined to return to a firmer attitude. Auriol deplored the fact that collaborators were confusing indulgence with absolution: "The atmosphere created by former collaborators . . . has not facilitated the clemency of the Commission for Pardons. . . . They do not want to acknowledge their faults. The guilty want to claim that after having been pardoned for their misdeeds they have been rehabilitated. This appalling atmosphere is going to ruin the clemency that was so necessary to restore calm."[60] Repression for other reasons against Communist machinations required the government to demonstrate coherence. Auriol refused to have his presumed clemency toward collaborators contrasted with his harsh conduct toward striking workers, which led him to reject some appeals.[61] That said, the exercise of the pardoning power offered the government a way of attenuating some excesses and discreetly imposing a policy of indulgence it would have been unseemly to reveal publicly.

The question of amnesty, however, soon made its presence felt on the political agenda because of the support it received from the conservative and liberal right. This political current called for national reconciliation and pointed out that the country in danger needed all its forces to ward off the Communist menace. From 1948 on, moderates made amnesty a central element of their political platform. On March 14, 1948, the "banquet of a thousand" that assembled notably former members of parliament of the Third Republic who had been barred from elected office called for the abolition of special legislation and the abrogation of the ostracism they faced. Propagated by the right-wing press, the campaign for amnesty grew in magnitude in 1951, when an Action Committee for General Amnesty united all the organizations who supported that measure. Of course, Resistance figures tried to launch a counterattack against this offensive. In 1948 the Communists created the Association of Combatants for Liberty, which included such members as Yves Farge, Jean Cassou, and Emmanuel d'Astier de la Vigerie, which provoked in response the establishment of an Action Committee of the Resistance bringing together the non-Communists—General Cochet, Louis Marin, and Rémy Roure. Nonetheless, the idea was gaining ground. The Gaullists were no longer against it, and the Christian Democrats were favorably inclined. "It was both the rules of tolerance contained in human rights and the generous virtues of Christian forgiveness that motivated a position that had ethical as well as political intentions."[62]

A first step was taken on January 5, 1951. The law granted full amnesty to individuals sentenced to fewer than ten years of loss of rank (*dégradation nationale*). It limited the sanction of national disgrace (*indignité nationale*) to twenty years and amnestied minors under the age of twenty-one found guilty of collaboration, on condition that their sentences had been limited to a fine or imprisonment for fewer than five years. Sanctions for collaboration could be removed by decree if those concerned had been sentenced to fewer than three years or if their punishment, reduced to that length by pardon, had been completed by that date.

This precedent opened a breach into which the right plunged. Armed with its success in the 1951 elections, it also intended to use that weapon to marginalize a Communist Party frozen in Stalinist rigidity. The debate opened on July 11, 1952, and concluded with the passage of a generous law on August 6, 1953, which granted amnesty to minors (except when they had committed murder, rape, torture, or denunciation), as well as those sentenced to national disgrace. Collaboration and dealing with the enemy were granted the same leniency—if the prison term was fewer than fifteen years. In short, "in 1953, excluded from the amnesty were only individuals over the age of eighteen who had been responsible for torture, death, or deportation, those who had worked for enemy police or espionage services, and those over eighteen who had been sentenced in the first place to prison terms longer than twenty years."[63]

The debates on amnesty were disrupted by the trial in Bordeaux of participants in the massacre of Oradour-sur-Glane. Opening on January 12, 1953, it targeted twenty-one members of the SS, including fourteen from Alsace, twelve of whom could be considered as unwilling conscripts. The emotion stirred up by the trial was all the greater because a law of September 15, 1948, provided that conscripts had to prove that they had been enlisted under constraint and that they had not participated in the crimes for which they might be accused.[64] This law was swiftly amended in January 1953, as the trial was already in progress. Despite this, the verdict, delivered on February 13, sentenced the defendants to penalties ranging from five years in prison to thirteen years of hard labor, with the harshest sentences for defendants from Alsace.

Alsace was up in arms; it considered the penalties unjust because almost all the SS had been conscripted by force. An Action Committee for the Defense of the Honor of Alsace and of the Forced Conscripts asked:

Humble foot soldiers of the Empire, obscure sacrificial victims of 1870, dead in distant campaigns, buried beneath the crosses of the cemeteries of the Great War, abandoned by the rear-guard combats of 1940, victims of the Nazi camps, unwilling conscripts fallen on the Russian front, dead in the battles of the Liberation, heroes of Indochina, your complaint joins that of the living. Has Alsace not given enough? Why this new wound?[65]

The violence of the reactions prompted the government to hastily grant amnesty to the defendants from Alsace on February 18, 1953, provoking sorrow in the Limousin. For many years a poster placed at the entry to Oradour-sur-Glane listed the names of the 319 members of parliament who had voted in favor of the amnesty. This affair is not only a particularly horrible war crime, the responsibility for which falls on a foreign totalitarian empire. Through an uncontrollable concatenation of circumstances, it became a confrontation between two French provinces, both equally convinced that their cause was just, equally loyal to the memory of their dead, equally outraged that the extreme nature of their tragedy was not recognized: in one place the massacre of children, in the other forced service in an enemy army.[66]

Above all, the episode revealed the difficulties the government had to face in handling memorial disputes following World War II. But by favoring Alsace, it gave in to arguments not inspired by justice alone. The region was, to be sure, richer than the Limousin; it voted more correctly than red Limoges, a traditionally Socialist area that had also been penetrated by the Communist Party; and elected officials from the east engaged in "blackmail around separatism or ingratitude, depending on who one listened to [that led] the Republic in 1953 to open a new breach in the defense of the memory of the Resistance and of the martyrs of Nazism, amnesty for the defendants from Alsace."[67]

In any event, with the amnesty laws a page had been turned. Their first effect was to empty the jails. Forty thousand people were in prison in 1945; only 1,570 remained in 1952, 62 in 1956, and 19 in 1958.[68] Their political consequence was to minimize the magnitude of the tragedy by pointing out that some Frenchmen may have allowed themselves to be drawn into the cataclysm although they were not out-and-out traitors. This peacemaking approach, which healed the gaping wounds of the war and the Occupation, was adopted by other institutions. The members of the Conseil d'État—who had hardly been shining examples of courage during the dark years—dismantled in part what the judges of the Liberation had constructed. Appeals to the council enabled many who had been purged to secure reparation. Between 1945 and 1950 the percentage of sentences quashed was always more than half, ranging from 50 to 73 percent. It even exceeded 80 percent in 1957, an indication that the Republic had chosen pardon for offenses over the law of an eye for an eye.[69] On the one hand, those who had been found guilty could therefore have their rights restored, and formerly prominent figures in the French State could again run for office. On the other hand, the authorities maintained the opprobrium attached to collaborators and refused to consider them as combatants like any others. In 1946 the directeur de l'état civil confirmed that "the requests received by the service to regularize the status of the French who served in the LVF [Legion of French Volunteers against Bolshevism] or in enemy units can be treated neither as concerning soldiers nor as concerning civilian victims of the war. . . . Necessary precautions will be taken so that the indication "MPF" never be attributed [to them] and that no certificate of exoneration be delivered."[70]

While paying tribute to the heroes of the Resistance, the leaders of the Fourth Republic thus favored appeasement, at the risk of shocking the supporters of a less consensual view of the dark years. The shifting circumstances obviously explain this politics of memory. The onset and solidification of the cold war produced rearrangements that, at the time of the Soviet threat, made the split between resisters and collaborators inoperative. From then on, the opposition between Communists and non-Communists functioned in part as the organizing principle of political debate, leading some former members of the Resistance to ally with former Vichyites and foster the emergence of new majorities prefiguring the government of Antoine Pinay in 1952.

Communism, Is That the Enemy?

This new pattern explains the battle under the Fourth Republic between the party of Maurice Thorez and the governing parties. The PCF, as we have seen, fought to establish itself as the active wing of the Resistance. With no fear of exaggeration, a party training manual of 1949 asserted: "It can be said that without the Communist Party, the 'Party of the Martyrs,' there would have been no real French resistance and as a result, France, liberated entirely from outside, would in fact have lost its independence."[71] This image corresponded in part to reality but was also intended to obscure the meanders of the line followed between 1939 and 1941, and even past that date. The "Party of the 75,000 martyrs" therefore strove to present its combat as a single entity: the confrontations of the dark years were a continuation of the antifascist fight launched in the aftermath of the right-wing riots of February 6, 1934, and followed by the refusal to ratify the Munich accords. From this perspective the alleged call to resistance launched on June 10, 1940, had a peculiar history after 1947. Its celebration "well and truly had the purpose of substantiating the idea that the party as a whole had joined the Resistance as early as July 1940 and, launching an appeal 'on national soil,' had nothing for which to envy the Gaullists."[72]

Of course, not all Communists followed this approach, and many red members of the Resistance would have greatly preferred to have memory celebrate the combats and martyrs of the cause rather than justify the rash positions adopted at the outset of the conflict. There was in fact a latent war between two tendencies within the party. "Whereas some leaders—Marty, and above all Tillon—unceasingly glorified the Resistance by emphasizing armed struggle, the higher leadership took pains to justify its policies in 1939 and 1940."[73] It is true that the PCF was facing a complicated situation. World War II had produced a threefold trauma. The unnatural alliance between Hitler and Stalin undermined its ideological coherence; the relative loosening of the control exercised by the Comintern had led each party in 1940 and 1941 to conduct an adventurist policy with sometimes burdensome aftereffects (the request that *L'Humanité* be allowed to publish provides a good example); and the victories of the Soviet Union and the prestige enjoyed by the "Party of the 75,000 martyrs" had produced a profound sociological change in party activists. To maintain their power and ensure the cohesion of their organization, Maurice Thorez and Jacques Duclos therefore had to "offer to the newcomers a communist identity based on a few decisive criteria of conduct: 'proletarian internationalism' (unconditional support of the USSR), 'party spirit' (total loyalty to the leadership), 'class consciousness' (absolute priority of the class struggle over any other type of political combat, including patriotic combat)."[74] This line required that resisters "for whom Stalin was chiefly identified with Stalingrad, armed with their past and the recognition they enjoyed outside the party, not acquire a dangerous political autonomy based on the 'common' memory of their particular experience."[75]

As an indication of this problem, the PCF refrained from emphasizing in its publications the sacred legacy of the Resistance, unlike what had prevailed at the Liberation and would be repeated after 1958. "In both cases, it was the rivalry with General de Gaulle that explained the greater or lesser vigor of communist historical practice."[76] The special issue that the *Cahiers du Communisme* dedicated to "30 years of history of the PCF" in December 1950 contained no articles on the army of shadows. In the same vein, the first volumes of the collection *Mémorial-Exemples*, intended to commemorate the heroes of the Resistance, were pulped in 1949. "In the end, all these constraints produced a low-key language full of ambiguity, which fit well with the muffled battle going on behind the scenes between those who, generally without afterthoughts, wanted to honor the sacrifice of the martyrs and celebrate the communist saga, and those who were outside that adventure and saw it as potentially dangerous for their own power."[77] The expulsion of historic members of the Resistance—Charles Tillon, Auguste Lecœur, Georges Guingouin—further confirmed the suspicion in which the apparatus held leaders who could mobilize for their benefit a legitimacy different from the international consecration conferred by Moscow. In April 1950 a preliminary purge removed historic members of the Resistance (Marcel Prenant and Jean Chaintron). "They were replaced either by young people who had come out of the Resistance but were still very malleable, or by prewar leaders who, although they were the first victims of the repression of 1939–1940, had nonetheless escaped from the vicissitudes of the Gestapo, deportation, and the firing squad because they had been interned in Algeria from 1941 on."[78]

Although the party glorified the Resistance in a minor mode under the Fourth Republic, it did fight legal battles to establish that the resistance battle had begun in 1940, not in June 1941. It strove, for example, to have the title of deportee or internee of the Resistance granted to men who, imprisoned in 1940 under the Daladier legislation, had obviously not joined the army of shadows. Its organizations therefore struggled to bring about the elimination of "the unacceptable clause of the link between 'cause and effect' introduced into the implementation decree of the law of August 6, 1948, that makes it impossible for hundreds of former members of the Resistance, their widows, or parents of those who died in deportation or disappeared to have their rights recognized."[79]

This unsubtle strategy was of course intended to present the Communists as a body that had resisted the defeat. The FNDIRP, the government noted, considers that "individuals who, starting in June 1940 (or even before), had been active in distributing the party press, its leaflets, and the slogans of the Third International have performed acts of Resistance and should be recognized as meeting the requirements of the status of Deportees and Internees of the Resistance (DIR). . . . The National

Front has been covering the activities of its members since June 1, 1940, and has furnished them with attestations of cause and effect between acts of Resistance, particularly in the National Front in June 1940."[80] As a result, the Ministry of Veterans Affairs and the National Commission charged with rendering its verdict applied the letter of the law very strictly.

This severity was, to be sure, not reserved for Communists alone. The National Commission of Deportees and Internees of the Resistance (CNDIR) refused, for example, to confer the title of DIR on Jules Santini, who had provided a foreign woman of Jewish origin with a Frenchwoman's identity papers—"an act that does not meet the requirements . . . of the decree of March 25, 1949, that concerns only the fabrication of identity papers for members of the Resistance."[81] Overall, the Commission considered that in many files, "the facts alleged as being the basis for arrest: aiding Jews or STO evaders, insulting the head of state, membership in a secret society, evasion of the STO, anti-German demonstrations and statements, insults of the German authorities, ownership of a hunting rifle or a revolver, and so on, cannot be identified as acts characterized as resistance against the enemy."[82] The statutes adopted thus produced particularly rigorous legal effects, perpetuating the military conception of the Resistance and maintaining the distinction the legislature favored between "political deportees" and "deportees of the Resistance." "Any interpretation of the legislative texts that tended to abolish proof of resistance activity and the existence of a relationship between that activity and deportation or internment . . . would end up unifying the two qualifications within the framework of political deportees and internees" and would therefore contradict both the spirit and the letter of the law.[83]

But the authorities applied the statutes with particular severity against the Communists. First of all, the CNDIR rejected the argument of the PCF and took into consideration "only evidence establishing services performed after May 1941 . . . (in fact, it considered that Front National resistance had effectively begun only in June 1941, when the USSR entered the war)."[84] The MAC also deemed that a militant arrested for distributing leaflets under the Occupation and deported for that reason could not be granted the status of a deportee of the Resistance, because his action was primarily political. For instance, on September 12, 1951, considering the case of Sabatier, arrested on August 28, 1942, the National

Commission pointed out that the claimant "invoked as the basis for his arrest: 'public demonstration outside a factory with distribution of leaflets calling on workers to sabotage airplanes.' No document in the file establishes that the leaflets emanated from a body recognized by the military authorities," it stated to justify its rejection.[85] Similarly, the men executed in Châteaubriant in 1941 were given the status of political internees, not internees of the Resistance, in 1955.[86] For their part the miners of Nord-Pas-de-Calais, deported because of the strike launched in May and June 1941, had to wait until 1962 to secure recognition of their status as deportees of the Resistance, a wait also endured by Émile Pasquier:

In March 1942, after the arrest of Monsieur Émile Pasquier, former secretary of the gas and electricity workers' union, the special forces of the Prefecture of Police apprehended 65 people. Accused of violation of the decree of September 26, 1939, 52 of them, whose arrest was upheld, were brought before the special section of the Paris Court of Appeal, sentenced to various prison terms, interned, or deported. CELTON and LENOIR were executed by the enemy at Mont Valérien.

The claimants, most of whom are political and union militants . . . claim membership in the Special Combat Organization of the PCF, which gave rise to the FTPF.

All, or almost all, hold certificates of membership in the RIF (National Front) or the FFI (FTPF) delivered by the military authorities.

However, the National Commission of Deportees and Internees of the Resistance rejected almost all the claims presented to the status of deportees and internees of the Resistance . . . on the grounds that this was a purely political activity.[87]

This interpretation held sway until the mid-1950s, and it went along with some petty gestures. It is well known that following the assassination of Lieutenant Colonel Karl Hotz, head of the Feldkommandantur of Nantes, on October 20, 1941, the Germans demanded that fifty hostages be shot. In the end forty-eight men were executed—sixteen at the shooting range of Le Bèle in Nantes, five at the fort of Mont Valérien, and twenty-seven militants taken from the Choisel camp were shot in la Sablière quarry near Châteaubriant. The young Guy Môquet, son of a Communist member of parliament, the deputy Charles Michels, and the union organizer Jean-Pierre Timbaud were in this group. For obvious reasons Châteaubriant soon became a central site of memory for Communist commemoration of the dark years, which led the PCF to conceal the presence of two

Trotskyites in the list of victims. At the Liberation a provisional monument was designed to celebrate these martyrs. The unveiling ceremony on October 22, 1944, was characterized by its ecumenicalism, bringing together the Communists Fernand Grenier and Henri Rol-Tanguy, the Christian Democrat Maurice Schumann, and the then Radical-Socialist commissaire de la République, Michel Debré. When the permanent monument was unveiled on October 22, 1950, this peaceful coexistence was only a memory—the prefect was conspicuous by his absence.[88]

The sectarian, to say the least, approach of the CNDIR and the Ministry of Veterans Affairs followed, of course, a political logic. The general secretary of the FNDIR, Jean Debaumarchais, for instance, prided himself publicly "on having personally secured the rejection of 75 percent of the requests [for DIR cards] from members of the National Front . . . and having invalidated requests emanating from participants in the 'housewives' demonstrations' organized by Communist women against Vichy's rationing policy."[89]

France, it should be noted, held no monopoly on these maneuvers. Although the law of September 18, 1953, in the FRG indemnified the victims of Nazi persecution, article 4 of the law excluded "anyone who combats the liberal and democratic constitutional order," a provision that amounted to depriving Communist resisters of an indemnity, because they intended "to substitute a 'totalitarian' Communist regime for the capitalist, liberal, and democratic order."[90]

The government gradually lifted this ostracism. Individual measures sometimes attenuated the Commission's rigor. For example, François Tanguy-Prigent agreed—disregarding the facts, as we will see—to consider Guy Môquet as an internee of the Resistance in 1956, although the decision was not made official until 1962.[91] Most important, the Conseil d'État often reversed rejections, beginning in 1954.[92] Although it ratified the government's position in the Pasquier case (Le Moullac decision, May 15, 1952), in a decision of November 17, 1954, it considered that in the Sabatier case a cause-and-effect connection had been established between arrest and deportation. Similarly, the Pasquier decision of March 25, 1962, finally established the cause-and-effect link between Resistance activity and deportation. The Conseil d'État also decided in favor of the miners of the Nord by refusing to consider that "the strike at issue was inspired by work-related concerns" (Dubois decision, May 4, 1962). The government finally acquiesced, accepting from 1957 on "the coexistence of political action and resistance action," which led it to accept "requests that in the past would have found the petitioners to have been political internees and deportees."[93] Yet the road had been a long one.

The desire to bring together all of the French by cauterizing the wounds opened by the war as a general rule impelled the state to favor an integrating memory that covered up the misdeeds of the former supporters of Philippe Pétain. By subscribing to the demands of the old guard, the government, disregarding the recommendations of its administrative services, won over an electoral clientele, strengthened the vitality of associations, and attenuated the resentments—founded or unfounded—of a portion of the French population.

Burying the Dead

This joint management of memory had real advantages. It strengthened the fabric of associations and helped the memory of World War II to take root in the population. Of course, the state did not merely respond to the requests of associations. Loyal to the principles established after World War I, it ensured that those who died in combat would have decent graves. Families, for example, could ask for the bodies of their loved ones and have them reburied in a place of their choosing at the expense of the government—a choice adopted in sixty thousand cases, covering more than half the losses suffered during the campaign of 1940. The others, often soldiers of the empire, were buried in necropolises or on communal land.[94] Soldiers who had been identified were given individual graves; unknown or inseparable (as, for example, tank crews) soldiers were grouped together in ossuaries. But this work remained imperfect: "The services of the Armed Forces believe that in France, ten to fifteen percent of the soldiers who fell between 1939 and 1945 are still listed as missing or have not been identified."[95] In any event, between 1950 and 1975 the Ministry of Veterans Affairs undertook a program of assembling the bodies in national necropolises, such as Condé-Folie (3,279 bodies), Cambronne-lès-Ribécourt (2,129 bodies), and Chasselay. In 1940, 188 Senegalese infantrymen, after being separated from their white comrades in arms, had been massacred by German forces in that small town of the Rhône—evidence of the savage racism that could drive the members of the Wehrmacht. The secretary general of the Office of Veterans of the department, Jean Marchiani, decided to give these victims a decent grave by burying them on land purchased with his own money. This big-hearted man had an enclosure built imitating the sacred enclosures (or *tata*) where warriors who die in battle are buried. Unveiled on November 8, 1942, the site became a national necropolis in 1966.[96]

That said, the authorities were intent on separating the wheat from the chaff. Beginning in 1948, the right to a grave site was restricted to civilians whose death was "the consequence of an act voluntarily carried out to fight against the enemy and [for whom] the notice 'Died for France' [was] written on the death certificate." Unlike civilians in the Great War, the families of hostages, of STO conscripts who died in Germany, and bombing victims could therefore not demand that they be buried in military cemeteries, despite their death having been certified as "for France."[97] For example, in Rennes,

in the cemetery of the East, carefully separated compartments hold the graves of those who "died for France" in the First World War and the different categories of the Second: bombing victims, Allies, all with white crosses or steles, executed Resistance fighters in civilian graves that display patriotic symbols and make the spatial connection between the military section and the city of the ordinary dead. Whereas almost two-thirds of the combatants of 1940 rest in the military graves of national necropolises (the same proportion as for the veterans of 1914–1918), the need to discriminate between victims, and for families to categorize them, has brought it about that barely 1,500 Resistance fighters who "died for France" have been interred in a permanent grave, out of the thirty thousand whose status was honored by that title.[98]

Plaques, Steles, and Monuments

It was the associations, sometimes towns and villages, and very seldom the state that took charge of the politics of memory under the Fourth Republic, for reasons that were primarily material as then Interior Minister André Le Trocquer pointed out:

A number of decisions by municipal councils favoring the erection of monuments intended to commemorate the memory of the sacrifices made during the occupation and Liberation of the territory by soldiers and members of the Resistance who died for France, by the executed, and by the victims of German barbarity have been submitted to my services.

Without failing in any way to recognize the indispensable and sacred character of these expressions, designed to glorify the significant participation of France in the defense of the great principles that are the very genius of our civilization, it is important to point out that, with regard to the material aspects of the execution of the work and the use of raw materials, the extreme scarcity of materials and manpower from which the country is currently suffering makes it inopportune in the coming months to divert the economic resources that remain at our disposal to accomplish this purpose.

This is the reason for which I ask you to intervene in all these delicate questions in the most persuasive way to make sure that the public or private bodies that present requests of this kind to you understand and accept this point of view. . . .

However, if because of very special circumstances you find yourself faced by exceptional insistence, it will be up to you to use all your authority so that public tribute, even provisional, will take a concrete form other than that of a monument.

For example, in a case like that, a plaque dedicated "to those who died for France" in a town or village could be temporarily displayed.

Conversely, no particular difficulty of a material order seems to stand in the way of displaying individual commemorative plaques.[99]

In other words, the central government, far from encouraging the commemorative fervor of associations and municipalities, took pains to rein it in and control it for base economic reasons. In this spirit it entrusted prefects with the responsibility for "deciding by decree on proposals for the erection of monuments to the memory of French heroes of the Resistance or commemorating the glorious deeds of the 1939–1945 war, on the condition, however, that these monuments contain no sculptural element, such as statue, bust medallion, bas-relief, figure in the round, and so on,"[100] and that their cost not exceed five hundred thousand francs.[101]

The prefects, it seems, were vigilant. The prefecture of Moselle, for example, declared that "the erection of monuments dedicated to the dead of the 1939–1945 war is to be proscribed wherever there is already in the locality a monument to the dead of the 1914–1918 war. In that case, the names of the victims should be engraved on the already existing monument."[102] The state also established, in addition to a national commission, departmental commissions for commemorative monuments charged with informing the authorities. Their activities were apparently limited since they were abolished on September 28, 1953. The decree of April 12, 1946, finally, specified that the prefect set the conditions for the attribution of public tributes by setting up individual plaques for the French, and the minister of the interior acted on behalf of foreigners.[103]

These measures were not free of political concerns. Indeed, the government soon had to fight on two fronts. It was not long in determining that General de Gaulle and his movement, the Rassemblement du peuple français (RPF), were enemies because de Gaulle, to secure popular support for his combat, deliberately exploited the chords of memory. The creation of the RPF, for example, was allusively announced in Bruneval on March, 30, 1947—a town where a commando unit had seized pieces of a German radar installation during the night of February 27–28, 1942—before being officially unveiled on April 7, 1947, in Strasbourg, a city that had been liberated by General Leclerc in November 1944. Many RPF posters also evoked the saga of France Libre by displaying the Croix de Lorraine. It was "ubiquitous in the forms of Gaullist representation, from the décor of rallies to printed propaganda documents (the monumental podium at Vincennes in October 1947; the platform at Marseille in April 1948, and so on). . . . An axis was thereby established that identified the man of June 18 with France, the RPF with the Republic, and the Gaullist symbol with the tricolor flag."[104]

The Third Force governments soon grasped the danger. Starting in 1948, they strove to cool the ardor of local officials, although they avoided prohibiting naming some public roads after the first resister in France. In May 1948 a note recalled that precedent restricted "this form of tribute to figures on whom history has been able to speak and the memory of whom, sheltered from polemics, is not likely to divide public opinion."[105] The Socialist Jules Moch advocated distinguishing between tribute rendered to the liberator and approbation expressed for the political man—a Jesuitical distinction that was rather difficult to apply concretely. Starting in 1948, the government refrained from commemorating the Appeal because in the view of the SFIO June 18 had become a partisan date.[106] The authorities merely laid a wreath at the Arc de Triomphe and did not grant the state's resources to the demonstrations that de Gaulle honored with his presence. But this offensive approach was softened when the Gaullists themselves muted the recall of the dark years. From 1950 and 1951 on, the anti-Communist battle focused the attention of Gaullists in general and of their young activists in particular. The press and leaflets recited the theme, "criticizing the Communist infiltration of the unions, denouncing the intellectual, political, and military grip of Moscow in Europe, or deploring the support of the PFC for Indochinese or North Korean fighters."[107] In these circumstances the memory of the dark years and the cooperation that had grown up between Gaullists and Communists would have been out of place.

Third Force governments were thus faced with a complex situation: in fighting against two camps that drew their legitimacy in part from the struggle conducted under the Occupation, they labored to derive credit from the memory of the Resistance, and consequently they chose the path of discretion. This is why, as we have just seen, reluctant to engage in a monument-building policy, the state restricted itself to supervising or channeling local initiatives. Indeed, following the Liberation, it was municipalities and associations that multiplied tributes, placing commemorative plaques and erecting the first monuments. At a minimum, they engraved the names or placed plaques listing those who "died for France" in the Second World War on the monuments of the First.

That said, not all countries paid such tribute. For example, "Dutch memorials seldom bore . . . the list of those who 'died for the fatherland'";[108] the authorities chose to adopt "a coherent policy of anonymous heroism that promoted the image of a nation of heroes in which patriotic virtue was collective and indivisible."[109] Local French authorities did not take this path. On the contrary, they multiplied monuments in homage to the victims at the cost of considerable effort "since nearly three fourths of the steles, plaques, and monuments date from before 1950."[110] For example, the first monument dedicated to the deportation, built in the department of Yonne, was the result of a local initiative launched in 1946 by the president of the departmental Association of Political Deportees and Internees of Yonne. His efforts were crowned with success, and the head of state, Vincent Auriol, presided over the unveiling of this sculptural group on April 3, 1949.[111] Similarly the Memorial to the Unknown Jewish Martyr was the result, as we will see, of an initiative launched by Isaac Schneerson in the early 1950s.[112]

Honoring Soldiers

Commemorations in honor of soldiers were, as one might expect, selective. Plaques and steles honoring the combatants of 1940 remained rare outside of cemeteries and necropolises. To be sure, an unknown soldier was interred in the national necropolis of Notre-Dame-de-Lorette—a ceremony intended to reproduce the precedent of the Great War. But "this tomb generated no cult, and the veterans of 1940, like their elders of 1914–1918, rekindled the flame of the Arc de Triomphe."[113] Otherwise, tributes were rather meager. Only 450 plaques and steles commemorate the sacrifice of those who fell in 1940. Indeed, the crushing defeat suffered by the French armies in the course of a brief campaign that had lasted for only six weeks did not provide much encouragement to glorify the great deeds of the badly equipped and badly led troops who were unable to resist the "Blitzkrieg hurricane," to adopt the term of the historian Jean-Pierre Azéma. Consciously or unconsciously considered responsible for the defeat, the soldiers of 1940 were also suspected of harboring Pétainist sentiments. The French State had indeed continually exalted the sacrifice of these men, whose ordeal in the Stalags was a prelude, so it was claimed, to the redemption of a guilty France. Cut off from what was happening in France, many of them were still following the cult of the Marshal in 1943, when they were not worshiping at the altar of Pétainist virtues. Finally, the ordeals endured in prison camps, bitter as they may have been, could not be compared to the suffering endured by Jewish or Resistance deportees. On their return the prisoners of war could therefore embody neither the archetype of the hero—monopolized by the figure of the Resistance fighter—nor the model of the victim—symbolized by the political deportee. Overall, the veterans of the campaign of France had very little memorial space in which to recall the meaning and value of their combat. As a result, the powerful National Federation of Prisoners of War, with more than a million members in 1945, chose to pursue claims for compensation rather than a politics of memory. It was not until 1958 that the Federation erected a National Memorial of Captivity in the necropolis of Montauville, unveiled on July 2, 1961, by Minister of Veterans Affairs Raymond Triboulet.[114]

The soldiers who had begun fighting under the Croix de Lorraine in 1940, then from 1943 on under the tricolor, were a little better served.

Some steles, for example, recalled the role played by French troops in the liberation of the territory, not omitting the participation of troops from the colonies. Founded in 1946, the La Koumia association of veterans of Moroccan units, for example, unveiled a monument dedicated to the Tabors in Basse-sur-le-Rupt in the Vosges on May 13, 1954.[115] But memorial traces were fragmented and remained limited.

Honoring the STO Conscripts?

The National Federation of Labor Deportees agitated with some extravagance to recall the suffering of the STO conscripts. Presenting the former workers as resisters, it did not hesitate to identify their fate with the ordeal endured by prisoners of war or even by deportees. In April 1946 *Le Déporté du Travail*, for example, stated:

Yesterday, hunted by the Gestapo, by the police in the pay of the enemy, 750,000 French citizens were constrained and forced to leave their Fatherland, victims of odious blackmail and under threat of very severe sanctions. Their attitude, both on the national territory and in the foreign countries to which they were taken as captives, never ceased being a constant battle against foreign domination and fascism. The heroic conduct of some of them even brought them to torture camps where the Political Deportees were already held; others were executed; and we have more than fifty thousand dead to mourn.[116]

The FNDT presented statistics that were at the least fanciful: if it was to be believed, fifteen thousand workers had been executed or died in concentration camps in reprisal for an act of resistance, eighty thousand workers had been placed in disciplinary camps, and more than four thousand workers found guilty and interned for sabotage.[117]

In the same vein, the Federation soon adopted the symbols and rites of the world of deportation. At the festival celebrating the liberation in Isère in 1947, its Verpillers section put a Labor Deportation float in the parade representing "a miniature barracks like those that deportees had lived in in Germany."[118]

The authorities were not deaf to the siren song of the FNDT. In August 1946 the Communist minister of veterans and war victims intended to celebrate the return of the stone of Rethondes that had denounced "the criminal arrogance of the German Empire vanquished by the free peoples it had tried to enslave." During their retreat the Germans had seized this stele and duly transported it to Berlin along with the railway carriage in which the armistices of 1918 and 1940 had both been signed. Wanting to avoid a repetition of this experience, the Third Reich had destroyed the carriage, but pieces of the plaque survived, suggesting to Laurent Casanova the idea of a solemn ceremony.

Indeed, Compiègne offered an ideal setting for holding a peaceable ceremony. The clearing of Rethondes recalled the days of the Great War. Further, the Royallieu camp had been a point of departure for the Frontstalag camps and had then become an internment camp where the Germans assembled political detainees before deporting them. It therefore evoked the twofold memory of captivity and concentration-camp hell. Finally, on August 11, 1942, in the Compiègne station, a train carrying workers heading for forced labor in Germany crossed the first convoy of liberated prisoners of war returning to France.[119] Everything should therefore have come together to ensure the complete success of days placed under the aegis of ecumenicalism. On August 15 tribute was to be paid to the veterans of the Great War in the clearing of Rethondes. On the sixteenth, sporting events and an air show would embellish the celebrations with a festive touch, crowned in the evening by an open-air film showing. On the seventeenth, a ceremony dedicated to political deportees would be held at the Royallieu camp, followed in the barracks by a commemoration devoted to prisoners of war. At four in the afternoon the STO conscripts would be honored at the railroad station in anticipation of the arrival of the plaque at seven. "Twenty structures had been erected along the route from Paris to Compiègne, each one evoking a station of the cross that France had gone through during the Occupation. In front of the station five structures symbolized the five federations participating in the event. That of the labor deportees represented a worker chained by the Gestapo, crushed between the Nazi hammer and the anvil of the Milice."[120]

Unfortunately, nothing went as planned. Rain forced the cancellation of the air show. And the tribute paid to the STO conscripts provoked anger. Of course, Minister Laurent Casanova delivered an amiable speech: "Dear comrades, I wish to salute you like all the others, because you deserve it. You, too, to the best of your ability, and in the conditions in which you found yourselves, helped France to defend its honor against the Traitors."[121] Through the intermediary of Rémy Roure—a Resistance fighter honored with the Croix de la Libération and a deportee to Buchenwald—*Le Monde* on August 20, 1946, was less amiable:

> Glorifying the Labor Deportees means praising collaboration. There were conscripts forced, mostly for material reasons, to go to work in Germany for the Great Reich. They can be forgiven for that failing, provided it is not turned into heroism. There were many who were half-forced. There were volunteers. . . . No political deportee or deportee of the Resistance can accept that the 25,000 survivors of the camps of slow death be confused with those who collaborated, through their labor, with the enemy. The "conscripts" are among them, and the reasons for this demagogy are easy to understand.[122]

Times had changed, and the FNDT gradually had to trim its sails. To be sure, an unknown labor deportee was interred on June 22, 1947, in Père-Lachaise cemetery in a ceremony presided over by Minister of State Yvon Delbos. An "unknown labor deportee" was also interred in la Guillotière cemetery in Lyon in March 1953. And a few plaques were placed to recall the departure of these young men—few in number, however, for easily understood reasons.[123] Indeed, what memory should be associated with these ordinary men, neither heroes nor martyrs, whose memorial status turned out to be problematic? "Torn between the stereotypes of hero and traitor, their experience in the final analysis fit neither. For no other group is it more difficult to distinguish between individual and collective responsibility, between submission and force majeure."[124] As a consequence, the Federation chose to battle to negotiate for material advantages, while taking care to facilitate the reintegration of its constituents, rather than engaging itself on the perilous ground of the battle of memory.[125]

Celebrating Resistance Fighters

Conversely, and this is hardly surprising, the celebration of Resistance fighters dominated, "making up from fifty to eighty percent of the tributes."[126] Seldom exalting positive acts—although they might evoke certain sites of meetings, parachute drops, maquis groups, or places where the underground press was printed—they celebrated primarily the martyrs of the army of shadows, who died in battle, in internment camps, as deportees, or were massacred or executed. A modest plaque placed in Bourg-en-Bresse in 1954, for example, indicates that "in this printing shop were published the Resistance newspapers *Libération-Sud* and *Bir Hakeim*, as well as a number of clandestine leaflets."[127] The memorial and national necropolis of Chasseneuil-sur-Bonnieure, built at the end of World War II to celebrate the memory of the Resistance fighters of the Charente and Charente-Maritime, were unveiled in 1951 by President Auriol.

These tributes to the army of shadows under the Fourth Republic seem to many of the French to be the legitimate homage that the country was obliged to offer. We should note that the example of Germany suggests that this rule enshrines a French exception. In the FRG, resisters at first were considered traitors and cowards, including the conspirators of July 20, 1944.[128] In 1956, 49 percent of the Germans questioned refused to have the name Stauffenberg, the man who had placed the bomb in Hitler's bunker, given to a school—only 18 percent were in favor.[129] Similarly, the Allies did not encourage glorification of the resistance, the memory of which "would endanger the conception of the collective guilt of the German people that justified the occupation policy. It might also enable the Germans to formulate political demands, concerning sovereignty, for example, or territorial integrity."[130] It was thus not until the late 1950s that the German resistance acquired legitimacy: the men of July 20 became models presented to future officers of the Bundeswehr. But although five barracks were named after former resistance figures in 1961—such as the Graf-Stauffenberg-Kaserne in Sigmaringen—others were named after "heroes" of the Wehrmacht, such as Eduard Dietl (one of Hitler's favorite generals) in Füssen and Ludwig Kübler in Mittenwald (Kübler had been sentenced to death in absentia in Yugoslavia in 1947 for war crimes).[131] Honoring German resistance was thus far from a universal norm.

Forgetting the Jewish Deportees

In contrast, racial deportation was seldom given a place of honor. It is true that it occupied a secondary place in the hierarchy of merit that had been established in the aftermath of the war. Moreover, despite the deep trauma created by the racial persecutions carried out by the Nazis and by Vichy, the great majority of the Jews of France could not or did not wish to demand a separate status among all the other victims of the Occupation. Their concern at the time was rather to rejoin the national community from which they had been excluded. In the postwar state of mind, except for a minority, the genocide was not grasped in all its uniqueness, whether in political discourse, in commemorations, in purge trials, or in historiography.[132]

The fragmentation of the world of associations, moreover, did not facilitate the emergence of a consensual meaning. Indeed, the National Federation of Resistance and Patriot Deportees and Internees, in the Communist orbit, grouped together all former detainees and was little concerned with singling out the fate of the victims of anti-Semitic persecution. Bringing together Gaullists, Socialists, and Centrists, the National Federation of Deportees and Internees of the Resistance, as its name indicated, included only former members of the army of shadows. The Association of Female Deportees and Internees of the Resistance, in which the Resistance fighter Geneviève de Gaulle, the general's niece, was active from the beginning, was even more restrictive, accepting in its ranks only former members of movements or networks. Overall, and despite the establishment of associations of former camp inmates that could to a degree bear their memory (beginning with that of Auschwitz), the survivors of the extermination camps hardly had the resources to make their voices heard and to point out the uniqueness of their fate. "The associations of Jewish survivors were places for mutual aid and solidarity, with no ambition to speak to anyone other than those who had lived through the same experience. The rare efforts to bring the memory into the public square remained futile."[133]

As a consequence, this memory was at worst covered up, at best subsumed in the general picture sketched by the memory of the deportation considered as a whole. At the time, Buchenwald, not Auschwitz, symbolized the world of the concentration camps. The crematorium, rather than the gas chamber, represented the hell of the camps. And although the ashes of the victims were often taken from the very sites of the crime to be brought back to France and interred in countless vaults, they most often came from concentration camps, not from the Polish death camps. The ceremonies the FNDIRP initiated did not violate this rule: they chose to commemorate Buchenwald rather than Auschwitz:

The "thousand French pilgrims" who attended the vast international gathering held at Buchenwald for the ninth anniversary of its liberation on April 11 [1954] brought back "urns of memory" containing earth mixed with ashes. Mixed with the earth of all the camps, of all the major sites of the Resistance, of the martyred towns and villages of all the countries of Europe, these symbols of Buchenwald are distributed in 90 urns, one for each department of France. On May 8, at a solemn ceremony held at Paris City Hall, the delegates of the departments received their urns, accompanied by the pledge made at the ceremony.[134]

This denial of uniqueness was to some extent compensated by religious communities that soon erected steles and plaques in cemeteries and synagogues. In Bordeaux a group of tombstones forming a large plaque was set up in the courtyard of the synagogue, bearing the names of six hundred deportees on steles in the form of the Tables of the Law.[135] Associations also took some steps. The association of former Auschwitz internees, for example, carried an urn to Père-Lachaise cemetery on June 30, 1946, an initiative repeated in 1947 by the Consistoire Central des Israélites de France. Most notably, at the beginning of the 1950s Isaac Schneerson launched an initiative that was destined to flourish. In April 1943 Schneerson had laid the groundwork for the Center of Contemporary Jewish Documentation (CDJC) in Grenoble, an institution designed both to trace the fate of Jews during the dark years and to collect evidence enabling them to obtain reparation from the courts after the war. But, believing that memory was better transmitted through ritual than through chronicle, he suggested building in Paris the "Tomb of the Unknown Jewish Martyr," whose first stone was laid in 1953.[136] Unveiled on October 30, 1956, the site received on February 12, 1957, an urn containing ashes from the extermination camps that was placed under the flame of memory. This was the first memorial in the world to recall the memory of the Shoah.[137]

But these accomplishments were exceptions; the uniqueness of racial deportation was still usually omitted. The plaque set up in the former camp of Nexon in Haute-Vienne noted that "here were interned many patriots," forgetting that many Jews had also been imprisoned before being sent via Drancy to the death camps. Similarly, the monument dedicated to the victims of Auschwitz unveiled at Père-Lachaise on June 26, 1949, bore the epitaph "To the memory of the 180,000 men, women, and children deported from France, exterminated at Auschwitz, victims of Nazi barbarity." Aside from the fact that the statistics were erroneous, the dedication failed to mention that the dead were generally Jews.[138]

Overall, the authorities were unable to impose, assuming they wanted to, a single monumental policy, unlike the situation that prevailed in the Netherlands. That country had, it is true, been spared by World War I, which gave it greater freedom to conduct a memorial policy unencumbered by burdensome legacies. As a consequence, as early as October 15, 1945, the Dutch authorities submitted the construction of "monuments of war and peace in public places or visible from public places" to prior approval by the Minister of Education, Arts, and Sciences. The state thereby intended to ensure a faithful representation of the dark years, respect the regional and political balance of all components of the resistance, and verify the patriotic credentials of the initiators to avoid having dubious figures tarnish the image of the army of shadows. Sculptors, moreover, hoped to manage a demand that, without control, risked becoming explosive.[139] Unlike in France, the authorities exercised their prerogatives with firmness. In May 1946 the monument of Koog-aan-de-Zaan, built without authorization, was destroyed—a brutal message to both associations and local communities. Because of this, the fifteen hundred monuments erected in memory of the occupation are characterized by great uniformity. "References to military events are rare and the pictorial repertory is either symbolic—with abundant pigeons, torches, and broken swastikas—or taken from the repertory of social realism—with anonymous heroes."[140]

The Commemorative Activism of Associations

The associations took charge of establishing the first museums dedicated to World War II, including the museums dedicated to the Normandy landings in L'Aigle (1952) and Arromanches (1954), the first memorial at Struthof, and even some sites. Victim of a massacre carried out by the *Das Reich* division on June 10, 1944, the village of Oradour-sur-Glane in the Haute-Vienne was with remarkable speed officially classified as a historic monument. Passed unanimously without debate, the law was promulgated on May 10, 1946. The vestiges of Oradour, "implacable in their silence," would stand as "the indictment drawn up by history against

every regime of oppression and violence."[141] This law simply crowned a series of local initiatives promoted by Doctor Pierre Masfrand—a regional
notable—and the subprefect of Rochechouart, Guy Pauchou. By October
10, 1944, Doctor Masfrand had already requested that the ruins, symbol
of "heinous Nazi barbarism," be classified as a historic monument, and
for that purpose he set up an ecumenical Comité du Souvenir to do battle
against the central government. Indeed, the Ministry of Fine Arts thought
it absurd "that the ruins of a country town should be counted as a national
treasure."[142] The comparison of sites so cherished by esthetes as Mont-
Saint-Michel, the Sainte-Chapelle, or the cathedral of Chartres with the
ruins of Oradour was hardly to the advantage of the ruins. Moreover, the
chief architect Creuzot, noting that "the houses of Oradour are largely
made of puddle clay [a mixture of sand and clay] or mud wall, materials
that readily crumble and cannot be conserved in a ruined state," doubted
the site could be permanently preserved as it was. But the support given
the project as early as November 1944 by Minister of Education René Cap-
itant and Charles de Gaulle's cabinet swept away this resistance, especially
after the first among the French honored the little town in Limousin with
his presence on March 4, 1945, enabling Doctor Masfrand to ask Minister
of the Interior Adrien Tixier to move the proceedings along—a request
that was granted.[143]

The role adopted by the associations on the issue was thus decisive.
More surprisingly, they ended up managing some cemeteries, a preroga-
tive generally reserved for the state. For example, the national sepulchers
of Saint-Nizier (1947) and Vassieux (1948) in Vercors belong to the Association of the Pioneers of Vercors who manage and maintain them; the
authorities merely provide financial support.[144]

Associations also sometimes shaped the national calendar that the
government hesitated to organize. The National Day of Deportation, for
example, instituted by the law of April 14, 1954, was the result of an initiative launched by the Network of Memory, headed by Annette Christian-
Lazard, who was concerned "with preserving through consistent and perpetual actions the memory of the Deportation and of its martyrs, in all
their diversity."[145] This initiative, it should be noted, was supported neither
by the FNDIRP nor by the Jewish community. The state also struggled
to settle on its doctrine concerning the celebration of the surrender of

Nazi Germany. The law of May 7, 1946, provided that the commemoration of the victory would be "celebrated on May 8 each year if that day is a Sunday, and if not, the first Sunday after that date."[146] This discretion provoked anger among veterans who, primarily through the intervention of Gaullist and Communist members of parliament, proposed eight laws between 1947 and 1951 to make May 8 an official holiday.[147] But it was not until March 20, 1953, that the law, following an initiative by Communist members of parliament, supported by their Gaullist colleagues, conferred on May 8 the status of an official national holiday, a status it maintained until 1959. Celebrated by the authorities, June 18 nonetheless disappeared from the calendar. "Having become in the eyes of the Socialists, the property of a party, [it] was no longer officially commemorated; all that persisted were the traditional ceremonies organized by the Order of the Liberation and the associations of the Free French."[148] The Gaullists continued to celebrate June 18 on their own, "showing that it is in the fight against the institutions of the Fourth Republic that the legacy of June 18 lay. . . . For the men of the Fourth Republic, the intent was to demonstrate that the legacy of the Resistance could go on against, without, or despite de Gaulle."[149]

A Biased View of History

The indecision that led the state to rely on associations would have had no consequences had it not given rise to two perverse effects. First, the associations, far from presenting a united front that defended if not a common then at least a universal vision of World War II, favored a corporatist conception of the dark years. To maintain or broaden their base, they defended the interests of their constituents, taking care to preserve their territories while not really presenting a general interpretation of the conflict. This logic marked the debates of 1945. In the "commission charged with determining the status of combatant of the 1939–1945 war," the representative of the UFAC asserted, for example, that "all armed forces enlisted or not in a unit defined as a combat unit or having participated in war operations between September 3, 1939, and May 10, 1940, have the right to the status of combatant." The delegate of the FNPG, for his part, claimed that "the combatant's card should by right be attributed to all the former prisoners of war, except for those guilty of acts of collaboration," and so on.[150] These corporatist arguments were soon combined with political disputes; the associations did not hesitate to take sides in contemporary ideological debates. The alignment of some associations with the positions of the French Communist Party, for example, brought about splits, resignations, and ideological conflicts that, undermining the unity of combatants, prevented them from speaking in one voice.

Second, and most important, the activity of the associations and their parliamentary spokesmen was often carried out to the detriment of historical truth. For instance, the Action Committee of the Resistance, founded in 1948 to preserve the memory of the army of shadows in the face of a renaissance of Vichy, protested against the scandalous award of medals of the Resistance, forgetting that nominations had been suspended in 1948.[151]

Similarly, through legislative activism, the French Communist Party hoped to obscure the meanderings of the strategy it had followed between 1939 and 1941. So it demanded that militants interned before the defeat of 1940 be granted the status of political internees and that volunteers on the Republican side in the Spanish Civil War be considered combatants.[152] As Mademoiselle Villeneuve of the Association of Resistance and Patriot Deportees and Internees explained, "the volunteers in Spain who were the first to fight against the principles of Nazism did their national duty not a duty external to the Nation, because we must not forget that the Spanish Republican Army was fighting against an army equipped by the Germans. Consequently, these combatants began their national duty at that time."[153] Coming from all political perspectives, the members of parliament who proposed countless laws forgot the most elementary historical truths. To justify its demand that the combatant's card be attributed to all prisoners of war, one group of deputies identified captivity with resistance:

Not only was the detention of prisoners of war in German camps for five years a striking affirmation of the combat that France never gave up, but the prisoners were also able to truly turn their activity into a new combat. Sabotage, rebellion, acts to demoralize the enemy, were countless and were not without serious risk; the number of prisoners of war daily traversing the roads of Germany has been estimated at forty thousand in the year 1942, attempting escape toward a freedom that too few of them were able to reach.

This was, through the long years of exile, a persistent struggle that the enemy many times recognized and denounced in the press, and that it brutally repressed by sending a large number of our prisoners to reprisal camps and disciplinary companies and by resorting to collective measures of constraint and deprivation of all kinds.

This struggle led to even graver dangers, sometimes a concentration camp and usually death. Of the fifty thousand who died in captivity, how many owed their fate to the abuses and summary executions carried out by the enemy? And how can one be surprised that, evoking our prisoners in Germany, the appeals of the French Committee of National Liberation spoke of a "third front"? In addition to many individual acts, the struggle was led by the collective and concerted action of almost all the captives.[154]

Did these falsehoods really help serve the memory of their constituents?

In the Service of Europe?

Did the memory of the war in general and of the Resistance in particular play a role in the construction of Europe? According to the historian Pieter Lagrou, "There is general agreement that the idea of Europe was born simultaneously in the different European resistance movements which, aware of the consequences of extreme nationalism, imagined a unified Europe before it was established, notably through the treaties of Rome and Maastricht," a view from which he dissociates himself.[155] In fact, veterans "individually in large numbers came out in favor of a European federation in order to abolish war in Europe forever."[156] But this romantic vision hardly corresponded to reality. Many members of the Resistance, to begin with, shared a solid hatred for Germany and had no intention of fostering its recovery. Moreover, the divisions engendered by the cold war complicated the situation by proposing antagonistic visions of the construction of Europe. Some rejected a Europe limited to the countries of the West alone, which, they argued, would be a betrayal of the antifascist ideal. Others, in contrast, saw in a "little" Western Europe a way of fighting against Communist totalitarianism. So the Communists mobilized the memory of Oradour-sur-Glane to oppose the European Defense Community (CED) and later German rearmament. Christian Pineau, in contrast, drew a radically different lesson from history:

With many of my comrades, I spent two years in a cell in Lyon and in a deportation camp. That means I suffered in Germany. Once again, I was not the only one, but among those who have come back I have noticed two tendencies. First there are those who have kept hatred in their hearts and, if not a desire for revenge, at least a profound revulsion against any future cooperation with Germany. I understand them, for suffering can engender feelings of that kind. For my part, the lesson of these ordeals was something entirely different. What I wish for is not revenge in any form but that we never again in our history have the occasion to experience these detention camps.[157]

The former deportees in the Socialist group in parliament were generally in favor of the CED (eight out of eleven), whereas prisoners of war were inclined to be opposed (eleven out of sixteen). Léon Boutbien considered that "the ideas of hereditary enemies and eternal Germanic souls should be relegated to the museum of nationalist mythology cherished by Barrès and the pitiful Maurras." But in 1955 Gaston Charlet judged the German people "infected by the Nazi virus."[158] Overall,

each one of these European orders and each one of these interpretations was thoroughly compatible with the reassertion of national sovereignty and the patriotic commemoration of the war. European myths and national myths were mutually reinforcing. On either side of the iron curtain, antifascist or antitotalitarian speeches served as templates for new nationalistic speeches, with the same heroes and the same martyrs. A European commemoration was not established at the expense of national commemorations: it served as a strategy of consolidation.[159]

Presenting the memory of the war as the matrix for the construction of Europe thus turns out to be at least an exaggeration—with one qualification. The Fourth Republic avoided reminding the West German authorities of the crimes committed by Nazi Germany while simultaneously masking the responsibilities of the Vichy regime. The National Defense delegate, for example, demanded that Alain Resnais eliminate from his 1955 documentary *Night and Fog* "the silhouette of the gendarme guarding the Pithiviers camp."[160] And the film, which was being shown at the Cannes Festival, was withdrawn from official competition at the last minute so as not to "offend the sensitivity of a participating country," explained Maurice Lemaire, junior minister of industry and commerce. In response to the feelings stirred up by this censorship, the minister nevertheless had it shown in the Festival Palace on the Day of Deportation.

The memory of the war should not be allowed to undermine the Franco-German rapprochement begun with the European Coal and Steel Community (CECA) in 1950, later consecrated by the Treaty of Rome. In the end the reference to the dark years served to support both the advocates of a Little Europe and its detractors. So much so that one might even reverse perspectives. Did the construction of Europe not deeply change the contours of the memory of World War II by calling on memory to support the march toward the unity of the Old Continent?

The Limits of Scholarly Memory

The government gave France an original organization that laid the groundwork for a scientific history of the conflict (long identified with the works of Henri Michel) by merging the Commission of the History of the Occupation and Liberation of France (established October 20, 1944) with the Committee for the History of the War (established June 6, 1945), a merger that produced the Committee for the History of World War II in December 1951.[161] The importance of this episode, however, should not be overestimated. Quantitatively, to begin with, books dealing with the army of shadows were far from abundant. More than 350 titles did appear between 1944 and 1951, but they were "for the most part testimony, 'books of immediate history' . . . whereas general pictures were rare and real studies belated."[162] Furthermore, very few books on the subject were published between 1951 and 1957. The major leaders were silent, with rare exceptions, including Charles de Gaulle. The Communists did not cultivate the legend, and the underground fighters fell into oblivion. In other words scholarly memory neither supported nor rectified popular memory or the memorial policies followed by participants, primarily the associations.

To be sure, by giving the associations free rein, the government made it possible for a vivid memory of the war to take root; this memory defended primarily the heroes of the Resistance and secondarily the soldiers, while it avoided fanning the flames of hatred among veterans of the two camps. But, assuming it wanted to, the government was unable to prevent dangerous excesses: memory became balkanized and politicized, the preserve of corporatism, and over time it moved away from historical truth. And the state in no way countered this development by speaking clearly about World War II. For example, the surrender of May 8, celebrated in 1946, forgotten from 1947 to 1953, was again officially commemorated only between 1954 and 1958. In 1954 Irène de Lipkowski and Henri Michel presented a major project for a museum of the Resistance, but it struggled to see the light of day.[163] The Fourth Republic did not place the development of museums at the top of its list of priorities. Out of the 204 existing structures, fewer than twenty were built between 1940 and 1959—a particularly small number.[164] Similarly, neither the central administration nor the municipalities followed in the footsteps of the Liberation—they stopped naming public thoroughfares after Resistance fighters. Finally, the war was not in the school curriculum, despite pleas from former combatants. In 1953 the Rhine and Danube Association demanded "immediate action to have school textbooks give proper space to the participation of the First French Army in the victory."[165] The plea went unheeded.

Partisan Divisions

This lack of activity on the part of the authorities was inadequately compensated for by the activism of the associations. They fought to preserve or conquer their rights and succeeded in the early years at least in partially organizing the memorial space. But they were unable to impose a memory that if not unique was at least unifying because they themselves were engaged in political debate.

The Communist galaxy vigorously embraced the cause of the Soviet Union, joining campaigns to defend peace, fighting against the CED and German rearmament. The cold war thus ended up fragmenting the associations who managed only infrequently to maintain their unity. These splits affected the deportees. In 1948 the ADIR asked Klement Gottwald, the president of Communist Czechoslovakia, to pardon a former female deportee. Marie-Claude Vaillant-Couturier then resigned from the board of directors and the administration, considering that it was outside the association's function to adopt such a position. In 1950 the same organization agreed to participate in an investigation of the crimes of the concentration camp system launched by David Rousset. Some members were troubled but agreed to have the ADIR participate in the work, provided it examined, in addition to the Gulag, other systems of internment, notably in Greece and Spain.[166] Similarly, the association of former inmates of Auschwitz came out in opposition to the CED, leading to the resignation of some of its members who thought the association was adopting Communist positions.[167] In 1949 Father Riquet refused to participate in a pro-Soviet congress for peace and supported David Rousset. He then left the FNDIRP and, with his friends, joined with the FNDIR in the National Union of Associations of Deportees, Internees, and Families of the Missing (UNADIF).[168] The FNDIRP remained faithful to its pro-Soviet position. Supporting the Stockholm Appeal, it denounced the repression that followed hostile demonstrations against General Matthew Ridgway, then opposed the CED, and called for a demonstration in Paris on February 15, 1951, with the slogan "No Nazis in Paris."[169]

The prisoners' associations were not spared from these debates. In October 1948 an eminent leader of the FNPG, Raymond Bossus, denounced the diktat of the Marshall Plan. "The Prisoners of War, Veterans who experienced the ravages of the policy of Kollaboration, will join the ranks of all the French who wish for the independence of France and for peace. . . . By supporting the friends and defenders of peace and by condemning the warmongers who are also the enemies of freedom, they will demonstrate that they cannot be counted on to make war against their liberators."[170] These positions, adopted by the departmental association of Seine, were disputed by the leadership, who demanded that the pro-Communist minority submit or resign. The dissidence fizzled out. At the Aix-les-Bains congress, April 13–16, 1950, the firmness of the leadership was approved by 93 percent of the delegates, leading to the removal of federal responsibilities from the minority.[171]

Finally, the Algerian War engendered deep divisions.

The Algerian War: A Mirror of the Dark Years?

The memory of World War II provided a frame of reference making it possible to identify the conflict that pitted the Algerian nationalists against the conscripts dispatched from metropolitan France with the struggle in the clandestine darkness between the Resistance and the German occupiers. By making wide use of torture, the French army strengthened both the reality and the value of a parallelism that was quick to identify the *paras* of General Massu with the SS of Reichsführer Himmler.

The forces on the ground made wide use of the comparison. The creation of the National Liberation Front (FLN), the National Council of the Algerian Revolution (CNRA), and the Provisional Government of the Algerian Revolution (GPRA) recalled the glorious days of war and Gaullism. The supporters of French Algeria were not far behind. For instance, Jean Moulin's successor, Georges Bidault, backed by the Resistance figure Jacques Soustelle, reenacted the clandestine saga by resurrecting in 1962 an ephemeral National Council of the Resistance intended to maintain the rights of Paris over the southern shore of the Mediterranean.

Far from being merely a propaganda weapon, this association was felt deeply by the various participants. Indeed, many of the French came to support the cause of Algerian independence for two principal reasons. First and foremost they rejected torture, which recalled the dark period of the Occupation. The geopolitical specialist Gérard Chaliand recalled: "For us, that is, the children of the Republic, it was a fantastic shock. The idea that the French army engaged in torture was for us an extraordinarily astonishing and revolting thing. For us, the torturers, according to what we had been taught, were the Nazis, the fascists . . . and not at all the democratic armies."[172] And the historian Henri-Irénée Marrou explained at the time: "I address all teachers who are like me educators, who like me have children and grandchildren: we must be able to speak to them without being covered by the humiliation of Oradour and the Nuremberg trials; we must reread to them the beautiful pages of our classics about the love of country, about our France, 'patron and witness (and often martyr) of freedom in the world.'"[173]

As an aggravating circumstance,

if the comparison with the Vichy regime was so insistent for the various participants, politicians, associations, or simple citizens, this was also because certain connections appeared between these two periods of recent history. The career of the high-level official Maurice Papon seemed an obvious example, making it possible to point out the continuity between official discriminatory practices instituted by the state against the Jews under Vichy (independently of any German demand) and those against the Algerians. That an authoritarian regime and a republican regime were able to follow policies that seemed similar in spirit was enough to cause disquiet and uneasiness.[174]

Moreover, despite or perhaps because of the coming to power of General de Gaulle, the fear of a disappearance of republican forms inspired many commentators. Jean-Paul Sartre, for example, asserted in 1960: "For the Algerian War has corrupted this country. The gradual dwindling of freedom, the disappearance of political life, the spread of torture, the permanent insurrection of military power against civilian power, mark an evolution that can without exaggeration be called fascist."[175] To be sure, the fear of dictatorship had many other sources; but the memory of World War II carried a good deal of weight.

In the second place, many participants believed in the right of peoples to self-determination, a principle that the Atlantic Charter had solemnly reaffirmed. In their view the Algerian rebels were conducting a fight identical to the one the Resistance fighters had led under the German boot to preserve national independence. But the supporters of French Algeria turned these arguments to their benefit. As a result all tendencies used "the same procedure to justify themselves and discredit their adversaries."[176] Suspecting the Algerian nationalists of having sought the support of the Third Reich during World War II, many political leaders did not hesitate to identify them with Nazis. On May 11, 1945, discussing the Sétif uprising three days earlier, Governor General Yves Chataigneau, for example, stated that "all steps have been taken for the Hitlerite terrorists to be mercilessly punished and order definitively restored."[177] Influenced by the proximity of the Occupation, this analysis, however, soon disappeared. Subsequently, the supporters of French Algeria situated their combat as a direct continuation of the commitments made during the Occupation, or even World War I, considering that giving away the three Algerian departments amounted to a resumption of the policies of surrender carried out by France, from Munich to the June 1940 armistice. Philippe Barrès, for example, declared: "The France that twice liquidated, in 1917 and 1944, the defeatism orchestrated by Germany is not today going to give in to the defeatism orchestrated by the FLN."[178] And Jacques Soustelle asserted: "From 1940 to 1944, I was among those who stubbornly and despite everything refused to surrender, and I have not changed. If now France is called upon, in the name of a medieval totalitarianism, to give up not only Algeria but in fact itself, I will not be an accomplice."[179] Whether they wanted to defend Christian Europe or preserve the empire under the French flag, the supporters of a greater France drew frequently from the repertory of the dark years to support their arguments.

But starting in 1956, this argument lost steam. Following the setbacks in Indochina, officers chose to brandish the specter of subversive and revolutionary warfare rather than waving the scarecrow of Nazism. Attributing the events in Algeria to the hand of Moscow, they weakened the identification of the independence fighters with Nazi Germany, particularly because in doing so they introduced anti-Communism into their argument, a reference that could only divide the Resistance camp. The FLN also oscillated, sometimes presenting its combat as a war of liberation, sometimes as a revolution, a view that could not coincide with the interpretive frameworks bequeathed by World War II.[180]

In any event the memory of World War II was widely exploited by all participants who intervened in the debate about the Algerian War. Within parties, as within associations, it provoked deep splits. In 1962 Anise Postel-Vinay, for example, resigned from the board and the administration of the ADIR, considering that the organization "which had judged it in conformity with its mandate to worry about the conditions of interrogation in the USSR, China, and Greece was qualified to follow closely what its delegates had discovered with horror in Algeria." The leadership replied: "The moral and humanitarian aspect in this circumstance cannot be dissociated from political support, which would lead the organization to take a position far from corresponding to the general feeling of all."[181]

This observation confirms, if confirmation is necessary, the multiplicity of meanings of a memory that opposing forces could also mobilize and illustrates the deep ambivalence of that memory. The dark years had certainly left their imprint on the French, leading them to shape their conduct according to their lived experience; but those years were also exploited by propaganda according to a logic that aimed to define collective interpretive frameworks. By this yardstick, memory was as much empirical experience emanating from the mass as it was an ideological model forged by the summit, a personal or family memory as much as it was a collective memory.

The memory of World War II in general and of the Resistance in particular was thus incapable of providing a consensual interpretive framework, which is hardly surprising. The Resistance had brought together individuals from the most diverse political backgrounds. In the clandestine darkness it had demonstrated admirable democratic vitality that rallying to General de Gaulle had done nothing to stifle. It was futile to hope that the unity celebrated at the Liberation would persist. In truth, it would have been able to survive only by becoming a moral tribunal, placing itself above the fray and issuing rejections while not claiming the right to formulate programs. "The solidarity of the shaken," wrote the philosopher Jan Patocka, "will not offer positive programs but will speak, like Socrates' *daimonion*, in warnings and prohibitions. It can and must create a spiritual authority, become a spiritual power that could drive the warring world to some restraint, rendering some acts and measures impossible."[182] The members of the Resistance as a whole could never ratify that austere line. Their commitment often derived from a democratic demand that impelled them to participate in public debate. Why, once peace had come, would they abdicate that right? They therefore entered the arena, paying for their intervention with the price of division and thereby barring themselves from proposing a single meaning for World War II. And through its policies, the state could not palliate that lack.

As a result, by refusing to speak a language of truth (about Vichy, for example) while being deaf to the suffering of some categories (the victims of the Shoah above all), the Fourth Republic contributed little to laying the foundations for a national memory that would carry meaning, in which the French as a whole would have been able, if not to restore the national values battered by four years of occupation, at least to reflect on the foundations of a civic community. From this perspective this short-sighted policy was a harbinger of rough times ahead.

CHAPTER 3

The Gaullist Republic,
a Golden Age? (1958–1969)

"I flew toward the complicated East with simple ideas." This lapidary formula that the general used on his way to disentangling the Middle Eastern mess in 1941 sums up to a large extent the politics of memory the government followed between 1958 and 1969. It was nonetheless subject to a degree of bias.

Debarment

Armed with the restored authority of the state, the regime of the Fifth Republic intended to put a brake on the demands made by veterans. For example, General de Gaulle, judging that "veterans should not be considered 'beggars,'"[1] halted the abusive extension of rights. In 1958 he abrogated the combatant's pension (restored in 1960), debarred further award of the titles of *resister* and *deportee*, and abolished the Ordre du Mérite Combattant. It should be pointed out that this policy was supported by the Ministry of Defense, which refused to support the claims of Resistance associations, on the basis of the following arguments:

(1) The time limits [for filing claims] initially adopted were periodically extended from 1948 to 1951. They were brought to the attention of the public in a timely manner. Notification of each change was made widely available in the press, on the radio, and on posters in town halls and police stations. Resistance associations, for their part, widely circulated these provisions.

With particular reference to the FFI, it should be noted that debarment was requested by the authorized representatives of their movement in the National Commission for Certification of FFI Ranks, the only official consultative body authorized to offer advice on the question. In 1951 that commission determined that there were grounds to set a definitive closing date for the filing of requests for certification; the period of six years following the Liberation had been judged sufficient to collect the affidavits to be produced in support of requests.

(2) The removal of this bar might enable a limited number of real but negligent resisters to restore their potential rights, but it would have the effect of provoking many collective or individual requests tending toward the recognition of new movements (or bodies) of resistance or new resisters. It would also be a way for those whose requests had been rejected to present a new claim.

(3) Liberation occurred more than sixteen years ago, and it is quite obvious that the further one gets from events, the more difficult it is to gather the necessary testimony and affidavits. Evidence that in many cases it was impossible to produce before the closing date (1951) will be no easier to produce in the future. It is therefore legitimate to fear the appearance of fraud that it would be difficult to detect.

(4) It may be granted that members of various RIF networks who took up arms had their services, rightly, validated as military service. But it would not be equitable that the majority of other members whose activities of a military character are practically indeterminable sixteen years after the Liberation be allowed to benefit from the same advantages.

(5) The removal of the bar would lead to the reestablishment at different levels of administrative and supervisory bodies that have been dissolved.

(6) Finally, challenging the time limitations for applicants for the national FFI certificate would not fail to bring about similar demands from other "major families" of the R[esistance] (FFC, DIR, etc.), which would multiply difficulties and broaden the scope of the arguments set forth in the preceding paragraphs.

In conclusion, the [Personnel Department of the Army] has determined that the time limitation now in force for the recognition of FFI services should be upheld.[2]

In other words, the Army Personnel Department feared that if it relaxed the time limits, it would witness a flood of claims from resisters with questionable war records. They had absolutely no intention of opening that Pandora's box.

A Builder-President

The Gaullist government also carried out a monument-building policy that, if not ambitious, was at least coherent; it was defined by the General Commission for Commemorative Monuments of the World Wars and the Resistance, an organization established in 1960 and presided by General de Larminat. As an indication of the interest he had in this question, in a letter to Prime Minister Michel Debré on March 21, 1959, Charles de Gaulle explained that

the absence of a competent body to stimulate and coordinate the building and maintenance of commemorative monuments to the dead of the two wars would limit government participation in this area to approval by the Minister of the Interior, which seems to me insufficient.

I wish to have established under the authority of the Minister of Veterans Affairs an "Inspection Service for Commemorative Monuments of the Two Wars and the Resistance" under the direction of General de Larminat.[3]

An order of June 24, 1960, appointed General Larminat to office and charged him with

a/ Supervising the maintenance of the Commemorative Monuments already erected by the French Government or French Communities . . . [and to] propose or prompt if need be the measures needed for their restoration.

b/ Supervise the maintenance of Monuments erected on French soil by Governments or communities of former allies. . . .

c/ Coordinate efforts with respect to the erection of new monuments, stimulate the appropriate initiatives and competitions, [and] suggest to the Minister measures beyond the scope of private initiatives.[4]

In the same vein, the state tightened its control over the erection of monuments and over public tributes by requiring prior approval, tempered by the "procedure of tacit approval with regard to the deliberations of municipal councils."[5] "This arrangement," explained Interior Minister Raymond Marcellin, "is obviously intended to institute a system of control that will make it possible not only to eliminate inopportune choices but also to avoid having the notion of public tribute lose a great deal of its value following an improper use of this procedure."[6] The state, in other words, had given itself the means to conduct a coherent memorial and commemorative policy that ended up, however, divesting members of parliament of their role. The government reversed the status of May 8 as a public holiday by decree; and the transfer of the remains of Jean Moulin to the Panthéon was also decided on without legislative participation.[7]

Now able to impose its views, the state, under the auspices of the General Commission, inaugurated an ambitious policy and launched a series of construction projects—Museum of the Provence Landing at Mont Faron, Museum of the Order of Liberation, Memorial of Struthof, Memorial of the Deportation on the île de la Cité, not to mention the rooms dedicated to World War II established in the Museum of the Army. "For the first time, the government is going to get involved in patriotic museography."[8] Along the same lines, the government supported provincial initiatives, such as the Museum of the Armistice in Compiègne (1962), and Museums of the Resistance that were established in Glières (1963), Grenoble (1966), and Lyon and Bordeaux (1967). In all, more than twenty museums were established between 1960 and 1969 (out of a total of 204 created between 1945 and 2008). A substantial increase in funds granted to ceremonies and commemorations followed along. In constant francs, state expenses increased from 88,383 francs in 1959 to 7,601,147 francs in 1964, and reached 8,977,986 francs in 1968.[9]

A Certain View of the War

These accomplishments did not contradict the major Gaullist positions. For one thing, the museums celebrated first and foremost the Free French Forces and the internal Resistance, in triumphant (Order of the Liberation) or martyred (Struthof, île de la Cité) forms. The government, in other words, did not recognize the special status of the Shoah, presenting Resistance and political deportation in the same spaces. Retrospectively, Prime Minister Michel Debré explained:

To the extent that they suffered in the same way, that's normal. It may not be a good thing, but it's a normal thing. This monument [on the île de la Cité] commemorates suffering rather than the causes of suffering. The cause of suffering, I agree, was different. And often, even so, I reproached myself for mixing the two things. But the misfortune and sorrow were identical and the common commemoration therefore is still justified.[10]

The only nuance to this attitude was that the government contemplated attenuating the contrast between political and Resistance deportees—a request that had been made by veterans' associations. At a meeting of the commission set up by Veterans Affairs Minister Alexandre Sanguinetti, the Communist Marcel Paul stated:

It would be a great relief to the families if we could agree that families of political and Resistance deportees should be treated in the same way, and I would say, with the same deference. The dead suffered in the same conditions; they all paid with their lives. In the great tragedy, the families suffered and are still suffering just as intensely. We very strongly wish that equality in this area be complete.[11]

He had adopted the argument traditionally put forward by the FNDIRP: "We speak of the 'merits' of Resistance deportees compared to political deportees, or else we compare the 'suffering' of internees with that of deportees. These arguments are totally extraneous to the principle of the right to reparation: people are not indemnified according to merit but according to the harm suffered."[12] The government backpedaled in the end but for financial not ideological reasons, as the minister's chief of staff acknowledged: "Morally, we are completely persuaded; unfortunately, we are constrained by financial imperatives."[13] In 1966 the cost had been estimated at 60.48 million francs.[14] But deportees and internees did obtain relaxation of time limitations in 1961, and again in 1965, thanks to the energy of Minister of Veterans Affairs Raymond Triboulet, who was determined to "persevere on the path that has been opened . . . for requests of other 1939–1945 war titles, particularly that of Voluntary Combatant of the Resistance."[15]

In contrast, the Gaullist regime maintained its traditional conception of the Resistance as a purely military phenomenon that united all of the French. Many films made between 1959 and 1969 "helped to firmly root in the fictional realm the image of a French population almost unanimously hostile to the occupying power and standing in fundamental solidarity with the Resistance."[16]

This view inspired for instance the quasi-official film *Is Paris Burning?* (1964), which presents the liberation of the City of Light as an enterprise involving Gaullists and Communists in a constructive spirit, united in the struggle against the invader—although the former are given more prominence than the latter. "Limitation of the forces of the Resistance to Gaullists and Communists alone and blatant lack of realism badly concealing the imbalance between the two camps are the two components of *Is Paris Burning?*"[17] The director had been so accommodating as to eliminate Georges Bidault from the screen because he was guilty of having defended l'Algérie française, and the former Communist Maurice Kriegel-Valrimont, who was a victim of the great purge of 1960. The Gaullist government thus reduced the Resistance to a face-to-face opposition between Gaullists and Communists, a view that excluded the other major Resistance movements—Combat, the Organisation Civile et Militaire (OCM), and Défense de la France, to mention only them. Similarly, *La grande vadrouille* (1966), a long-running national hit, presents the France of the dark years in bright colors. In their escapades Bourvil and Louis de Funès encounter no collaborators—all of the French, from hotel keeper to nuns, do their best to help them. Despite the class barrier, the two men cooperate to save an English airman with the greatest of ease because the Germans, cartoonishly stupid, cannot manage to arrest them. The only divergence from the Gaullist legend is the fact that the heroes dream of nothing but saving their skin by crossing the demarcation line, which makes Vichy into a space of freedom, a "free zone" in the full sense of the word.

The government also tended to identify the army of shadows with Gaullism, an ambition lying behind the transfer of Jean Moulin's remains to the Panthéon in 1964, as the speech by André Malraux suggested: "To attribute little importance to so-called political opinions, when the nation was in mortal peril . . . to see in the unity of the Resistance the most important means of fighting for the unity of the nation—to hold these views was perhaps to affirm what has since been called Gaullism. It was certainly to proclaim the survival of France."[18] To be sure, the ceremony, which took place in two stages, distinguished "between the commemoration of a unified resistance and the commemoration of the roots of Gaullism, which now traced its origins back to World War II and sought to identify itself with France in its entirety."[19] It is nonetheless true that the Gaullist government was seizing a legacy: "The man who in 1943, under the orders of the General, was 'above' parties and movements, had to serve the same cause twenty years later when France was once again fighting for its national independence."[20]

A Scholarly History That Raised Few Questions

This memorial policy was seldom challenged by scholarly memory. The period was, of course, marked by a historiographical revival epitomized by the "Esprit de la Résistance" series published by the Presses Universitaires de France under the direction of Henri Michel. But the books published in this series—centered on Resistance movements (OCM, Défense de la France, Combat), Gaullist institutions such as the Conseil national de la Résistance (CNR), or "the currents of thought in the Resistance"—were not very critical of the ruling mythologies. For instance, the authors paid little attention to the *maréchaliste* or even Pétainist inclinations of some organizations (Combat or Défense de la France) and hardly analyzed them. The tensions between London and the internal Resistance were also attenuated, which reinforced the image of a Resistance France unanimous in its refusal to submit. The process of joining the Resistance provoked little interest, and the sociology of organizations took up, at most, a few pages.

Several factors explain why the process of historicization gave way before the power of myth. First, almost all writers, following the example of Arthur Calmette, Henri Michel, and Daniel Mayer, had actively participated in the adventure of the Resistance, which did little to guarantee a healthy critical distance. The Resistance, moreover, was such a powerful myth that historians were wary of chipping away at it. A writer as shrewd as Lucien Febvre presented a curious argument:

Historians will say what they can say, being men of the year 2000, living in the climate of the year 2000. . . . All the more reason for us to provide them . . . in all honesty, with our version of events, which they will of course interpret in a different way. . . . And we cannot say whether they are right and we are wrong. At least our version of events is based on living evidence. It is countersigned by thousands of sacrifices.[21]

Coming from a major historian, the advice had a certain piquancy. But it explained the fact that historians had internalized limitations to the extent that they based their investigations on witnesses more than on archives. It is true that researchers were barred from collections of archives. But they showed little determination in exploring private collections, choosing to rely on the precious words of veterans. As a form of the pursuit of knowledge, history can shape memory only if it contradicts memory's predicates. Before the 1970s it tended rather to reinforce them.

School curricula were not exempt from this rule. World War II was taught for the first time in the final year of the lycée in 1962–1963, following a decision made in 1959—a measure extended to first-year students in 1969–1970. But textbooks perpetuated a conventional approach. "The 'Aronian' view of Vichy, with its questionable distinction between Pétain's reactionary and Laval's collaborationist regime, is uniformly favored," even though the collaboration began to be mentioned. Moreover,

although most of the texts are careful not to understate the complexity of the Resistance, they generally respect a similar hierarchy, always giving priority to the appeal of 18 June and the organization of Free France. It is as if resistance activities within France only discovered their true identity through the person of General de Gaulle. Last but not least, the specific nature of French antisemitism and French initiatives in enacting anti-Jewish laws are generally ignored.[22]

To be sure, some expressions were able to disturb this view. *Night and Fog* was shown widely in collèges and high schools during the Gaullist republic. But the film served a primarily moral purpose, contributing to the civic education of the students rather than fostering truly historical thinking about the hell of the concentration camps. Similarly, the Resistance competition was sometimes out of harmony with official discourse. Created by the CNCVR in 1957 the Prix de la Résistance, after approval by the Gaullists, became the Concours national de la Résistance in 1961. With heavy participation by associations, although it was administered by the services of the Ministry of Education, the competition might offer another version of the dark years because of the variety of participants and the major role played by direct witnesses.[23] While contributing to the circulation of the ideals of the Resistance, this enterprise, which was very popular among secondary-school students, seems not to have shaken the pillars of the temple—indeed, that was not its purpose. Overall, then, the Gaullist vision was virtually untroubled by challenges, with one exception.

The Communist View

The Communists indeed tried to impose their view of the Resistance, "authentic expression of the will of the people, in the face of the maneuvers of the bourgeoisie, that is, the BCRA [Bureau central de renseignements et d'action, Central Bureau of Intelligence Information and Action] and the 'fence-sitters' of metropolitan France."[24] The PCF hewed to its orthodox line, whose broad outlines were restated by Jacques Duclos in a February 1968 lecture at the Institut Maurice-Thorez. In 1939, he asserted in substance, war was conducted against the Communists, not Hitler. The party therefore had every interest not in supporting it but in interrupting it by forging a general agreement including the Soviet Union. But by June 1940 the party had occupied the "front lines of patriots fighting to defend the independence, honor, and future of the nation." June 1941 marked not the inauguration of a commitment but an intensification of combat, "despite instructions from London," which enabled the Communists to become the primary architects of the liberation of the country.[25] This approach, as one might imagine, minimized the eminent role of General de Gaulle, against whom the PCF formulated two grievances. De Gaulle had used the Resistance "to establish his personal power," said Pierre Juquin.[26] He had also loyally served the interests of the bourgeoisie:

It was not a question simply of relativizing the role of De Gaulle during the war, but of discrediting the adversary by showing that he had always single-mindedly, before and during the war, been as they wanted to see him in the present, a "representative," by nature and out of choice, of the particular interests of his class. Moreover, the denunciation of Gaullist lies also enabled them to point out in contrast that only the PCF had the vocation of embodying democracy, the people, and France.[27]

These attacks carried little weight. To be sure, the Communist memory of the Resistance was still intact—in contrast to what happened in subsequent years:

Nothing of what contravened the established arrangement of themes brought up by this reference to the past—the unity and loyalty of the working class, the courage and sacrifice of the Communists, the betrayal of the property owners, the determination of the Soviets—emerged, neither the Nazi-Soviet pact and its consequences, disturbances, and defections, nor the postwar tensions and conflicts over legitimacy between the Communists who had been members of the Resistance and the others, nor even any doubt about the costs of armed struggle.[28]

Paradoxically, even

conflicts of memory and polemics, the duel and the duo of Gaullist and Communist memories, also caused to emerge among the Communists a homogeneous, conflict-free memory of the Resistance, despite internal tensions and disputes provoked within the organization by the memory of the Resistance.[29]

The death of Maurice Thorez in 1964, moreover, fostered a renewed glorification of the army of shadows, which the former general secretary, a deserter in 1939 who had found refuge in the Soviet Union during the dark years and was granted a humiliating pardon by de Gaulle at the Liberation, had not been very eager to celebrate. By the same token, the commemorative revival that was perceptible in the mid-1960s confirmed, "if that were necessary, that it was indeed the general secretary and his entourage who had transformed the period of the war into a taboo subject."[30] Jacques Duclos, in contrast, particularly in 1968 and 1969, succeeded in embodying "the difficult synthesis of the Communist generation of the twenties and thirties, the generation of the Resistance, Soviet demands, the expectations of the French working class, and the sensibility of post-May 1968 militants."[31] But although the restored image of the dark years remained intact in the eyes of Communist militants, the PCF lost influence. By the end of the 1960s it drew only one voter out of five, whereas it had captured more than one-fourth of the electorate at the Liberation. Its view of the Resistance was also challenged by veterans, often expelled from the party, in the 1970s, making the preservation of the dogma at the very least uncomfortable.

De Gaulle Loyal to Gaullist Dogma?

The Communists, however, did not hold exclusive possession of loyalty to the legacies of the Liberation. De Gaulle, who harbored long-standing grudges, had his own manias: he insisted on excluding the Allies from the spectrum of commemorations. For example, he refused to attend the commemorations marking the twentieth anniversary of Operation Overlord, sending only Minister of Veterans Affairs Jean Sainteny to the

Normandy beaches. By a decree of April 11, 1959, he abolished the official holiday status of May 8—an event that minimized the weight of France—but restored it for an exceptional occasion, the twentieth anniversary of the German surrender in 1965. In 1964, however, the head of state honored with his presence the ceremonies dedicated to the landing in Provence, in which the French forces had played a significant role, it is true, providing two thirds of the expeditionary force. The president of the republic also often took pains to couple the memory of the Second World War with the memory of the First; in this he was continuing a long-standing tendency, since René Coty in 1954 had associated the Battle of the Marne with the Normandy landing: "40th anniversary of the Marne, 10th anniversary of the Liberation, two battles, a single cause: the freedom of the nation." In addition, the Gaullist government sometimes merely co-opted preexisting initiatives. The Memorial to the Deportation on the île de la Cité, for instance, was the result of an initiative launched in 1953 by the Réseau du souvenir, which wanted to erect a monument to the martyrs of the deportation. The city of Paris granted land to the association in March 1956, and it obtained the right to launch a public subscription that made it possible for the memorial, the work of the architect Henri Pingusson, to be unveiled by Charles de Gaulle on April 12, 1962. The association did give it to the state on February 29, 1964, and the Ministry of Veterans Affairs took charge of maintaining and guarding it. But it would be at the very least erroneous to make this crypt a product of the architectural ambitions of the Gaullist government.[32]

Similarly, the desire to preserve the camp of Struthof—the only concentration camp on national territory—went back to the Fourth Republic. The camp's land and its gas chamber were classified as historic monuments in 1951, and a decree published on October 14, 1953, provided for the erection on the site of a memorial to the deportation, financed by public subscription.[33] It is therefore advisable not to overstate the break represented by a Gaullist Republic that, in memorial policy, often continued or completed works undertaken during the previous regime.

In any event, during the period of triumphant Gaullism the memory of the war was based first and foremost on the memory of a glorious and martyred Resistance, which was incidentally confirmed by the inflation of streets given the name Jean Moulin. Between 1964 and 2004, General de Gaulle's former representative monopolized 70 percent of newly named streets.[34] In 1995, 37 monuments and steles, 119 plaques, and 281 educational establishments were dedicated to him.[35] In contrast, although not occluded, military operations conducted by the regular army occupied a subsidiary and hierarchically organized position. The necropolis of Colmar, for example, was to bring together the remains of veterans of the First Army. But it was in danger of being disfigured by the construction of factories, which disturbed the widow of Marshal de Lattre de Tassigny. She persuaded the president of the republic to assign the site in Alsace, which lacked prestige, to the dead of 1940, and the soldiers of the First Army were given a space "commensurate with the grandeur of the sacrifices willingly made"—Sigolsheim.[36] Similarly, to commemorate the Italian campaign, the Gaullist government merely assigned the name *Garigliano* to the bridge opened in Paris on September 1, 1966. In the hierarchy of military value, Leclerc, a Gaullist from the outset and the liberator of Paris, occupied the first rank. De Lattre, despite his initial acceptance of the Vichy regime, followed him, because of the resistance he demonstrated against the invasion of the free zone on November 11, 1942, and considering the glorious campaign of Provence, followed by those of Alsace and Germany. Juin, finally, came in third, because of his past as a follower of Pétain and because he had fought in the Italian theater of operations, considered, rightly or wrongly, as secondary.

Vichy occupied an ambiguous place in this memorial configuration. Of course, Charles de Gaulle maintained his principled position, holding that the French State had had no reality. When he visited the spa town, he minimized its effect on national history by submerging it in the stream of time. "I am obliged to say that I feel somewhat stirred to be officially in Vichy. You understand the reasons for this, but we are carrying on with history, we are a single people, whatever the course of events may have been; we are the great, the only, the unique French people." Similarly, he refused to allow General Weygand to be buried at the Invalides in January 1965, an indication that the time of forgiveness had not yet come, but on November 10, 1968, he had four wreaths laid at the tombs of Joffre, Pétain, Gallieni, and Clemenceau, and he did not pursue the condemnation of former collaborators: Returning to France, Abel Bonnard, who had been tried in absentia at the Liberation, had his sentence commuted to ten years exile.

The same ambivalence was found in the memorial relations bringing together France and Germany. De Gaulle, indeed, had promised a
politics of reconciliation, which had been anticipated by some initiatives
from associations. On May 27, 1962, the first stele of reconciliation was
unveiled at Stonne in the Ardennes—"a simple concrete cross carved with
two hands shaking, the hands of yesterday's enemies."[37] But the initiative
was not greeted with unanimity, and the oak planted at the ceremony was
uprooted six times.[38] This points to the fact that the actions of the man of
June 18, receiving Konrad Adenauer at Colombey, or freeing the architects
of the final solution in France (Karl Oberg and Helmut Knochen were
discreetly removed to Germany in 1962) were not anodyne. No former
enemy of Nazi Germany followed this path, neither Poland nor Yugoslavia
nor Russia, another indication that one cannot characterize the effort of
reconciliation that was crowned by the Élysée Treaty in 1963 as a gesture
of no importance.[39]

On the contrary, Gaullist signals had a stimulating effect. For instance, the hitherto limited Franco-German sister cities grew in number.
Although a first agreement had been signed between Montbéliard and
Ludwigsburg in 1950, only twenty-five pairs of communities had been
joined together in the seven following years. By the eve of the Élysée
Treaty, 133 pairings had been agreed. The relaunching of the construction of European unity along with the improvement in Franco-German
relations expanded this form of reconciliation. In 1969 more than four
hundred agreements were signed—they were more than one thousand in
1981. Overall, Franco-German entente took the lion's share: pairings across
the Rhine accounted for 69 percent of European agreements in 1970, a
proportion that fell to 37 percent in 2007.[40]

But this voluntarist policy did not mean that France had forgotten.
Paris, like a dozen other countries, secured indemnification from Bonn
for the victims of National Socialism, a question that the Yalta and Pots-
dam conferences had not broached. Negotiations were arduous. "Despite
requests from the French, Bonn refused to take into consideration . . . former Resistance members, especially Communists, even if they had been
deported to concentration camps. The German negotiators considered
that to be a domestic political problem." Moreover, "German money was
not to honor after the fact acts of resistance against the Occupation in

France."[41] In the end, by virtue of the agreement reached on July 15, 1960, France received four hundred million marks, which it distributed primarily to deportees and internees, although some funds did go to Resistance members.[42] That said, the services of the Ministry of Veterans Affairs were surprised by the "avalanche" of requests (27,472 were admissible in 1965), due, they believed, to a change of attitude: "Deportees, after having often declared that they would never touch German money, suddenly realized that they were going to receive a significant sum."[43]

Saying he was ready for "direct and special cooperation" with Bonn, de Gaulle settled the irritating problem of German war graves. On July 19, 1966, an agreement granted the former enemy free and perpetual use of land for military cemeteries; the agreement also offered a reduction of 50 percent in transportation expenses to eligible parties to visit the graves of the dead, although this liberality was limited to one thousand people annually.[44] The stakes were not trivial: some 240 German military cemeteries had been established after 1871, 1918, and 1945 to inter the million victims resting in French soil.

But accommodation had its limits: parliament adopted unanimously the nonapplication of the statute of limitations to crimes against humanity in 1964, which could fan discord between a France determined to obtain reparation and a Federal Germany not very inclined to prosecute war criminals. But this decision should not be overstated. The law had primarily symbolic intentions, and its drafters probably did not measure the concrete consequences of their action. Paradoxically, it chiefly enabled the initiation "of prosecutions of former high officials of Vichy who had played a role in the application of the 'final solution' in France."[45] Western Germany, for its part, was less inclined to protect its former Nazis. For example, the Frankfurt trial in 1963 had a profound effect by confronting twenty-two members of the SS who had worked at Auschwitz with their victims. In this respect times had changed.

Finally, with respect to the fate of men who had served in the French army, relations joining France to the former territories of the empire experienced the consequences of decolonization. In 1958 and 1959 the Gaullist government decided that troops called up from the colonies would continue to receive their veterans' pensions as well as military disability pensions, but they would be changed into annuities calculated on the basis of the rates and legislation in force at the date of the change, then "crystallized" (that was the word) at that value. This measure was not the result of a dark plot hatched by a Gaullist government determined to punish the populations who had emancipated themselves from metropolitan France; nor did it derive from a desire to mask the very real participation of indigenous populations in the battle waged under the tricolor banner. It resulted, more simply, from new conditions created by decolonization and responded to the wishes of newly independent countries. The new governments feared that their army pay could not rival the amount of the pensions paid by France.[46] But these measures displeased veterans—for obvious reasons. And beginning in the 1980s, they harbored suspicion, especially because the integration of immigrant populations and their children was becoming an issue of primary importance. The image of a France cultivating ingratitude tended to come to the fore, even though the motives that had led to the "crystallization" had been purely prosaic.

The results of Charles de Gaulle's memorial policy are, all things considered, hard to evaluate. The regime certainly brought a halt to some demands set forth by combatants, offered a coherent view of World War II, built a group of museums, and reaffirmed the values of the Resistance. At the same time, it was partisan, failing to celebrate the veterans of 1940, ignoring the specificity of the Jewish genocide, denying the reality of the Vichy regime, and, with regard to the punishment of war criminals, conducting a policy that was at the very least timid. It also strongly identified the internal and external Resistance with the Gaullist saga—not without cunning. The design of the Colmar necropolis, originally intended for the burial of veterans of the First Army, took on the form of the Croix de Lorraine and displayed the insignia of the Second Armored Division, which troubled General de Lesdin when he visited the site in November 1959. He considered that "neither one nor the other corresponded to the wishes of the veterans of the First Army, nor for that matter, to historical truth."[47] Nor did the government seek to include the specifically French aspects of World War II (starting with Vichy) in school curricula.

That said, this view stirred little debate. Although those nostalgic for Vichy constantly demanded the transfer of the remains of Philippe Pétain to Douaumont, the memorial disputes that had marked the Fourth Republic—notably the opposition between Gaullists and Communists—lost force. Indeed, the PCF had no intention of giving a government whose foreign policy suited Moscow a hard time. It also hoped to exploit the centrality of the Resistance, from which it rightly drew some memorial benefits. In addition, the other components of the Resistance were too weak and dispersed to have their voices heard. And the Jewish world, despite the Six-Day War and the emotion provoked by the general's notorious statement (calling Jews an "elite people, sure of itself and domineering")[48] did little to restore the importance of the Shoah, assuming it wanted at the time to revive that memory.

Nonetheless, the Six-Day War did produce a shock. Fearing that the Jewish state would disappear, many Jews suddenly (re)discovered their Jewishness while simultaneously fearing a resurgence of anti-Semitism. Moreover, by his language, the president changed people's views. "The Jews were no longer 'French of Jewish faith,' but 'a people,' clothed in national characteristics, existing from the dawn of time."[49] This new awareness laid the groundwork for the awakening that a few years later led some Jews in France, now inclined to think of themselves as a community, to demand that the Vichy episode be thoroughly investigated.

On a totally different level, the anti-Semitic policies carried out by the Polish government created a stir in Communist organizations, particularly the FNDIRP. Beginning in 1967, "survivors were confronted with a choice between their Communist and Jewish allegiances, so conflicted had these solidarities become. The commemorations at Auschwitz of the Jewish martyr, the antifascist martyr, and the martyr of the Polish nation became, explicitly, incompatible."[50]

In the end the Gaullist view, generally speaking, stood up. Although it might retrospectively provoke a critical view because of its ideological biases, despite its limits, it favored consensus over dissension, unity rather than division. It would be difficult to say as much for the memorial policies carried out by Georges Pompidou and Valéry Giscard d'Estaing.

CHAPTER 4

Stormy Weather (1969–1981)

The presidencies of Georges Pompidou and Valéry Giscard d'Estaing signaled a shift in the memorial policy implemented by the authorities. Far from coming to a consensus, the memory of the dark years provoked conflicts, disputes, and controversies for two distinct but related reasons. For one thing, the government followed a policy that was, to say the least, peculiar. Rather than considering memory as a rallying point likely to rekindle public-mindedness and patriotism, the two presidents seemed intent on burying the memory of those hard times in the sands of oblivion, which led them, for reasons badly (or well) understood by public opinion, to carry out risky policies. For another, groups that had previously had only marginal influence on memorial policy began to make their voices heard, demanding primarily that the truth be finally told about Vichy and that the Shoah no longer be relegated to the fringes of national consciousness. Veterans had, of course, affected memorial policy from the Liberation forward by mobilizing their organizations. But civil society now entered the arena by creating ad hoc associations (following the lead of Serge Klarsfeld), by staging debates about films or books such as *Le chagrin et la pitié* and *La France de Vichy*, in short by taking up subjects that had been monopolized and shaped by the government, political parties, and officially recognized associations.

Georges Pompidou and the Resistance: Indifference or Aversion?

Although he had not behaved reprehensibly under the Occupation, it is well known that Georges Pompidou had belonged neither to the internal Resistance nor to the Free French Forces, which at the time distinguished him from the Gaullist notables whose Resistance credentials were generally solid. Michel Debré did not consider this particularity shocking in any way, "since General de Gaulle was not troubled by it," a feeling shared by Jacques Chaban-Delmas, who was not inclined to blame those who "as Sieyès said after the Revolution 'had survived.'" Pierre Messmer, however, thought that "at the beginning that created a slight problem between us. Neither one of us was embarrassed, but we felt a sort of reserve, the reserve between two men who had followed different paths from 1940 to 1945."[1] Whatever the differences of judgment, the fact remains that Georges Pompidou probably felt no sympathy for the men of the Resistance and equally probably did not think that the values of the army of shadows could cement a national consensus.

The reasons for this attitude are still mysterious. Perhaps he felt some remorse for not having participated. After being demobilized, he had merely continued teaching until the Liberation, conduct that might not merit opprobrium but could be contrasted with the brilliant military exploits of the historic Gaullists. Perhaps the veterans' tales of former underground fighters bored him. Perhaps, out of an inclination to compromise, he felt the need to heal the wounds of the Occupation. The historian is reduced to conjecture, but one observation is indisputable: the president followed a schizophrenic policy. By refusing to shed light on the Vichy episode, he was essentially following the lead of his predecessor; however, whereas Charles de Gaulle had balanced the veil thrown over the French State with a glorification of the Resistance, Georges Pompidou did nothing to celebrate its virtues; quite the contrary. Public opinion could only be surprised by this imbalance, which in the end led to a disavowal of the Resistance and, rightly or wrongly, gave the feeling that the government was coddling the ghosts of the French State.

For example, despite growing pressure, the Pompidou government refused to help, in other than conventional ways, to shed light on the

Vichy episode. Commissioned by French television, the documentary *Le chagrin et la pitié* was banned from broadcast; the head of the French national broadcasting service, Jean-Jacques de Bresson, himself a former Resistance fighter, explained to the Senate Cultural Affairs Committee in 1971 that the work "destroys myths that the people of France still need."[2] The government similarly refused researchers access to the archives they sometimes requested. Conducting research on the Special Sections (special tribunals created by Vichy), the writer Hervé Villeré was denied access to the archives; Minister of Justice René Pleven, a former member of Free France, informed him that the legal provisions "are intended to reconcile the administration's obligation to preserve privacy with the public's right to be informed, when these archives are studied for historical purposes. But you will acknowledge that it is appropriate to adopt the greatest circumspection in such matters. It is in fact important to avoid as much as possible causing harm to private interests and awakening passions in public opinion."[3] In the same vein, the government censored a film presented on television by Maurice Clavel in which he denounced "the aversion and annoyance" that the Resistance provoked in Georges Pompidou. At the request of the government, the first term was withdrawn, whereupon the philosopher stalked out of the studio with the resonant remark, "Goodnight censors!"

More embarrassingly, Pompidou pardoned the *milicien* Paul Touvier in November 1971, an affair that, when revealed in May 1972, created an uproar. Large demonstrations were held, bringing together left and right, resisters and deportees, Jews and Catholics. And the justification Pompidou provided was unconvincing. "Are we going to keep the wounds of our national discord bleeding eternally? Has the time not come to draw a veil over the past, to forget a time when Frenchmen disliked one another, attacked one another, and even killed one another?"[4] Even though a segment of the public wanted to go beyond the simplistic view of the past forged by de Gaulle and maintained by his successors, this was an unfortunate mistake.

It was particularly untimely because Pompidou spoke of the Resistance in unflattering terms. Interviewed by the *New York Times*, the president admitted to "detesting medals": "I detest decorations of all kinds." Indeed, he did little to encourage the development of a real politics of memory. The General Commission for Commemorative Monuments of the World Wars and the Resistance was dissolved in 1969 and the idea of a national museum for World War II abandoned the same year.[5] In the same vein, commemorations of the conflict became discreet, to say the least. The Communist deputy André Tourné was disturbed: "We could not help but be hurt when we realized that the day before yesterday, about six in the evening, wreaths had been laid at the war memorials, almost in secret, as though there was something shameful in commemorating the day that saw the end of the most horrible tragedy, imposed by Hitlerite fascism, that humanity has ever known."[6]

Moreover, the president strove to distance himself from the burdensome shadow of his predecessor. In August 1969 the commemorations of the Liberation of Paris glorified the figure of General Leclerc, sending an implicit message to public opinion: "We must shift the history of the Gaullists away from the history of General de Gaulle alone."[7] And the stamps issued that year honored the battle of the Garigliano, the head of the Second Armored division, the Normandy and Provence landings, and the Normandie-Niemen squadron but failed to celebrate the first resister in France.

Thus, "General de Gaulle's resignation in 1969 created a real break in the state's politics of memory. Established organizations were gradually dissolved. The government now intervened only through procedures for the classification of sites and oversight of museum construction. Central government powers were distributed to the prefects of each department, and initiatives again became primarily local."[8]

The government did nonetheless work to promote some projects. The law of July 9, 1970, for example, although it did not abolish the distinction between political deportees and deportees of the Resistance, attenuated it by harmonizing the methods of calculating disability payments for the two categories. To accomplish this, a good deal of reluctance had to be overcome. For although the FNDIRP had always fought to abolish the distinction between "politicals" and "resisters," the UNADIF-FNDIR did not accept that principle until 1966. In any event this measure made it possible to partially relieve the destitution sometimes suffered by the few survivors of the extermination camps. Between 1947 and 1958, social services had swallowed up 37 percent of the slender resources of the association of former deportees to Auschwitz and Upper Silesia.[9] The only remaining difference lay in the fact that only the DIR were considered to be military. As a result, "the small quota of Légions d'honneur reserved for deportees and internees benefited only those whose deportation or internment had been a sanction taken against them because of their participation in the fight against the occupying forces. Similarly, the decorations awarded to the disabled whose disability resulted from a war wound can [now] not be given to political deportees whose disability resulting from illness is not identified as a war wound."[10] That said, the difference in status between the two categories was obviously diminishing. This was all the more the case because, following the Dubois and Pasquier decrees, the awards committees and the Veterans Affairs Ministry were less restrictive in granting the title of internee or deportee of the Resistance. Whereas in all 17,340 internee cards and 32,289 deportee cards had been issued by 1959, the total climbed to 34,434 and 37,801 respectively in 1985.[11] The greater indulgence of the authorities no doubt served the Communists, who could identify their detention as a Resistance rather than a political internment.[12] But these technical measures—applied gradually because of the cost incurred to harmonize indemnities—were not enough to calm concerns. The feeling that the government was denying the values of the Resistance while at the same time maintaining silence about Vichy could not fail to outrage a public opinion that was newly stirred by a thirst for knowledge.

The Thirst for Knowledge

Several developments helped shatter the simplifications bequeathed by the Liberation. On the left, to begin with, dissident Communists challenged the party line by calling into question both General Secretary Georges Marchais and the line the party had followed between September 1939 and June 1941. In July 1970 a polemic was launched about the past of Marchais, who presented himself as a victim of the STO, whereas he had gone to work in Germany voluntarily. It was revived during 1977 and 1978 in the course of a suit Marchais brought against a former Communist official, Auguste Lecœur, who had revealed the affair after he was expelled from the party. Similarly, in his memoirs published in 1975 the former leader of the Francs-tireurs et partisans français, Charles Tillon, also expelled from the party, presented a view of the Resistance that did not conform to the orthodox Communist version. The incomplete de-Stalinization begun in 1956, the strategy adopted in May 1968, and the repression of the Prague Spring, halfheartedly disapproved by the party, explain why, in memorial matters, the "Party of 75,000 martyrs" was finding increasing difficulty in presenting itself as the intransigent defender of the camp of freedom, especially because the publication in France of *The Gulag Archipelago* in 1974 threw a harsh light on the reality of the Soviet Union.

At the same time, former resisters from movements that had been neither Communist nor Gaullist began to speak out. Between 1946 and 1969 these groups had been relatively discreet, allowing Gaullist and Communist orthodoxy to occupy memorial space. Their leaders now gave expression to a discordant voice, following the lead of the head of Combat, Henri Frenay (*La nuit finira*, 1973) and Claude Bourdet (*L'aventure incertaine*, 1975). By emphasizing the fact that the army of shadows was a minority phenomenon, pointing out the tensions that had existed between London and the internal Resistance, and launching serious attacks against Jean Moulin—accused of having played into the hands of the Communists—Henri Frenay helped to make the discussion more complex by shattering the legend of a massive, fraternal Resistance united behind the man of June 18.

To be sure, scholarly history made little progress before the late 1970s, with a few exceptions. Henri Noguères published a history of the Resistance whose intentions were critical. It brought out the prevarications of the line followed by the French Communist Party, pointing to its missteps and its attempts to infiltrate Resistance movements. The book also challenged the biases of Free France, which had been intent on placing the internal Resistance under its control, without regard for effectiveness—London demanded that it control operations, whereas command should have fallen to the men in metropolitan France who were closer to the facts on the ground.

But these challenges remained limited. The numbers of attacks and sabotage actions the PCF claimed to have carried out were again taken at face value, although the archives were not consulted to verify these deeds of war. And although Colonel Passy and the Gaullist special services were stigmatized, Charles de Gaulle was singularly spared. The historicization of the Resistance therefore remained a work largely yet to be accomplished: witnesses continued to dominate publications.

Vichy: A Revised History

The Vichy regime, however, had an entirely different fate. Until the 1970s a soothing version of the French State prevailed. A member of the Académie Française, André Siegfried argued, for example, that the State was divided between Pétain's Vichy—patriotic—and Laval's—the embodiment of evil. Enjoying wide success, the history by Robert Aron (1954) dominated the field; it asserted that behind Philippe Pétain, Vichy had made unstinting efforts to resist German demands and had thereby played the role of a "shield" protecting the French from the rigors of the Occupation.[13] These arguments could not help but attract a majority of the French who, having joined neither the Resistance nor the collaboration, could recognize themselves in the essentially reassuring portrait of a Marshal subjected to pressure from the Third Reich, having like them negotiated around constraints, bending though not breaking. This comforting view had only one defect: it was false. Robert Aron relied only on biased sources, the high court trials above all, in which the accused, whose lives were at risk, had exaggerated their opposition and kept silent about their compromising acts.

Against this background one can imagine the shock created by the work of the young American scholar Robert Paxton. A revolutionary work, *Vichy France* (1971; French translation, 1973) shattered the myth of Pétain the resister openly or secretly resisting German pressure. Relying primarily on German archives, Paxton showed that collaboration was not the result of German demands but had always been called for by the French authorities intent on negotiating the country's place in a Nazi Europe. He brought out especially the close link between diplomacy and domestic politics: the protection granted by the Reich guaranteed the permanence of the French State, which explains why Vichy leaders always associated their fate with that of their German masters. These analyses had, of course, been formulated by some precursors. In his *Vichy année 40*, Henri Michel had pointed out as early as 1966 that collaboration met a

French demand, an argument supported by the work of Eberhard Jäckel. Stanley Hoffmann had also formulated brilliant hypotheses, showing in particular that Vichy signaled the revenge of elites that the Popular Front had marginalized and also that the regime, considering the contributions provided by the traditional right and by outliers from the left, put itself forward as a "pluralist dictatorship." It can also be argued that the American historian and his followers "rediscovered something that had been obvious to the Gaullists and for many others in France who had the same reflex as General de Gaulle, refusing to collude with Nazism: Vichy had never intended to defend specifically French interests against Nazism."[14] But this remark fails to note that for the man of June 18 Vichy had represented nothing but an epiphenomenon, whereas the American historian demonstrated its centrality, its relative autonomy in domestic politics, and its popularity, while at the same time—and this was relatively novel— considering its actual operation.

Did scholarly memory help change perceptions of the dark years? This question leads one to consider the impact of research on what I will call, for want of a better term, public opinion. In quantitative terms decisive books were far from best sellers. The first year, Robert Paxton sold only 11,845 copies of his book, and 13,382 copies between 1973 and 1985. This respectable figure is, however, hardly comparable to the 53,000 sold by Robert Aron between 1954 and 1981.[15] Less fortunate, Eberhard Jäckel sold only three thousand copies in ten years, although his book "marked a real advance."[16]

The influence of research on changing views of history should not, it seems, be interpreted in quantitative terms, which does not mean that its role was secondary. To begin with, it had the effect of bringing the debate into the public square insofar as the new knowledge it contributed challenged common belief. Reported in major newspapers, Paxton's book fostered a controversy that was echoed in the media. One might also point out that, despite the oft-proclaimed death of the book, most disputes about the dark years were launched by books (Paxton provides a good example), less often by radio scoops or television broadcasts. Moreover, scholarly history had a legitimating function by providing advocates of revision the support of science. The arguments set forth did not depend on opinions or impressions; they were articulated around the search for knowledge, which guaranteed their validity.

Changes in the Memorial Landscape

The memory of World War II had thus been oddly reconfigured. Up to 1969 it was focused on the view of a glorious France, an exaltation of Resistance fighters, and a denial of the effect of Vichy and the particularity of the Shoah. It now incorporated darker realities, recognized the fact and the popularity of the French State, and discovered the fate the Nazis and their Vichy allies held in store for the Jews living in France between 1940 and 1944. In the past centered on heroism, memory now emphasized the turpitude of the population and its leaders, identified en masse as *collabos*. The figure of the hero gave way before that of the victim. Buchenwald had symbolized the phenomenon of the concentration camps, a place now assumed by Auschwitz. The Resistance had stirred public opinion; it now found Vichy intriguing. The people of France had frequently been united by legend; they now demanded the truth and turned into prosecutors. The government had previously adopted a rather syncretistic view of the past, defending, in language if not in law, a broad conception of the Resistance, considering together as consequences of Nazi barbarity the tragic fates of deportees, prisoners, and even forced laborers. New times encouraged the making of distinctions. The dark years had occupied a relatively minor place in public discussion; in the 1970s they became an important feature of it, although not devoid of ambiguity. The thirst for knowledge was sometimes mixed with less noble motives.

Retro fashion, to begin with, was a great success, inspiring films and novels. A memorial tourism also developed. The phenomenon, of course, was not new. The battlefields of the Great War had attracted thousands of pilgrims in the aftermath of the conflict, among them Charles de Gaulle, who wanted to show his son Philippe the major sites of battle. The defeat of 1940 had not produced a similar fad. But beginning in 1970, some locations developed a strong attraction, particularly the Maginot Line. The Ministry of Defense had decided to get rid of its blockhouses, and the government property office put them up for auction. Individuals, municipalities, and associations joined in the bidding. For instance, in Bas-Rhin five sites out of seven became town properties, four of them managed by associations. After restoration the sites opened their doors to the public, which flocked to them. By the late twentieth century the seven sites in

Bas-Rhin were attracting 105,000 annual visitors—Four-à-Chaux alone (an underground artillery installation) accounted for 43 percent of visits.[17] That said, visits seem to have arisen more from an interest in military art and technique than from a hypothetical duty of memory.

In any event the mnemonic landscape had changed. The causes behind the change are not easy to define, although several points are worth suggesting. The entry into adulthood of the generation born in the aftermath of the war probably weighed heavily in this change in the memorial paradigm. Expressing a generational revolt that exploded in May 1968, these young people were all the more dissatisfied with the Gaullist-Communist myth because the forms of power in the Gaullist republic and in the French Communist Party remained hierarchical and authoritarian, rejected diversity, paid little attention to the rank and file, and distrusted what they saw as troublesome youth. The oil shock of 1973 also plunged France into distress. The population renewed its acquaintance with mass unemployment—a phenomenon that had been forgotten since the 1930s—inflation, and job insecurity. The authorities seemed powerless to protect the people of France against the deleterious effects of this stagnation, which may have had two effects on the forms of memory.

For one thing, the crisis inaugurated an age of suspicion toward political, economic, and intellectual elites, who had until then managed to lead the country on the path to modernization. This suspicion extended to former heroes whose glorious past was now called into question. Myths were revised; a good illustration of this is provided by the 1974 film *Lacombe Lucien*. In recounting the story of a young man who is rejected by the Resistance and decides to join the Milice, Louis Malle desanctified joining the Resistance by reducing it to a series of chance events in which the desire to act was much more important than any ideological conviction. This process of debunking heroes went on in the following years with a series of ad hominem attacks on Jean Moulin (1978) and Georges Marchais, the general secretary of the PCF. Critics now attacked not the general, impersonal line of a party; they attacked men whose past they subjected to scrutiny.

The triumphalist discourse of the people in Resistance had not been contradicted by the experience of the thirty years of postwar prosperity (the Trente Glorieuses). Heroic in the past, France recaptured its grandeur in the sky (Caravelle, Concorde) as on land (the development of civil and military nuclear power, major industrial projects). Gaullist diplomacy also ensured that the country held an eminent position. But the crisis fostered doubt and raised questions about the capacity of France to remain in the group of great powers. In the light of this situation, identifying the French as a spineless people wallowing in Pétainism and collaboration could not fail to harmonize with the sensibility of a society that was plunged into a crisis and doubted that its elites could lead it out of the storm. Decolonization had, of course, already begun this process. But economic growth and successes achieved on the international scene by the Gaullist government had masked what rightly or wrongly appeared to be a weakening of French power. Times had changed as the decade of the 1970s began. And the unblinking gaze cast on the dark years, a reflection as much as it was a syndrome, was only one facet of the crisis of national identity that the country was going through.

It should be added that the gap between legend and historical truth, which was now better known because of witness testimony and scientific research, became impossible to sustain. The soothing language about Vichy used by the authorities could no longer be heard after the revelations presented by Robert Paxton, among others. Ernest Renan remarked: "Forgetting, even historical error, is essential to the creation of a nation, and thus the progress of historical study is often a danger for a nationality."[18] The government had previously followed that maxim, but over time its position became untenable. The Giscard government tested that at its own expense.

False Steps and Advances

Valéry Giscard d'Estaing conducted a memorial policy whose assumptions increased questioning rather than dissipating it. To begin with, the government seemed to reject the legacy of the Resistance and of the combatants of World War II. In 1975 the president decided to no longer officially celebrate May 8. This token of Franco-German reconciliation could, however, appear a deliberate sign of the intent to slight the heroic memory of the dark years. This initiative provoked anger among veterans. Thirteen bills were proposed in the National Assembly, five in the

Senate. On June 27, 1979, the Senate voted unanimously to restore May 8 as an official holiday, but the junior veterans affairs minister objected that the measure was inadmissible.[19] The president's initiative, however, did not shock the mass of the French population: 48 percent deplored it, but 43 percent approved, with 65 percent of the right in support.[20] In the same vein, in 1974 Giscard invited the ambassadors of East and West Germany to participate in ceremonies commemorating November 11. More discreetly, the government offered some tokens to former Vichyites: the president paid tribute to Pétain at Douaumont on June 13, 1976, and laid a wreath at the Marshal's tomb on November 11, 1978. Far from satisfying the emerging demands of the Jewish community, the authorities took many false steps. First, they ordered television networks not to broadcast the American miniseries *Holocaust*, on the pretext that it was too expensive, which provoked a general uproar. After the bomb attack on the synagogue in the rue Copernic on October 3, 1980, Prime Minister Raymond Barre denounced "a heinous attack against Jews in a synagogue that struck four innocent Frenchmen crossing the street." Only Simone Veil went to the site of the attack; Giscard spent the weekend hunting.

The Removal of Debarment

Aware of the unease its initiatives were creating, the government, of course, took countermeasures. To appease the anger of Resistance figures who had been shocked by the abolition of the May 8 holiday, it removed the debarment that de Gaulle had imposed, satisfying the keenest wish of the associations. But this decision, taken by decree on August 6, 1975, forced the Ministry of Veterans Affairs to revise its regulations, since a law could not be changed by decree. This operation especially troubled the administrative services; fearing an avalanche of false declarations, they alerted the ministry: "Experience has shown that neither the solemnity of the form in which witness statements must be produced nor the obligation to provide in addition authentic documents has prevented some petitioners from producing affidavits containing false statements. For example, one affiant asserted that an individual had been with him in a particular camp from one date to another, whereas merely consulting the file of the affiant proved that he himself had not been in the camp."[21]

This danger, it is true, had haunted the administration from the beginning, driving it on many occasions to grow vehement. As early as 1948, the ministry was deploring the fact that certificates proving the status of member of the Resistance issued by departmental services were not

attributed under the same conditions in every department. Fairly often, it appears that Federations, private bodies, had been left in charge of operations, whereas they played only a consultative role in Departmental Commissions. The central administration was able to see only appeals from individuals to whom the requested status had been denied, but it was not in a position to rectify all the abuses because files had not systematically been sent to it.[22]

In an instruction issued May 16, 1976, André Bord explained that

each time it seems to you that a witness['s] statement has obviously been prepared in a way that twists the truth in order to permit a petitioner to obtain a title he does not deserve, it will be up to you to immediately inform me under official seal—I reserve the right to bring the matter to the attention of my colleague in the Ministry of Justice—about this kind of fraud that must be denounced publicly and punished. . . . However, our action is likely to be limited by the operation of article 6 of the Code of Criminal Procedure, according to which the statute of limitations for misdemeanors is three years. In this case, the time would run from the date of the false statement. It is thus to be feared that when we are in a position to react, the statute of limitations will already have run.[23]

To appease the anger of veterans, Valéry Giscard d'Estaing overrode these reservations, choosing to open the Pandora's box of debarment rather than to brave the wrath of the associations.

But were the ministry's fears justified? By December 31, 1975, 227,531 cards of voluntary combatants of the Resistance had been issued. The removal of debarment and the more indulgent approach to the criteria defining the status of resister did not lead to a relative inflation. Between 1976 and 1987, 28,956 new cards were issued, a limited increase of 10 percent. At the end of 1997, the total had reached 261,533, and it culminated at the end of 2008 at 262,730. Just as interesting, the number of rejections remained considerable. By the end of 1997, 184,765 requests had been denied, a number that rose modestly to 184,803 by the end of 2008.[24] In other words, 58 percent of resisters, or those who claimed to be resisters, have had their claims recognized from 1945 to the present.

Satisfying Prisoners of War and Residents of Alsace and Lorraine

In the same vein, the Giscard government strove to meet the expectations of prisoners of war. To have their status as combatants recognized, these prisoners either had to have belonged to a duly recognized combat unit or to have manifested an "attitude of rejection in the face of pressure from bodies serving the enemy" (article R227). Up to 1977 the interested party had to provide evidence; but an instruction of December 22, 1977 decided to opt for "the *FAVORABLE PRESUMPTION* constituted by the fact that the interested party is not subject to any opposition."[25] This provision could only increase the number of prisoners considered combatants, a proportion that was already high, with 90 percent of former prisoners of war enjoying that precious status in 1977. It is nonetheless true that this instruction "perceptibly increased the possibilities for access to the combatant's card for prisoners of war."[26] The minister, Jean-Jacques Beucler, was all the more open to this long-standing demand from former prisoners because he himself had endured five hard years of detention in Vietminh camps.

The president also sought to clear up the dispute between the French forced to serve in the German army and the German Federal Republic. The draftees from Alsace and Lorraine received military pensions, combatants' cards and—in case of death—the notice "Died for France." These rights could even be granted to volunteers, on condition of providing proof that the enlistment had been imposed by the threat of reprisals against them or their families. But this arrangement excluded any pecuniary reparation for moral, material, or professional damages, which provoked the anger of the veterans. After long negotiations in which Giscard was personally involved, an agreement was finally reached on March 31, 1981. The FRG promised to contribute 250 million marks to a foundation for Franco-German understanding that would indemnify the draftees and also work to strengthen friendship between the two peoples through ad hoc programs. The Socialist Jean Laurain proceeded to establish the institution in Strasbourg on November 16, 1981.[27]

In an entirely different register, the *Holocaust* miniseries was finally broadcast, albeit grudgingly, in November 1978.

The Awakening of Jewish Memory

The false steps referred to above led Jewish associations to react. As early as the 1960s, Serge and Beate Klarsfeld had undertaken to pursue the unpunished perpetrators of the final solution, whether French or German, particularly by using the weapon of the media. In November 1968, for example, inside the Bundestag, Beate Klarsfeld slapped Chancellor Kurt Kiesinger, who had a heavy Nazi past, and then in 1970 she opposed the appointment of Ernst Achenbach to the European Commission. An assistant to Otto Abetz, this Nazi dignitary bore heavy responsibility for the deportation of two thousand Jews from France in February and March 1943. At first, the couple focused on the pursuit of former Nazis. Serge Klarsfeld later undertook the work of a historian, setting out to write the *Mémorial de la déportation des Juifs de France*, published in 1978, "because it was not possible for us to participate in the trials of the perpetrators without having gathered the names of all their victims."[28] It is a work of history, as well as of piety. "*Le memorial* brings out of night and fog, calling by name the countless anonymous ghosts annihilated by their executioners. To name these pale shades is already to summon them forth," said the philosopher Vladimir Jankélévitch.[29] Finally, in 1979 the lawyer created the association Sons and Daughters of the Jewish Deportees from France in order to perpetuate a battle that was now focused on the French accomplices of the final solution. It is worth emphasizing that the torch had been transferred to the children, guaranteeing that the next generation would continue the fight.

The activities of Serge and Beate Klarsfeld took place in a context that had changed considerably since the Liberation. Jewish memory had awakened following the Six-Day War and the unfortunate press conference during which de Gaulle called the Jews "sure of themselves and domineering." Above all, painful reminders of the past fostered the reactivation of this memory. In October 1978 an interview of Louis Darquier in *L'Express* created a great stir. The former commissioner for Jewish affairs asserted that "only lice were gassed" at Auschwitz. Driven by Robert Faurisson, Holocaust denial found an unexpected audience in the years between 1978 and 1983. And the first indictments of high Vichy officials for crimes against humanity (the deputy to the secretary general of the police, Jean

Leguay, was indicted in 1979) explicitly connected the French State to the Shoah and therefore stimulated a revision of the history of the dark years.

The figure of the Jewish deportee came to dominate the memory of the hell of the Nazi concentration camps. In a ruling on February 13, 1978, for example, the Paris court of appeal barred former STO conscripts from using the term *labor deportee,* a decision affirmed by the Cour de Cassation on May 23, 1979. The Federation of Labor Deportees had done everything to avoid this decision, which appears surprising in retrospect. It was essentially a "semantic battle with the peculiarity that it was decided by a judge, not the Académie Française. . . . The battle drained some of the energy of the associations, but also money that could have been used for other purposes, to serve history or memory, for example."[30] But something was at stake in this dispute. By claiming the status of deportee, labor conscripts hoped to benefit from the aura of the resisters' courage or Jewish suffering and thus to escape from the historical status of ordinary men who deserved "neither admiration nor opprobrium."[31] The fight revealed above all a change of paradigm: the deportee—particularly the Jewish deportee—was on the highest rung of the scale of respect and feeling.

Following a well-tried process, associations also filled in the deliberate or involuntary gaps left by the state. They undertook the task of naming the Jewish victims and numbering them with the most rigorous precision, data that the Ministry of Veterans Affairs still did not have, although more than thirty years had elapsed since the surrender of the Third Reich. They also persisted in launching or relaunching prosecutions that successive governments had been reluctant to pursue. This process also set the deportation of the Jews of France within the frame of a national memory that had previously been afflicted by a strange amnesia.

The Question of Archives

Despite the gaps in his memorial policy, Valéry Giscard d'Estaing benefited historians with the law of January 3, 1979, simplifying access to archives.

From 1945 to 1970 the Archives de France carried out two tasks, the collection and conservation of documents. Although that mission was accomplished, "there was a total embargo on the materials gathered. The possibility that they would be opened was considered neither in professional publications nor in circulars issued by the Archives management. The 'rule of fifty years' customary in most countries was applied with no qualms. . . . Access to materials of whatever kind was rigorously denied to individuals, including historians."[32] That meant that the law of January 3, 1979, marked a major advance. It opened the archives and liberalized the system by authorizing consultation of documents after thirty years and especially instituting a system of exemptions that many historians were able to use.

Despite this real advance, the Giscard regime followed a tortuous path, refusing to pay tribute to the cult of the Resistance and doing little to encourage reasoned understanding of the facts of the Vichy regime and the anti-Semitism of the dark years. Of course, the same evasion of Vichy and anti-Semitism had taken place during the Gaullist government. But the cult of the underground and regular combatants of World War II had had a balancing effect, the golden legend of a people in resistance compensating for the lies perpetuated about the dark side of France in the 1940s. This was no longer true in the 1970s, particularly under the presidency of Valéry Giscard d'Estaing.

This situation was unquestionably the result of personal factors. The president's family was hardly characterized by its commitment to the Resistance—his father Edmond and his uncle René had been close to the Marshal—and as a lycée student he had not joined the underground. He no doubt felt some regrets, if not remorse, since he asked Marie Granet, who was then writing a history, *Défense de la France*, to interview him as a veteran of the movement, although his service credentials were rather thin. In the same vein, his joining the First French Army in December 1944 can be read as an attempt to clear his name. While not decisive, these factors explain why the president felt no sentimental attachment to a cause from which he and his circle had been distant. But more crassly political reasons also played a role. Giscard had built his political career against Gaullism, for which he felt little sympathy. The memory of World War II provided ideal ground for powerfully expressing the gap that separated his camp from the supporters of the General.

This political factor also led the Communist Party to inflect the harsh judgment it had made of de Gaulle. Aside from the fact that the death of the former president, depriving the party of a major adversary, encouraged it to be indulgent, the party leadership counted on deriving political benefit from this revision; it hoped also to tap a portion of Gaullist prestige and perhaps bring a fringe of Gaullists to join the union of the left. "For the Communists sought to turn their former adversary's strength to their own advantage, to benefit from the favor and authority of a figure whose legend seemed no longer open to erosion, and to find a place for him that would be useful for current struggles while not tarnishing the luster of the Communist past."[33] But the party hesitated about the line it should adopt and its view of the war's Gaullism remained incoherent: sometimes the PCF summoned positive references; sometimes it brought up negative examples to strengthen its own positions.

In any event, the distance the new government took from the Resistance could not help but attract the president's party. Indeed, the Independent Republicans contained in their ranks both Pétainists and Resistance figures. Setting aside the legendary tale therefore satisfied men, most of whom thought that Vichy in the end had not been wanting, on this point matching a rather indulgent public opinion. In 1976, 35 percent of the people of France still thought Pétain should have been acquitted (or that the sentence had been too harsh), 27 percent had no opinion, and 38 percent stated that his sentence was justified.[34] It should be added that a fringe of Giscard supporters were friendly to the far right; the future president had even hired members of the movement to organize his security detail in the 1974 campaign.

These factors explain why, all things considered, the memory of World War II was muddled. Having lost the clarity of the legendary tale, it divided rather than bringing together, and this fragmentation led to memorial demands that were all the stronger because the groups that made them believed—rightly or wrongly— that they were not being heard. This confusion was intensified under the two presidential terms of François Mitterrand.

CHAPTER 5

The Ambivalences of the
Mitterrand Era (1981–1995)

The period that began in 1981 and ended in 1995 was marked by a certain complexity. Many of the battles launched in the preceding decade had, of course, been won. The memory of the Shoah had gained legitimacy; the defense of the Vichy regime collapsed under the attacks carried out by historians and artists; the production of scholarly history increased; and France acquired museum resources of major importance. But these victories were accompanied by a degree of discomfort. Attacks against the Resistance and Jewish memory proliferated, usually emanating from a right that had forgiven de Gaulle neither for his battle against Vichy nor for the "loss" of Algeria. Above all, the policies carried out by François Mitterrand produced a confusion of memory, explained in part by the sinuous path of a president who had frequented the corridors of the French State before joining the camp of the Resistance.

The Settlement of Memorial Disputes

Until 1969 successive postwar governments had tended to ignore both Vichy and the Shoah. In the 1970s the demands expressed by civil society had shaken the government although they had not forced it to give way. During François Mitterrand's two presidential terms, memory focused on the French State and on the Holocaust, both of which acquired a central place. For example, school curricula that had given an important place to World War II under the Gaullist republic now emphasized two points: the study of France during the dark years, beginning in 1983, and the history of the Shoah, but not until 1985.[1] In addition, in 1994 the destruction of the European Jews took up between 6 and 15 percent of textbook space, whereas it had previously been given scant attention. In this regard France was hardly precocious when compared to Germany or Italy. The Third Reich had entered the school curriculum in the FRG in 1959, and in 1980 the Ministers of Culture of the various *Länder* requested that the Resistance, "the key of democracy," be included in order to sharpen "the students' political consciousness."[2] Likewise in Italy a presidential decree required that the Resistance, the Liberation, and the Constitution be taught in all secondary schools, a provision that was strengthened by the 1962 unification of secondary education.[3]

In the same vein, research focused on Vichy and the Shoah, producing the publication of conference proceedings and important books. The last surviving French and German criminals were tracked down and held accountable by the justice system. Extradited and indicted for crimes against humanity in 1983, Klaus Barbie was tried and sentenced to life in prison on July 4, 1987; indicted for crimes against humanity on several occasions (November 1981, May 1989, November 1989), the former *milicien* and fugitive Paul Touvier was arrested in May 1989 and sentenced in 1994. Indicted in 1983, the high-ranking civil servant Maurice Papon was tried in 1997 and sentenced in 1998 to ten years in prison for complicity in crimes against humanity. In the view of Henry Rousso: "Despite the legal, political, and historical problems they posed, despite the fact that their "pedagogical" value was not always evident, these belated trials, centered solely on Vichy's anti-Jewish policy, not only provided a form of "reparation" to the victims, but also played a not inconsiderable role in the evaluation and public consciousness of the specific responsibilities of a French government in one of the greatest crimes in history."[4] Apparently determined no longer to spare former Vichy leaders, the government also intended to celebrate World War II and the Resistance in a more positive way. For example, on the day of his inauguration François Mitterrand went to the Panthéon, simultaneously paying tribute to the abolitionist of slavery Victor Schoelcher, the Socialist thinker Jean Jaurès, and the unifier of the Resistance Jean

Moulin. And the law of September 21, 1981, restored the commemoration of May 8, 1945.

Significantly, the government encouraged the creation of museums and memorials overseen by an ad hoc group. An interdepartmental committee of museums of the two world wars, presided over by the minister of veterans affairs, was established on April 24, 1985, to examine requests for support and issue opinions on the appropriateness of state aid. The government likewise rationalized the organizations channeling its politics of memory, which was entrusted to a succession of administrative bodies and finally to a permanent mission. Revitalized because of the fortieth anniversary of the Liberation in 1984, the memory of the Resistance gave rise to a flowering of museums and memorials, in Neuvic (1982); in Agen, Lyon, and the Memorial for Peace in Caen (1988); and later creations in Vercors and Grenoble (1994). Aside from the memorial of Izieu constructed by the public works service, these creations usually resulted from local initiatives; the state, following tradition, intervened only to subsidize projects directly, or indirectly with European funds, as with the Museum of the Resistance in Saint-Marcel (1983), the first one it subsidized. Overall, more than 110 museums (of a total of 204) were built between 1980 and 1999. This fervor was encouraged by the laws on decentralization that abolished the requirement of authorization from the prefect for the installation of commemorative plaques, thereby encouraging local initiatives.

Furthermore, the government strove to defuse memorial disputes. For example, it tried to incorporate the memory of former STO conscripts into the national memory, not without some hesitation. On the one hand, the government refused to have a conscript appear beside a deportee and a prisoner of war on the stamps and posters commemorating the fortieth anniversary of repatriation.[5] On the other hand, on September 3, 1989, junior Minister of Veterans Affairs André Méric unveiled a plaque on the former Gare d'Orsay, recalling that "between April and May 1945, a large number of survivors from prison camps, concentration camps, forced labor camps, all victims of Nazism, were welcomed in turn at the Gare d'Orsay, the most important French center of repatriation." *Le Déporté du Travail* hailed this initiative, considering that the gesture proved "that the family of misfortune can be united in memory and agree about words while respecting historical truth."[6] On February 27, 1993, government minister Louis Mexandeau repeated the signal when he unveiled a plaque at the Gare de l'Est recalling that "Victims of Nazism and the special laws of the Vichy Government of September 4, 1942, February 16, 1943, and February 1, 1944, that instituted the Forced Labor Service, several hundred thousand young French citizens left from this station under constraint and threat. To the memory of the tens of thousands who did not return and of all those who did not survive this tragedy."[7]

The government was also determined to pay tribute to the indigenous troops in the empire. A stele celebrating the liberation of Notre-Dame-de-la-Garde basilica in Marseille by the Seventh Algerian Infantry Regiment was unveiled on August 30, 1992; in the Vosges a monument celebrating the Fourth Tunisian Infantry Regiment was erected on Mount Hockneck in 1991. The original plaque with the inscription "The Sidi Brahim of the Snows: in memory of the night of December 14, 1944," was replaced by a more precise inscription: "Fourth Tunisian Infantry Regiment: combat from December 5 to December 14, 1944. To the glorious memory of the combatants of the Fourth Tunisian Infantry Regiment, supported by other units of legionnaires, Moroccan Goumiers (auxiliaries), cavalry, combat engineers, fallen for the liberation of Orbey in December 1944."[8] A memorial to the army of black Africans was unveiled at Fréjus by then Defense Minister François Léotard in 1994. The *Indigènes*, in other words, acceded to a form of memorial recognition, although it did not destroy stereotypes. The Fréjus monument displayed black soldiers, exhausted and staring into space, surrounding their white leader proudly carrying the tricolor flag.[9]

Most strikingly, deportation on racial grounds, previously given little attention by the authorities, now occupied a place in public memory. In February 1993 a decree instituted "a national day to the memory of the victims of racist and anti-Semitic persecutions committed under the de facto authority known as the 'government of the French State'"; following this initiative, a plaque or a stele was supposed to be set up in every department to inscribe, in the marble of memory, the names of the victims of this criminal policy. On July 17, 1994, the monument commemorating the Vélodrome d'Hiver roundup was unveiled, and many commemorative inscriptions were amended. The plaque placed in the Nexon camp in the Limousin had not mentioned the deportation of the Jews. It was corrected on September 12, 1993, specifying that "from this station departed for Port-Vendres, in March 1941, to be deported to camps in North Africa, longstanding antifascist Resistance patriots called undesirable Frenchmen and interned by the governments of France and Vichy. Victims of fascist repression, they were the first to show us the path of Resistance. Later, Jews, Resistance fighters, and patriots were deported to Germany. Let us never forget their suffering, their courage, their sacrifice. Let us remain vigilant; remember."[10] Similarly, the monument dedicated to the victims of Auschwitz unveiled at Père-Lachaise cemetery in 1949 failed to mention that most of the dead were Jews. The plaque unveiled in 1995 specified that "Victims of the anti-Semitic persecutions of the German occupier and the collaborationist government of Vichy, 76,000 Jews of France, men, women, and children, were deported to Auschwitz. Most of them perished in the gas chambers. Victims of police repression, 3,000 Resistance fighters and patriots suffered and died in Auschwitz."[11] The government finally agreed in 1985 that the notation "Died in deportation" would be included in public records and launched the construction of the memorial house in Izieu.[12] These reminders were imperative because the National Front kept alive the flame of anti-Semitism that some of its troops had never stopped feeding. On September 13, 1987, Jean-Marie Le Pen asserted, for example, that the gas chambers represented "a point of detail in the history of World War II" and then a year later indulged in a dubious joke targeting Minister of Public Service Michel Durafour (September 2, 1988). François Mitterrand was determined to show that he would give no ground in this area.

These developments should have helped turn the memory of World War II into a pacified domain, offering civil society a single message, hailing the courage of Resistance fighters, honoring the sacrifice of soldiers, mourning the victims of the Shoah, denouncing the crimes of Vichy. But this was not the case, for a multiplicity of reasons.

François Mitterrand: Troubled Career, Troubling Past

First and foremost, the head of state had a complex personal relationship with the period of the Occupation. Coming from the extreme right, an escaped prisoner of war, a Vichyite for a time, a belated but genuine adherent to the Resistance, after 1958 he developed a militant anti-Gaullism. These factors led him to carry out policies that were to say the least complex. No doubt, he paid tribute to the saga of the Resistance, although he refused to place it under the aegis of the man of June 18. What's good for the goose is good for the gander: in 1986 the Association of the Free French launched the "plaque of June 18" operation, which consisted of placing enameled reproductions of the appeal in towns throughout the country. Between 1987 and 1990 more than one thousand plaques were placed, indicating the vitality of a Gaullist memory not much to Mitterrand's liking.[13] The president also refused to condemn Vichy. Favorable to trials of the "criminal underworld," in which he included Paul Touvier, he showed less enthusiasm in urging the judicial authorities to bring Maurice Papon or his friend René Bousquet before the tribunals of the republic. Nor did he hesitate to lay a wreath at the tomb of the Marshal on the île d'Yeu in September 1984, a gesture he repeated every year from 1986 to 1992.

The revelations presented by the journalist Pierre Péan shed new light on this action, which showed that François Mitterrand had not entirely broken with his "French youth." After escaping from prison camp in December 1941, Mitterrand had found a modest job in the research department of the Directoire de la Légion, showing no distaste for Pétainist ideology, some of whose ideological orientations he shared at the time, with the notable exception of anti-Semitism. He resigned in April 1942 and took a position at the Commissariat for Rehabilitation of Prisoners of War, while at the same time trying clandestinely to help escapees and war prisoners, with no contradiction between these two approaches. "He had no position of authority, but all his activity, including his clandestine activity, was in no way opposed to the Marshal's policies."[14] In January 1943, however, a *maréchaliste*, Maurice Pinot, was dismissed from the Commissariat and replaced by a man closer to Pierre Laval, André Masson. Mitterrand then tried to infiltrate the Commissariat while getting more deeply involved in the Resistance. He was awarded the *Francisque*, the highest decoration of the Vichy regime, in early 1943, while simultaneously setting up a Resistance movement among war prisoners. During a trip to Algiers, he met the Commissioner for Prisoners Henri Frenay and the head of the French Committee of National Liberation (CFLN), Charles de Gaulle, who agreed to have Mitterrand unite under his own authority the three organizations active in the Resistance among prisoners. Thus was born on March 12, 1944, the National Movement of Prisoners of War and Deportees, which brought together Mitterrand's movement (RNPG), the MRPGD of Philippe Dechartre, and the Communist-leaning CNPG of Robert Paumier. *Morland* (one of Mitterrand's cover names) then became a full-time member of the Resistance.

These revelations, published by Pierre Péan in 1994, triggered violent controversies, and the president was called on to explain his past activities. Although it was not exemplary, his career had nothing out of the ordinary. In 1940, millions of French people, stunned by the defeat, considered Philippe Pétain a providential man. Others looked favorably on the National Revolution, hoping that the Vichy regime would clean the Augean stables and carry out the reforms that were particularly necessary because the Third Republic had postponed them for decades. But the slipshod performance of the French State, the atmosphere of civil war that it fomented, and its shameless collaboration with the Third Reich had gradually turned them away from Philippe Pétain; the majority placed their hopes in Charles de Gaulle and the forces supporting him, the Resistance above all. François Mitterrand, in other words, had held common, if not trite, convictions. Of course, his actions and his friendships were less ordinary. He had, however, never collaborated, and his conduct under Vichy had nothing reprehensible, although his writings demonstrated the depth of his affinities with Pétainist ideology. Carried out at the risk of his life, his Resistance activity above all brilliantly redeemed these divagations.

The problem, in other words, lay not on the factual plane—the discovery of an ordinary career—but in the realm of memory—the image of his past that François Mitterrand had constructed. He had always claimed that he had carried the banner of the internal Resistance, a political force over which, in his view, Charles de Gaulle had seized control:

I have always argued, something that is now more accepted, that the Resistance was twofold: internal Resistance and external Resistance coexisted. And a hidden struggle between the two played itself out. General de Gaulle feared that the Resistance might produce men who would later symbolize and lead the country. I think that many things were done to make sure the internal Resistance was without a head. Most major Resistance leaders who had been in Algiers did not come back. Frenay, d'Astier de la Vigerie, ten others. I myself, who was not a major leader, had a great deal of difficulty in getting back. I had to really will it and make the decision myself. . . . That is why I have a position that diverges from that of the majority of the French on the role of General de Gaulle. I acknowledge his work and his great actions. But . . . in 1940, De Gaulle's envoys to metropolitan France, courageous and loyal men, were at the same time controllers. And since De Gaulle and the external Resistance very quickly achieved mastery in the field, everybody fit the mold, including some Resistance fighters who might have asserted themselves: Chaban, Bourgès-Maunoury. The others are dead.[15]

For many years, Mitterrand had thus presented himself as a qualified representative of the internal Resistance destroyed by de Gaulle—an argument repeatedly developed in his speeches as in his books. To perfect the construction, he did not shrink from using expedients. For example, a decree of April 27, 1992, identified the MNPGD as a combat unit in the internal Resistance, a recognition the authorities had refused in March 1951. Beyond the symbol, which counted, this measure made new rights available to members of the movement. The decree concluded backroom maneuvers that had begun in 1984. A first decree, on March 1, 1984, had reopened the question of recognition for units that had not been certified after the war. Three decrees followed in March 1986 identifying the CNPG and the RNPG as movements of the internal Resistance, while the MNPGD was recognized as a combat unit. But these decrees referred to the transcript of a meeting that had not yet been drafted. The president of the committee, Colonel Francis Masset, was outraged and filed a demand for invalidation with the Conseil d'État on April 22, 1986. After extensive deliberation, that body nullified the decrees on March 11, 1991. Unruffled, the government reissued the decrees in 1992.[16]

François Mitterrand also strove to transform the Pointe de Beg-an-Fry into a site of memory. It was known that during the night of February 26–27, 1944, the future president, then using the pseudonym M. Jacques, had landed on this beach after having traveled from Algiers to England. Before 1985 he had seldom frequented the spot, having visited it in 1954 and again in 1978. The presidential journey of 1985 enabled him to shape his image as a unifying president, at a time when he was anticipating governing with a prime minister of the right because of the probable defeat of the left in the coming legislative elections. It also provided the opportunity to create a Mitterrandian counterpart to the île de Sein, a mecca of Gaullist memory. But the effort had limited results. Although the left, beginning on January 11, 1996, met at the site at regular intervals—the Socialist Federation of Finistère decided to celebrate the memory of May 10, 1981, there—the site did not succeed in achieving national recognition, unlike Solutré.[17] But these two affairs confirm that Mitterrand took care, sometimes in great detail, to polish his image as a Resistance figure. *De minimis curat praetor.*

Mitterrand's memorial (re)construction in fact reactivated a threefold split. It revived the muffled or explicit conflict between the internal and external Resistance that Henri Frenay had earlier heralded. It revived the flame of the anti-Gaullism for which the author of *Le coup d'état permanent* had been a crusader. And it restored the rights of Socialists to invoke the legacy of the dark years, a legacy of which Gaullist and Communist memories had cruelly dispossessed them. The massive commitment of Socialist officials in the Resistance had been totally neglected by the SFIO in the aftermath of the war. The party had chosen instead "the path of expiation." And the dispersion of Socialists in networks and movements made their actions less visible. Whereas the Communist rival claimed the aberrant figure of seventy-five thousand martyrs, the Socialists refused to "beat a drum roll on the coffins" of their heroes who had fallen on the field of honor, in the words of Daniel Mayer.[18] The (re)discovery of an embarrassing Vichy past thus undermined a carefully constructed memorial edifice that had made François Mitterrand into a symbol of the internal Resistance, a herald of anti-Gaullism, and a rebuilder of French Socialism.

The risk in terms of collective memory turned out to be real. There were also personal considerations. François Mitterrand had always manifested a strong interest in history in general, placing himself particularly in the memorial traces of captivity and Resistance. He detested de Gaulle, who had a quality that irritated a psychic wound of Mitterrand's. Despite his education and the tacit rules of his milieu, the general, a conformist personality, living like a bourgeois in Colombey-les-deux-Églises, had been able to make a startling break. Far from seeking any kind of agreement with Vichy, he had launched his famous appeal as early as June 18; far from temporizing with a hostile majority, he had resigned from office on January 20, 1946. Moreover, he had never feared breaking with companions when he thought service to the country required it. Mitterrand, conversely, had thought he could exploit the Vichy apparatus during the dark years. He later stayed in governments whose Algerian policies were questionable. Throughout his life he remained loyal to old friends, who were sometimes quite embarrassing. The sudden reappearance of his Vichy past personally reminded him of these facts.

That said, Pierre Péan's revelations were not entirely new. That François Mitterrand had received the *Francisque* was public knowledge: the extreme right press had frequently commented on the Vichy past of the future president. Roger Frey, interior minister in the Debré and Pompidou governments, also kept his files up to date. Possessing the famous photograph in which Pétain is shaking the hand of the young Mitterrand and knowing of the friendship that tied him to René Bousquet, he suggested that the general use this information during the 1965 presidential campaign. "You're not telling me anything," de Gaulle retorted. "Mitterrand and Bousquet are returning ghosts: the ghost of anti-Gaullism that arose from the depths of collaboration. I don't need you to tell me that Mitterrand is an impudent careerist. Mitterrand is a scoundrel." But he refused to follow Frey's advice, scorning "dirty politics" that could "undermine the office in the event he were to occupy it."[19]

But although they were public knowledge, these compromising elements were simply not believed. The left, for example, presented the award of the *Francisque* as a supreme trick: Mitterrand sheltered his Resistance activity behind a façade of Pétainism. Pierre Péan's revelations, in other words, were accepted only when public opinion was inclined to believe them. From this point of view the end of Mitterrand's second presidential term was a propitious time. François Mitterrand had accomplished his historic mission, first by renovating the Socialist Party and then by bringing the left to power. The storm could batter a man who was now of no use. Moreover, his government had had mixed results: the last years of his reign had deeply disappointed a portion of his electorate. His former admirers could accept that the statue be torn down. The president's attitude, finally, did a disservice to his defense. Weakened by illness, shaken by scandals, he took refuge in clumsy denials that did nothing to increase his stature, particularly since Péan's book was stirring the embers of suspicion. It shed light on the private motives of a man who had wreaths laid at Marshal Pétain's tomb in his name and demonstrated obvious bad faith in refusing to acknowledge the responsibilities of the Vichy regime for the deportation of the Jews of France. On July 14, 1992, he asserted:

The republic has always been the republic that extended its hand to avoid racial segregation. So let us not ask the republic to defend itself! But in 1940, there was a "French State," the Vichy regime, that was not the republic. And from this "French State" we must demand an account, I agree, of course, how could I not agree? I totally share the feeling of those who address themselves to me, but precisely, the Resistance, the De Gaulle government, the Fourth Republic, and the others were founded on the rejection of that "French State"; we need to be clear about that.[20]

This was quibbling with words, for officially acknowledging the crimes of the French State did not lead to a condemnation of the Republic, contrary to what the president suggested.

François Mitterrand tried to make up for all of these missteps by instituting the commemoration of July 16 dedicated "to the memory of the racist and anti-Semitic crimes of the French State" (decree of February 3, 1993), then, on April 24, 1994, inaugurating the house of Izieu, where forty-four children and seven teachers had been rounded up on April 6, 1944, on the orders of Klaus Barbie, and finally by unveiling the monument to the Vélodrome d'Hiver on July 17, 1994. Furthermore, as I have noted, the government gave both the Vichy regime and the destruction of the Jews of Europe substantial attention in school curricula.

But the harm had been done, and the image of François Mitterrand was lastingly affected, even though the Socialist Party failed to raise questions about his dark side. The duty to make an inventory of the past promised by Lionel Jospin trickled away in the sands of the desert.

François Mitterrand was more fortunate in his international memorial policy. He significantly affected the commemorations of the Normandy Landing, so much so that he established the framework that still prevails today.

The Renewed Commemoration of D-Day

The commemoration of the Normandy Landing now brings together heads of state and government; this phenomenon, with its attendant media presence, is relatively recent.

Of course, the importance of D-Day was obvious to contemporaries and to the inhabitants of Normandy. As early as May 22, 1945, the first subprefect of liberated France, Raymond Triboulet, created a committee on the Landing charged with organizing commemorations on the Normandy beaches. The committee took on a threefold mission. First, it would take care of the material organization of the celebrations. It also wanted to protect the material traces of the operation, which was the subject of a law passed on May 21, 1947. And it hoped that the anniversary of June 6 would strengthen ties between former allies.

To some degree these choices turned out to be problematic. For one thing, they amounted to excluding the Normandy countryside as a whole and favoring the coast at the expense of the interior as the setting for the ceremonies. Consequently, this choice excluded the approximately twenty thousand civilian victims of Allied operations and minimized the French authorities because of the small role French forces played in the operations. It granted preeminence to the Allies and their veterans, as suggested by the inscription carved beginning in 1947 on the "signal monuments" erected in the Normandy region: "Here on June 6, 1944, the heroism of the allied forces liberated Europe." Conversely, the Soviets were excluded from the spectrum of commemoration, although the weight of the war in Europe had largely rested on their shoulders until 1944.

This view generally prevailed until the 1980s, and the participation of French officials was therefore, as a general rule, rather modest. Throughout the postwar period, the state as such participated in the ceremonies on only six occasions (1954, 1969, 1984, 1994, 2004, 2009). Moreover, it was usually represented by a secondary figure. Although President of the Republic René Coty honored the 1954 commemorations with his presence, he was careful, as I have noted, to link World War I to World War II, reinforcing the Gaullist view of a "Thirty Years' War." Charles de Gaulle, for his part, always refused to participate, sending only Minister of Veterans Affairs Jean Sainteny in 1964. The same scenario was repeated in 1969 and 1974. Neither the prime minister nor the president of the republic attended the ceremonies on June 5 and 6, having their ministers, Henri Duvillard and then Jacques Soufflet, join General Omar Bradley. Gaullist France carried a grudge. Excluded from the preparation and conduct of the landing, Charles de Gaulle judged that the operation had in no way been French. By his pointed absence, he showed that he held to this accurate but rather narrow view. Britons and Americans consequently tended to take over the commemorative space. In addition to the numerous veterans who took advantage of the opportunity to return to the scene of their exploits, officials intended to use June 6, in the context of the cold war, to celebrate their unity and emphasize the role their nations had played in the defense of the free world.

But this official memory ended up excluding the civilian victims, a view ratified by the local authorities, because their first projects were aimed primarily at exalting the deeds of the Anglo-American forces. For a long time, therefore, the general population had few monuments to recall their suffering. To be sure, the burial of an "unknown civilian victim" on the grounds of the château of Caen was worth acknowledging; but this reparation in 1964 was, at the very least, belated. Similarly, the few monuments dedicated to the civilian population were practically never included in the tours conducted by officials. When ceremonies in homage to civilian victims were held, they were always confined to the sidelines, looked down on by the state, and usually organized and conducted by local communities. Until very recently, moreover, associations of victims, were never invited to participate in official commemorations.[21]

A variety of factors explain this apparently surprising eclipse. During the war Normandy had been relatively spared in comparison to other regions. It had seen little fighting in 1940, unlike the Nord, and its small number of Jews, Communists, and Resistance fighters had preserved it from Nazi repression—in contrast to the Limousin and the Savoy region, for example. Its rich farmland, moreover, had made it possible to maintain a decent food supply, even in the terrible period of July and August 1944. In many respects and despite real problems—absence of prisoners of war, prohibition of access to the coast, German requisition of men and material—the zone well and truly looked like a privileged area. Starting in April and especially after June 1944, the situation was reversed, and Normandy suddenly became a victim. Combat and bombing caused death and destruction; the civilian population was often forced to leave battlegrounds in a pathetic exodus; finally, the presence of Allied troops, who caused disturbances and sometimes crimes, was particularly resented, during and after the Liberation.

These elements organized the personal memory of the people of Normandy, and it was not channeled by official vectors—museums, commemorations, monuments. Indeed, preserved under the Occupation, Normandy experienced some difficulty in presenting itself as a victimized region, particularly because it had had the notable privilege of having been the first region liberated (not counting Corsica). Moreover, it was impossible for the population to blame the Allies by deploring the combat, the bombing, or the abuses committed. This attitude would have been considered an inappropriate sign of ingratitude toward the "boys" who had risked their lives to liberate France. Complaints and recriminations would also have risked damaging memorial tourism, which, by attracting American and British veterans, provided comfortable income for the region. Finally, civilians could hardly attribute a meaning to their mourning. In a period that favored heroes over victims, they were obviously out of step; and the death of civilians carried no lesson except to confirm that in contemporary conflicts civilians are affected as much as, if not more than, soldiers. For many years civilian victims were therefore confined to the sidelines of commemorations and official memory.

Not that they did not try to influence that memory, by forming associations (Ceux de la Bataille de Caen, for example). Moreover, participants and witnesses raised questions very early about the appropriateness of Allied strategy. In the words of Pierre Daure, the Gaullist prefect of Calvados:

Because I have always been a friend of your country, I feel I can speak frankly. The need for large-scale air bombardment [of Caen] was not understood by the inhabitants, as so few Germans were directly in the town. There could be no comparison between the losses of the civilian population and those of the enemy, the latter being very few. The Germans hide in the woods and not the towns. As for the argument [that] the bombardment was necessary to block the roads, my answer is that in this part of France there are so many alternative routes and tracks that it made little difference. The power and destructiveness of the bombardment made some people compare it to the well-known methods of the enemy. However, the extensive looting by the SS that followed helped to redress the balance and there is not the slightest doubt that the people are delighted to be liberated.[22]

This theme had an interesting history. While not challenging the operation as a whole, by questioning the appropriateness of the bombing strategy, it made it possible indirectly to reintroduce the martyrdom of civilians. "Did the people of Normandy in the summer of 44 suffer for something?" asked Claude Quétel, research director of the Memorial of Caen, and he pointed out that "the tactical imperative of the bombardment of the towns of Normandy in 1944 will find little support."[23] This event, however, had a lasting effect on the memory of the city of Le Havre, which was destroyed by a series of bombardments between September 5 and 11, 1944. But these nuances could hardly affect a dominant memory supported by the commemorative policies adopted at both local and national levels.

Mitterrand's two presidential terms changed the equation. In 1984 the president endowed the fortieth-anniversary ceremonies with unusual luster. Invitees included the monarchs of the United Kingdom, the Netherlands, Belgium, Norway, and Luxembourg, and President Reagan made an unprecedented appearance, for, except for Jimmy Carter on January 5, 1978, no American president had yet come to the beaches of Normandy. The equally impressive ceremonies in 1994 brought together, in addition to representatives of the Western powers (Queen Elizabeth, Bill Clinton), representatives from the nations newly emancipated from the Soviet yoke (Lech Walesa from Poland and Vaclav Havel from Czechoslovakia). The previously military commemoration was becoming political or geopolitical.

This change in participants was matched by a change in discourse. It is true that as early as 1972 Pierre Messmer had placed the commemorations under the auspices of the construction of European unity:

For twenty years, after being materially reconstructed with American aid, Europe has been organizing and attempting to become itself. The time has come for the governments of the Six, and tomorrow the Ten—as the president of the republic said recently—to have "the will to act to give voice to the distinct voice of one Europe." Experience has taught us that this is a difficult task. We will not forget that, if it is possible, it is thanks to the sacrifice one day in June 1944 of those we honor today.[24]

This language was echoed in 1979 by the junior minister of veterans affairs and war victims who, comparing Normandy to the cradle of Europe, asserted that on this site was "founded the Europe that is our concern today."[25]

François Mitterrand extended the theme: "Yesterday's adversaries have been reconciled and are together building the Europe of Freedom. Let them now dare to go beyond themselves . . . to dominate the contradictions of a common victory that has brought us peace," he said in 1984.[26] And he confirmed this in 1994: "Europe saved could not but be another Europe. With others waiting in the wings, 340 million Europeans have adopted common laws. Armed conflict between them has become inconceivable. Reconciled adversaries are now marching in step." An indication of this change was the fact that the Germans, undesirable in 1984 and absent in 1994, were represented by their chancellor in 2004. In 1984, however, Helmut Kohl had rejected that prospect, stating that there was "no reason for a [German] chancellor to celebrate a victory in a battle in which tens of thousands of Germans [met their] death."[27] In 1994 he was surprised not to have been invited to the ceremonies, considering that "that had been an ideal occasion to celebrate before the world the reconciliation of the various belligerents, that the ceremonies would amount to an official pardon by the Allied nations." But former Minister of Veterans Affairs Louis Mexandeau considered an invitation to Germany "on the same footing as the other nations" to be "unthinkable."[28] In 2004 these objections fell by the wayside, and President Jacques Chirac in turn associated D-Day with the construction of European unity. "The European idea and the progress that embodies it were in fact born here. With the end of the Third Reich. With the feeling that we owe it to our dead to give meaning to their sacrifice by resolutely committing ourselves to the only path that would guarantee peace in Europe: the path of reconciliation between our two countries," he said.[29] Gerhard Schröder replied: "The victory of the Allies was not a victory over Germany, but a victory for Germany."[30]

This evolution confirmed the fact that the construction of European unity had substantially changed the contours of memory. Many participants frequently claimed that Europe was born out of the horrified memory of the torments of World War II—an overstatement to say the least, as I have noted. A completely opposite argument could be made: the progress accomplished in unifying the Old Continent led to considering the confrontations of the past as the prelude to reconciliation in the present. From Charles de Gaulle to François Mitterrand, diplomacy exploited memory, seizing hold of the disputes of the past in a teleological perspective as the matrix for an *entente cordiale*. Operation Overlord was aimed neither at ridding the Germans of Nazism nor at laying the groundwork for European unity—a vision that would no doubt have astonished its commander, Dwight Eisenhower. But through commemorations the landing became a symbolic marker on the road that linked the Treaty of Rome to the Treaty of Maastricht. This particular example is not the only one, and other events were given the same treatment: the battlefields of the Great War and the liberation of the death camps.

By conferring special luster on the Normandy Landing, François Mitterrand also intended to celebrate the Western alliance, a prospect that probably did not trouble a man who had often been criticized for his Atlanticism. By inviting representatives of the great powers to the Normandy beaches, France became for a day the epicenter of the world, and its president raised his stature to match that of these leaders, something he must have found gratifying. It should be added that, by commemorating June 6 with pomp, he launched an indirect critique of Gaullism, in keeping with the views he had expressed in *Le coup d'état permanent*.

Respected internationally, but challenged for his national memorial policy, Mitterrand helped to muddy the image of the Resistance. The army of shadows would have been happy to avoid the controversies surrounding the president's career. In fact, it had been facing a storm since the 1980s.

A Resistance on the Defensive

Indeed, despite the museums devoted to it, the Resistance found itself to some degree on the defensive. The 1982 film *Papy fait de la résistance* had already opened the way by caricaturing the great memorial myths of the dark years. In addition to mocking Gaullist grandiloquence, Jean-Marie Poiré presented a hilarious satire of the principal Resistance types (the rich bourgeois woman, the young hothead) while simultaneously dynamiting the stereotypes of the occupying forces (the brutal Nazi, the proper German, and so on). In less frivolous fashion, in 1989, Daniel Cordier published the first volume of his biography of Jean Moulin, whose secretary he had been. The book caused a great stir because it revealed that some Resistance figures had been devotees of the cult of the Marshal and even shared some of the ideological orientations of Vichy. Far from accepting a dispassionate debate, veterans of the Combat movement, explicitly targeted in the book, took shelter behind declarations that were especially ineffective because they were based not on evidence but on value judgments. Similarly, in 1993, a journalist named Thierry Wolton asserted, on the basis of sources that were questionable because they were not referenced, that General de Gaulle's former envoy had in fact been working for the Soviet secret services. Behind these arguments lay an attempt to increase the stature of Jean Moulin in one case and a desire to attack, through a Gaullist symbol, the general who was forgiven nothing by those who were nostalgic for Vichy, Giraud, or French Algeria in the other. Added to the revelations about Mitterrand's past and, in the case of Cordier, pointing to the ambivalence of some movements, these books could not fail to stir up trouble and prevent the definition of a unified commemoration of the French Resistance, assuming that the authorities wanted one.

Scholarly memory, moreover, strengthened this tendency. The opening of the archives and the decline in timidity among university scholars led to a renewal of research that focused on movements and political organizations (chiefly the PCF and the SFIO) but also on women and the excluded—Jews, immigrants, or rank and file Resistance members—the "stokers" to whom Pierre Brossolette had paid a remarkable tribute on the BBC. Carried out by researchers who refused to rely on oral testimony and who, because of their age, had no desire to relive the battles of the dark years, these works provided a more complex image of the Resistance. They pointed, for example, to the roots of a phenomenon that, although tied to immediate circumstances, had a close connection to a set of past practices (poaching, insurrection against established authorities) that had been mobilized for this new battle. Research developed a view of the Resistance as a social, not merely a military, phenomenon, which encouraged the sociological analysis of various organizations. The cultural approach also shed light on the influence of worldviews—for instance, some Catholics identified their combat with the heroic age of the primitive Church, when a handful of the faithful, convinced they were bringing truth to the world, had accepted martyrdom in order to bear witness.

The delicate question of commitment was also revisited. It had garnered little attention in a period governed by the model of Sartre, when commitment was a matter of course, since everything was political. By asserting that the great majority of the French had participated in the underground struggle, although under different banners, Gaullists and Communists had done little to focus attention on conduct that might well be considered outside the norm. As a result, historians had been satisfied with defining involvement in clandestine organizations in a relatively rudimentary way, contrasting patriotism, supposed to explain involvement by the right, with antifascism, a notion supposedly explaining the mobilization of the progressive camp. This simplistic view did little to help clarify why so many patriotic or antifascist French citizens had adopted a wait-and-see attitude, when they had not supported the Marshal, *perinde ac cadaver*. That is to say, other causes played a role. Ideologically, the ability to identify the enemy played an essential role—it was easier for a man of the left than for a man of the right to consider Vichy an enemy. The same political background, however, might lead to diametrically opposed positions. Even though they came from the same background—the intensely Catholic Republican Federation—and shared the same patriotic fervor, Philippe Henriot and Henri Becquart followed radically opposed paths. The former won fame on Vichy radio and wore the uniform of the Milice; the latter broke ties with the French State as early as the Montoire episode, even though he shared its domestic political orientations and supported the Resistance. Henriot, to be sure, had placed anti-Communism at the summit of his concerns, whereas Becquart had chosen to give pride of place to national independence. In other words, everything depended less on political orientations themselves than on the hierarchy among them. In the same vein it was necessary to distinguish opinion from the logic of action, for although individuals might share refusals or hopes, they were not necessarily inclined to sacrifice their lives for them. For them to move forward, action had to be considered effective, which again brought up the cultural approach. A soldier might judge that distribution of the underground press was a completely puerile gesture, because you don't win a war by distributing paper; weighing the importance of words, Christians and intellectuals did not share this cut-and-dried opinion. Commitment therefore depended on the view of its effectiveness, a clearly subjective notion. Less exalted considerations also played a role—the taste for adventure, the wish to escape from the daily routine, whose effects cannot be considered negligible.

In general, historians countered the simplistic views of memory with more complex realities that disturbed the pious arrangements of the Liberation. They showed, for example, that Vichyites, after a latency period, might have joined the Resistance, and challenged the Manichaeanism of Resistance versus collaboration by exploring the gray area that so many of the French had inhabited. But by the same token,

the reexamination of the Resistance seemed to take a turn toward a suspicious view of everything and almost everyone. The constant and sometimes obsessive return to Vichy and the Occupation ended up putting the Resistance in the hot seat; it was accused, for example, of having done nothing to prevent racial deportations, and even suspected of sharing the same antipathies as the regime. . . . Political guidelines were shaken, because there was collaboration on the left as well, and the right had met the call of the Resistance. The French Communists, indicted for their attitude to the MOI [immigrant work force], were now confronted with piles of evidence revealed in the ex-Soviet archives and especially with the decay of a system and an ideology that led to a summarily negative— and anachronistic—reinterpretation of their entire history.[31]

Scholarly history thus helped to shake the columns of the temple. But it did little to facilitate the reshaping of the contours of memory by offering a clear, if not a single-minded, view of the past.

Flourishing museums and memorials did little to build up a pedagogy of memory, although this was often the ambition behind them. For example, the memorial of Vercors celebrates the figure of Arlette Blanc, a child martyr of Nazi barbarism. "The Resistance in general, and in Vercors in particular, here became the pretext for a general discourse on suffering, human rights, and the duty of memory, that necessarily put the accent on the innocent victims rather than the combatants, on death suffered rather than death anticipated."[32] Similarly in the Memorial of

Caen, the spaces dedicated to the France of the dark years shed little light on the period:

This section of the museum, abandoning the Resistance view of the French history of World War II, despite everything, seeks to suppress the absence of glory of Vichy France by merging it with the history of Europe. Every European country, we are told, had its collaborators and its resisters. All of them in the end are said to have been merely witnesses to an event whose outcome escaped them. From this point of view, the patriotic value of the Resistance, that is, the attachment to the name of a people and to the meaning it can assume in the history of "patriots" is absent. Collaborating or resisting might appear to be a purely individual and random choice. . . . French war museums confront us with this fearsome question: if the conflict is no longer speakable, if it no longer has any meaning, to what political regime have the wars of the twentieth century opened us up?[33]

In the same vein "a prohibition still seems to cover heroizing representations; soldiers of 14–18 at Péronne or Resistance fighters at Caen, they are indistinguishable from the figures of martyrs."[34] Unlike the United Kingdom, France, in other words, is having trouble handling the glorious side of its past by offering positive models with which to identify.

Conversely, it has also refused to present the dark side of that past: for example, neither collaboration nor the Vichy regime have given rise to museums. Of course, the effort would be arduous. As a general rule, museums and commemorative monuments are constructed in homage to the victims, and the murderers rarely speak. But the Germans took up the challenge by building the memorial to the victims of the Holocaust in Berlin, unveiled on May 10, 1995, and by establishing, also in Berlin, a Jewish museum that opened in 2001,[35] evidence that yesterday's guilt is not necessarily an obstacle to the construction of memorial edifices.

The development of a discourse functioning in the realms of both memory and history has turned out to be an arduous task, as suggested by the avatars of the Center of Memory of Oradour. Burned by the Germans, the town had been preserved as they left it. But the idea of creating next to the martyred village an area explaining the tragedy soon gathered momentum, placing the men in charge at the heart of contradictory tensions. "Since local elected officials were not indifferent to the tourist attraction, they looked for a balance between the constraints of pilgrimage, the local economy, which needed development incentives in order to prolong tourist visits, and the pollution inevitably associated with mass tourism."[36] But the composition of the message that the permanent exhibit should present was not self-evident. For example, should the Vichy regime be mentioned?

Wasn't there a risk of bringing up matters always difficult to handle, such as anti-Semitism, the roundups, and the many camps in Haute-Vienne? The respective fields of history and politics, amalgamated by memory, could at any moment lead to conflict. Indicating that context did not seem indispensable to those who considered that the misfortune of Oradour had its source in 1942, at the time of the invasion of the free zone.[37]

In charge of the scholarly aspect of the project, Jean-Jacques Fouché encountered formidable obstacles:

We confronted the obligation to reconcile readers of archives with pressure from witnesses and elected officials. We recognized our inability to express equitably the suffering of the victims in all their diversity. We came up against exploitation of the founding memories of the weight of the dead on the living, that is, an immutable form of the sacred. "History catching up with memory" might not satisfy the promoters of the Center of Memory.[38]

Indeed, Jean-Jacques Fouché was quickly replaced.

The museums built under the two presidential terms of François Mitterrand and in their immediate aftermath are a mixed bag. The state, however, made unstinting efforts. Between 1988 and 1998 the financing (French and European) mobilized for the memory of contemporary conflicts amounted to a cumulative total of 250 million francs, more than half of which was spent on six major operations: Caen (1988), Péronne (1992), Izieu (1994), the World Center for Peace in Verdun (1994), the National Historic Site of the Resistance in Vercors (1994), and the Center of Memory of Oradour (1999).[39]

Mitterrand's two presidential terms shed little light overall on the meaning that World War II should bear in the name of the state, which according to the accepted formula embodied the general interest. But the period that began in 1995 provided no clearer answers.

CHAPTER 6

Memory Assuaged? From Jacques Chirac to Nicolas Sarkozy (1995 to the Present)

Elected in 1995, Jacques Chirac confronted a memorial situation that was at the very least complex. The ambiguities of the Mitterrand era had helped muddy the image of the Resistance because the reintegration of those who had served both Vichy and the Resistance into national history had blurred the previously clear prevailing distinction between collaborators and resisters. While public opinion had called for scores with Vichy to be settled, President Mitterrand had held fast to stubborn denial, inflaming passions and provoking exasperation that transcended the left-right divide. Some French Jews, appalled by the contradictions of a man who laid a wreath at the Marshal's tomb one day and the next unveiled the memorial to the Vélodrome d'Hiver, finally demanded their rights. Hence, the new president had to strive mightily to calm passions. Although he succeeded in pacifying the memory of World War II, he failed to give it a shared meaning, assuming he wanted to do so.

Removing the Obstacle of Vichy

As soon as he was elected, Jacques Chirac undertook to remove the obstacle of Vichy. On July 16, 1995, the president spoke the words that many had been waiting for by recalling the assistance Vichy had provided in deporting French Jews. "Yes, it is true that the criminal insanity of the occupying forces was backed up by French people and by the French State," he acknowledged:

France, land of the Enlightenment and of Human Rights, land of hospitality and asylum, France, on that day, committed an irreparable act. It failed to keep its word and delivered those it was protecting to their executioners. . . . But there is also France, a certain idea of France, upright, generous, and faithful to its traditions and its spirit. That France had never been at Vichy. It had long since been absent from Paris. It was in the sands of Libya and everywhere the Free French were fighting. It was in London, exemplified by General de Gaulle. It was present, one and indivisible, in the heart of those French people, those "righteous among the nations" who at the risk of their lives and in the darkest hour of the storm, as Serge Klarsfeld has written, saved three-fourths of the Jewish community living in France and gave life to the best in this country: the values of humanity, of liberty, of justice, and of tolerance. They are the foundation of French identity and our obligation for the future.[1]

This important speech might have been open to criticism. Jurists had been troubled by the petition from a "Vél d'Hiv' 42 Committee," with two hundred signatures, published in *Le Monde* on June 17, 1992, demanding that

the head of state, the President of the French Republic, officially declare and acknowledge that the Vichy French State is responsible for persecutions and crimes against the Jews of France. This symbolic act is demanded by the memory of the victims and by their descendants. It is also a demand of France's collective memory which suffers from this silence. Ultimately it is the very idea of the French Republic, faithful to its founding principles, which is at stake.[2]

This demand posed two problems. With respect to the law, in the view of jurist Dominique Rousseau, official acknowledgment of the crimes of Vichy should be accompanied by "an abrogation of the ordinance of August 9, 1944, 'concerning the reestablishment of republican legality over the territory of mainland France.'"[3] From the legal point of view the ordinance of August 9, 1944, meant that the Republic had never ceased to exist as a matter of law. All the actions taken by "the de facto body calling itself the government of the French State" had thus been invalidated at a stroke, an interpretation undermined by the president's speech. But the July 16 speech also posed a political problem. Since the founding act of the Appeal, Charles de Gaulle had denied any legality to the Vichy regime. This position had led him to reject—despite the suggestion by Georges

Bidault—the idea of proclaiming the Republic from the balcony of Paris City Hall on August 25, 1944. The Republic, through the state that embodied it, never having ceased to exist, such a proclamation, he had asserted, was superfluous. In this sense Jacques Chirac's speech broke with Gaullist orthodoxy by asserting that the French State had, to some degree, embodied France.

The legality and even the legitimacy of the Vichy regime can be endlessly debated, of course, a temptation avoided by neither jurists nor historians, not to mention contemporary witnesses. But isn't this a false debate? For "in reality, the Vichy regime was illegal not so much in its forms as because of its goals."[4] Sticking to the question of legality, Jacques Chirac's speech did not undermine the edifice constructed at the Liberation, unless one were to accept the fallacious hypothesis that presidential words create norms. From the political perspective, however, Chirac was repudiating the Gaullist legacy. But, as I have noted, the general's view was itself a construction that in no way intended to reflect reality. De Gaulle was fully aware of the reality of a regime that it was hard to reduce to "a handful of scoundrels." Whether or not it had been legal, for four years the Vichy regime had mobilized its police and its judges to carry out a bloody repression against the Resistance and republicans, assisting the German occupying forces in their criminal designs. On July 10, 1940, a very large majority of deputies and senators had approved its formation. Besides, the French State did not come out of nowhere. It was the continuation of a French right-wing tradition that had long had a place in the national political debate. It is, of course, possible to believe that "making of Vichy the inevitable outcome of French national feeling was to confer on it a legitimacy that the entire effort of true French antifascists had been bent on denying it."[5] The Pétain regime nonetheless embodied an old political tradition that, from Boulangism to the Dreyfus Affair, had commanded a certain audience. In other words, it was hard to compare Philippe Pétain and his accomplices to a junta seizing control of a banana republic. The French State perhaps did not embody "true France." It certainly denied the founding principles of the Republic and betrayed the essence of the country of the Rights of Man. It nonetheless represented a certain France and not, as the Communists and Gaullists asserted, a band of traitors. By the end of the twentieth century, a large portion of the French population expected the authorities to acknowledge that obvious truth, which Gaullist discourse had symbolically long denied.

In this connection the example of Germany provided a precedent. It is well known that on December 7, 1970, Willy Brandt had kneeled before the memorial to the Jewish ghetto of Warsaw erected in memory of the victims of Nazism. In personal terms the chancellor had nothing to reproach himself for. He had left Germany to fight in Norway and later taken refuge in Sweden so that he was untainted by any compromises. Similarly, the German Federal Republic was in no way a successor to Nazism, although it agreed to pay compensation for Nazi crimes. Willy Brandt's gesture therefore was an element of a whole that he brought to a striking conclusion, particularly in light of the fact that Konrad Adenauer, although he had proceeded to indemnify the victims of the Third Reich, had not always given the impression that he was vigorous in his pursuit of former Nazi dignitaries. Through his symbolic act Brandt acknowledged the barbarous occupation of Poland by Hitlerite Germany, a situation for which he bore no responsibility. He thus fit into one of the four categories of guilt identified by the philosopher Karl Jaspers, who distinguished between criminal, metaphysical, moral, and political guilt, and stated that in the case of political guilt, "the citizens of a state have to bear the consequences of the deeds of the state."[6] All things being equal, Jacques Chirac's speech fit into this framework. And the president was able to find the appropriate words. Indeed, 72 percent of the French population approved of his remarks. By sentencing Maurice Papon to ten years' imprisonment, the Gironde criminal court provided an epilogue to this internal French war.

Chirac's speech and the Papon trial put an end to the controversies that had repeatedly shaken up the political calendar, and they also solidified a genuine consensus, since the question of Vichy seems to have been settled. Only a handful of the nostalgic steadfastly demand that Philippe Pétain be laid to rest at Douaumont among his soldiers. But neither public opinion nor the government now believe that Vichy played the role of a shield, defending the French against the occupying forces and facing the demands of the Third Reich with the silence of Antigone.

Stitching Up the Wounds

The Jewish community had been appalled by François Mitterrand's memorial policies, although his balanced Middle East diplomacy and his friendship with Judaism had long earned him that community's support. Jacques Chirac strove to calm the remaining anger.

On March 27, 1997, his prime minister, Alain Juppé, launched a mission intended "to shed light on a twofold historical process, the despoliation and pillage of the possessions of the Jews of France during the Occupation, and the restitution and indemnification the Jews may or may not have received."[7] Many thought that the state had inadequately indemnified the Jews at the Liberation. This mission, known as the Mattéoli mission, presented its conclusions in April 2000. Its report countered these concerns. After a long investigation, it established that 90 percent of the possessions had been restored, or their equivalent value paid at the end of the war. "The restitution arrangements were not put in place as quickly as they should have been, but they covered the bulk of the harm. Overall, the restored Republic did its duty."[8] It is true that 1.5 billion francs remained that a commission for indemnification for the despoliations resulting from anti-Semitic legislation in force during the Occupation took charge of distributing starting in September 1999. In five years it responded favorably to fourteen thousand petitions, and distributed a total of 176 million euros.[9]

The mission had also recommended the creation of a Foundation for the Memory of the Shoah, to which it assigned a threefold "mission of history, education, and solidarity."[10] Established in April 2001 and at the beginning presided over by Simone Veil, a former deportee and prominent political figure, this organization supported the Memorial of the Shoah, unveiled on January 25, 2005. Merging the CDJC and the Mémorial du Martyr Juif Inconnu, and endowed with substantial resources, it joined a scholarly mission intended to encourage research with a memorial purpose. Testifying to the Americanization of the forms of memory, a wall presents the engraved names of the seventy-six thousand Jewish deportees, "tribute to the victims" as well as "introduction to the visit by restoring their identity to the victims, beyond anonymity and cold numbers."[11]

Crowning all these initiatives, on July 13, 2000, Prime Minister Lionel Jospin decided to indemnify the children "whose mother or father had been deported from France in the framework of anti-Semitic persecutions . . . and died in deportation."[12] Formulated by Serge Klarsfeld and adopted by the Mattéoli commission, this provision was initially intended to fill a legal gap. Orphans who were under the age of twenty-one at the time of the events and whose parents were foreigners on the date of their deportation were excluded from the right to reparation, a failing that this decree was designed to remedy. The measure bore fruit. In 2001, 11,200 requests were accepted out of the 14,000 filed.[13]

These spectacular initiatives were a break from the dilatory approach adopted in this area by Valéry Giscard d'Estaing, followed by François Mitterrand. They put relations between the government and the Jews of France on a new footing. They also stimulated the mobilization of associations that conducted an active memorial policy, for example putting up plaques at schools to recall the barbarous fate that had afflicted Jewish schoolchildren.

The Primacy of the Shoah

These developments also led to placing the memory of the Holocaust in a central position. But although this primacy strongly sensitized public opinion to the misdeeds of anti-Semitism and racism, it may have had the side effect of exacerbating competition among victims.

This approach no doubt explains the bitterness of some groups, members of the internal Resistance or Free French Forces, who sometimes used harsh expressions in deploring this polarization. A modest example suggests as much. In 1997 a demonstration by the Sons and Daughters of Jewish Deportees from France demanded that the Star of David appear on the banners of the île de la Cité. But the Foundation for the Memory of the Deportation obtained instead the abolition of the red triangle, because the authorities preferred absence to accumulation. According to the Sons and Daughters of Jewish Deportees from France, "the presence of the red triangle on the banners dedicated the Mémorial de facto to Resistance deportees alone and perverted the message intended by the network of Memory in 1962. This abolition was experienced by many associations of former deportees as a slight to the deportation of members of the Resistance. They vigorously demanded a return to the status quo ante, judging that the red triangle can represent all deportees from France."[14]

Similarly, the decree of July 13, 2000, indemnifying the orphans of the Shoah provoked anger among a portion of Resistance deportees or their descendants. Some were surprised at the disparity it created. The spokesmen of one association wrote: "We are aware of the appalling situation of the Deportees of all categories. We cannot accept a disparity contrary to our Constitution, contrary to the high regard in which the government and its leaders hold those who gave their lives for our country."[15] Other letters presented more dubious arguments. For example, the child of a Resistance fighter noted that "the death of a father or a mother is a difficult ordeal to live through in any circumstances and for any child; it seems logical to treat all cases in the same way without incorporating a religious or ethnic aspect in the matter. If I understood correctly, the reason for not attributing this indemnity is linked to inclusion or non-inclusion in 'the status of Jew,' and I could thus not help but denounce a sectarian and racist position of which I would be the target."[16] The son of a deported Resistance fighter who had died in Neuengamme protested: "I am simply ashamed that I am subjected to such an affront, and I wonder whether in the country of the rights of man we will soon not have to wear the Star of David in order to be treated and respected like anyone else (ordinary, normal French person) who has spent decades fighting against injustice, racism, and anti-Semitism."[17] These complaints were heard: the decree of July 27, 2004, instituted "financial assistance in recognition of the suffering endured by orphans whose parents were victims of acts of barbarity during World War II."[18]

Even so, the Conseil d'État issued an opinion on February 16, 2009, that put an end to any further claims. It pointed out that the measures benefiting the victims of Nazism and of Vichy "should be viewed, insofar as possible, as having permitted the indemnification, in accordance with the rights guaranteed by the European Convention for the Protection of Human Rights and Fundamental Freedoms, for the harms of all kinds caused by the actions of the state in connection with deportation." It also specified that "reparation for the extraordinary suffering endured by the victims of anti-Semitic persecution could not be limited to measures of a financial nature. It [the reparation] called for solemn acknowledgement of the harm collectively suffered by those individuals, the role of the state in their deportation, and the memory that their suffering and that of their families must forever leave in the mind of the nation." But, it went on, "this acknowledgement has been carried out by a set of actions and initiatives by the French authorities," such as the law of December 26, 1964, concerning the nonapplicability of statutory limitations to crimes against humanity, the declaration by Jacques Chirac, and the creation of the Foundation for the Memory of the Shoah.[19]

Beyond these demands, symbolic as well as material, the fear of seeing racial deportation eclipse Resistance deportation haunted the Resistance associations. For example, at a meeting of the Haut Conseil de la Mémoire Combattante on November 10, 2004, Mme Valmy

reminded the President of the Republic of the current organization of the day of deportation and asked that the President of the Republic participate in the ceremony that should concern all deportees and not only the victims of the Shoah. She asked that the associations of deportees be consulted on the content of the ceremony. . . . Mme Vernay and Mme Rol-Tanguy urged that all victims of deportation be honored and that the Resistance fighters who were deported not be forgotten.[20]

But, more generally, these demands reflected an erosion of Resistance memory, which had for many years been placed on the defensive.

Manifestations of Resistance Memory

Of course, Resistance fighters enjoyed—and still enjoy—deep respect, especially because their image had been profoundly modified. In the immediate aftermath of the war, a Resistance fighter had been considered a soldier by default, a view that led to an underestimation or even disdain for the effects of "civilian resistance." But starting in the 1980s, the Resistance fighter was identified as a pioneer of human rights who had combated not eternal Germany but Nazi totalitarianism. For example, in 1992 Socialist Minister of Veterans Affairs Louis Mexandeau asserted: "In relation to democracy and human rights, the actions of Resistance fighters amounted to a kind of anticipation of what has come about particularly at the instigation of France and is known as the humanitarian duty to intervene. It has taken sixty years for minds to follow this path and for this duty to be recognized. Well, we should not forget those distant pioneers."[21] At a time when human rights were imposing their presence on political and diplomatic calendars, this view was in step with society's expectations. By updating the terms of the combat conducted in the clandestine darkness and by consecrating the contemporaneity of their values, it could place Resistance veterans at the heart of civic debate.

Violent disputes contradicted this optimistic view. For example, in 1997 the journalist Gérard Chauvy published a book about Raymond and Lucie Aubrac.[22] Reconsidering the 1943 arrests that, in a fatal sequence, had led to the arrest of Jean Moulin on June 21, he pointed to the multiple contradictions peppering the testimony of this mythic couple after Moulin's arrest. Although it acknowledged that no archive document validated the accusation of betrayal made by Klaus Barbie, Chauvy's book might "give the impression that it was toying with suspicion or even insinuation."[23] The author was in fact found guilty of defamation, although the aura of doubt was not totally dissipated. The detractors of the Resistance stepped into the breach, anticipating that discrediting a symbolic couple would undermine the legend of the army of shadows. In a situation in which the National Front was progressing, this attack could not fail to weaken the position of the Aubracs, who were intensely involved in the fight against the resurgence of the old racist and reactionary demons. The jacket copy of the book, written by the publisher, was a model of casuistry. Within the Resistance "the purest heroism and the most guilty weakness continue to keep company." And it went on to ask: "Beyond the saga, which *may have* had its legitimacy . . . is it not time to abandon patriotic exaltation for the serenity of historical study?"[24] The reader, however, might judge that the Resistance *had* had its legitimacy.

At the same time, Gérard Chauvy dismantled a memorial reconstruction created by the Aubracs that forced readers to consider "the account of events . . . experienced like a simple, partially subjective narrative, a narrative that added some embellishments to the account of verified facts and left certain matters obscure."[25] In other words the problem did not lie in the area of the facts. In a round-table discussion sponsored by *Libération*, historians generally agreed that the couple had not betrayed

Jean Moulin. They were more skeptical about the accounts developed after the fact. And if Resistance fighters had embellished their stories and preserved some mysteries, how much trust could be placed in their words? Coming after the clumsy defense conducted by the members of Combat who had been quick to support their former leader, Henri Frenay, despite the archival evidence, the Aubrac affair disturbed relations between historians—increasingly inclined to rely on the archives—and witnesses—hurt that they were no longer taken at their word. Until the 1990s the history of the Resistance had long been based, as the work of Henri Noguères indicates, exclusively on the testimony of witnesses. This period was definitively over.

A few films reflect the blurred image that now characterized the Resistance. In *Un héros très discret* (A Self-Made Hero, 1996), Jacques Audiard described the career of an impostor who managed to pass himself off as a hero in the aftermath of the war. This brilliant film suggested that posterity had perhaps consecrated false heroes and that memory really did not coincide with history. Conversely, films adopting the received view were notable for their mediocrity, like *Lucie Aubrac* by Claude Berri (1997), which presented a cartoonish image of the army of shadows. Opening with a train sabotage—something the Aubracs had never done—it tried to link history to personal anecdote (namely, the couple's private life) and succeeded neither in moving the audience nor in helping it understand the saga of the underground. Were filmmakers more adept at dismantling the legend than at reinforcing it?

The government was unable to contain this memorial disturbance. Able to resolve the dispute around the Vichy episode and to soothe the pain of the Jewish community, it was unable to provide the nation with a positive view of the Resistance. Its policies, moreover, were suspected of producing perverse effects.

Was Too Much Attention Given to the Shoah?

The emphasis placed on the Shoah in both media and teaching did indeed give rise to hostile reactions on the part of certain fringes of French society, particularly among the children of recent immigrants. "Recent troubling reports from the [Education] Inspection [Agency] have . . . indicated the points of friction, particularly the revival of anti-Semitism in some educational establishments," according to Jean-Pierre Rioux, a historian and an educational inspector.[26] So much so that one might question the effectiveness of a memorial policy that is so quick to invoke "the duty of memory."

Similarly, the activism of some Jewish groups, demanding rights and conducting an active memorial policy—for example, by putting up plaques recalling the deportation of children—could and did sometimes cause irritation. By constantly recalling the crimes committed between 1940 and 1945, these actions helped to confer on the Shoah a centrality that seemed to strip the other participants in the war—Resistance fighters, the Free French, prisoners—of their memory.

To be understood, however, this fervor has to be seen in context. The destruction of the European Jews had for many decades been not only forgotten but subjected to a kind of euphemistic treatment by the state. The dead had no sepulcher reminding the living of their names, and no one was troubled by that. Jewish deportees, too small in number to carry any weight, found it hard to make their voices heard. Favoring a policy of unity, associations had no intention of distinguishing among the dead: "all united and in the end mixed together in the smoke of the crematoria."[27] They also identified deportees as combatants. The survivors, according to Charles Joineau, general secretary of the FNDIRP for thirty years, should "display the values for which we fought and suffered and so many of us died. In that sense our testimony cannot consist solely of the expression of the suffering we endured."[28] This approach put the racial deportees in an awkward position: "How could one consider the millions of innocents gassed in the death camps whose only crime was to be Jewish as anything but victims? Where is the heroism proclaimed in so many speeches and so much testimony?"[29] In addition Jewish deportees received pensions in amounts substantially lower than those received by Resistance deportees—an injustice not corrected until 1970. Foreigners younger than twenty-eight at the time of their naturalization had to fulfill their military obligations, even if they had been deported (they were then exempt from the last six months of service).[30]

Associating Jews and Resistance fighters in its memorial policies, the government had also long striven to mask the responsibilities of the

Vichy State in the deportation of the Jews of France—a choice reflected in governments from Félix Gouin to François Mitterrand. For many years school curricula also offered a complacent reading of the dark years. "Little by little, the difficulties linked to the Nazi regime and the war— undernourishment, anti-Semitic persecutions, great sums of money levied for the costs of occupation, arrests of patriots, executions of hostages— created increasing irritation." "The dignitaries of the Freemasons and the Jews—under pressure exerted by the Nazis—were subject to a census, and later excluded from holding employment in the public sector. The Nazi authorities carried out mass arrests of Jews in the occupied zone: 4,000 children from two to twelve years old arrived in the span of two weeks at Drancy. While the government remained silent, Pastor Boegner and the Cardinals and Bishops of France protested vigorously." This was the language that could still be found in two textbooks at the dawn of the 1980s.[31] Added to that was the fact that research on anti-Semitism in general and the destruction of the European Jews in particular was little encouraged by the authorities. For many years the historian Léon Poliakov was an isolated figure. And in order to make a census of the Jews deported from France, Serge Klarsfeld had to rely on volunteer students from Jewish schools—the Yabné school and the ORT establishment in Montreuil—to type the names. Besides, the *Mémorial de la déportation des Juifs de France* was originally published in 1978 at the author's expense.

These factors explain and justify the activism of some Jewish groups in France. In the face of the magnitude of the trauma suffered and the silence, or even the denials, of the authorities, energetic action was called for. Under these circumstances the memorial excess that some deplored, if not condemned, was only a response to the void that had until recently characterized the memorial policy of the state. Moreover, "the duty of memory" was a relatively recent program. The phrase itself dated from 1995 and was taken from the title given the French translation of a posthumous interview of Primo Levi by two Italian historians.[32]

To be sure, as I have noted, under Jacques Chirac the government issued a clear and unambiguous condemnation of the Vichy regime. The half-measures of François Mitterrand were succeeded by a clear policy based on the rejection of any ambiguity (there were no more presidential wreaths at Pétain's tomb on the île d'Yeu) and on a desire for clarity that led Prime Minister Lionel Jospin to authorize access to the archives of the dark years in 1997:

The text [of the decrees] prescribes the multiplication of general dispensations, the availability to the public of all inventories, and acceleration of the processing of dispensations. After negotiations between the Archives de France and the departments concerned, the great majority of materials held in the Archives Nationales are completely open, by decree, including files containing letters of denunciation and directly accusing individuals, which it had been impossible to open earlier out of fear of acts of vengeance. Other decrees, like the one issued by the Ministry of Defense, limit the field of application of the general dispensation to general documents, to the exclusion of documents mentioning names, reducing the scope of a decree whose legal validity it has called into question.[33]

The authorities also granted the memory of the Shoah the place it deserved, particularly in school curricula. As a result textbooks and teacher education were substantially modified, integrating the most recent research results:

It is with respect to "crime against humanity," "genocide," and "Shoah" that the strongest efforts for educating teachers, providing documentation, and improving pedagogical practices (in and out of class: in this regard, favoring visits to "Memorials" will continue to be useful) have been made. It is on the subject of World War II that we have noted the most significant improvements in the wording of lycée curricula and their accompanying documents and that the most useful notions and concepts have been clarified, whereas the question of the curriculum for *collèges* is open and that of the primary school curricula should be reviewed in the immediate future.[34]

The supposition that the focus on the Shoah contributed to the revival of anti-Semitism thus seems dubious. It would amount to arguing that the hatred of the Jews has its source in a rationality fostered, for example, by abnormally vivid memory or the presumed behavior of some imagined "Jewish community." The reality seems to be more complex and sordid. It is possible that the Palestinian Intifada and the 2003 Iraq War created tension in some schools. In the absence of a precise accounting, however, it seems premature to deduce from that that teaching World War II in general and the Shoah in particular is impossible today in so-called sensitive schools.

But this observation should not obscure some disturbing facts. To begin with, far from behaving calmly, the government merely reacted to the demands of civil society on memorial matters. Instead of anticipating the movement, for example by granting the Shoah a prominent place, it equivocated for a long time. But World War II was not the only subject affected by this lack of will; it touched equally other conflicts:

The state [a fortiori since the 1990s] has never taken a position on the Algerian War unless it was forced to by the pressure of public opinion or certain groups. It is as though the state's chisel carved the bronze plaque of official recognition according to the pressure exerted by various interest groups. Indeed, the lights and shadows of that plaque reflect rather various social demands than the expression of a policy of recognition or eclipse of the past. The recognition of the past is in the end primarily the recognition of the legitimacy of the demands of one group or another. The state's role is not so much to take a position on the past as to construct, for today or tomorrow, a relationship with a given group.[35]

This policy, not very well thought out, also led the government to misconstrue the demands made by other groups, particularly the Free French and the internal Resistance. Merely reacting to the immediate situation and arbitrating among contradictory demands, it did not define a rigorous politics of memory, which explains the frustration that overcame some groups. In reality, this lack of will reflected a deeper uneasiness:

The memory of our nation indeed remains incapable of giving a unified historical account. For on the one hand, there was a common destiny which linked all the French people and all the foreigners who had taken refuge on French soil. This was a population that experienced the same ordeal: the ordeal of the war, the defeat, and the enemy occupation. But on the other hand, there were radical differences in the situations to which various groups were subjected.[36]

It should also be noted that the demand for truth imposed by historical investigation sometimes produced perverse effects. The reminder of compromises or even crimes committed by France might contradict the underlying purpose of the teaching of history, which, since the beginnings of the Third Republic, has always been designed to forge a civic community that shares common values illustrated by the national saga. This contradiction fosters the fears felt, for example, by Jean-Pierre Rioux:

It is . . . inconceivable to allow [some students] to lodge in their memories a negative representation of France, which would risk having them internalize the "hatred" of what they are when they witness the spectacle of such an avalanche of crimes attributed to the nation that is offered to them. How could they recognize themselves in this wicked stepmother? Their integration would be compromised, which is far from the goals of the school, whose underlying purpose, of course, is the individual emancipation of each student and his civic integration in a continuously vital relationship between different individuals and between the whole and each one of them.[37]

The primacy granted the Shoah also accentuated the tendency of exalting victims at the expense of heroes. Positive models gave way in favor of martyrs.

The Disappearance of Heroes

The memorial approach to the Normandy Landing was a clear indication of this development. Until the 1980s the authorities had paid little attention to the victims of military operations in Normandy and preferred to glorify the exploits of the Anglo-American armies. As time went by, however, the victims were heard and even listened to. And monuments have been unveiled in recent years. An exhibition titled *En regard de Guernica* recalled the price paid by the population during the bombing. Also for the first time, a regional ceremony was organized at Saint-Lô in 2004. Many vigils were held in the same year in memory of the men and women crushed by the military operations of the summer of 1944—a phenomenon picked up by the media (notably the press and local radio). Pressure from survivors and their families led historians to turn their attention to the history of civilians; starting in 1994, they carried out vast investigations of the bombing that produced a statistical survey of the operations.[38]

This development was the result of many factors. For historical and memorial reasons, but also for tourism, the authorities decided in 2004 to expand the commemorative framework of June 6, 1944, to the eighty days of the Battle of Normandy. This expansion meant the inclusion of the victims previously left out because of the primacy given the landing in the narrow sense. The transformations that had occurred on the international scene magnified this tendency. With the disappearance of the Soviet threat, the Anglo-Americans reduced their symbolic exploitation of June 6, replacing the logic of the cold war that had prevailed in the 1950s. By changing the meaning of a commemoration that had been frozen in the patterns set at the Liberation, leaders opened up a memorial space that made it possible to recall some of the suffering endured by the population. But we should not exaggerate. This memory is still situated at the fringes of official memory. "It seems that as soon as they want to go beyond the framework of local commemoration, these celebrants do not dare engrave that memory in stone, give it visible form, and are content with presenting it in the ephemeral form of speech."[39] Above all, celebrants tend to give heroic form to the attitude of the victims, "evoked as active martyrs who sacrificed themselves for the noble cause,"[40] which integrates them into the overall picture of the Battle of Normandy but denies the specificity of their fate.

The French and Colonial Subjects

The authorities also were committed to incorporating the colonial troops into the national memory. Their participation in the Italian, French, and German campaigns had, it is true, been rather slighted. This memory had at first been confiscated by those who were nostalgic for French Algeria, inclined to dedicate roundabouts and public squares in localities to General Salan, a way of celebrating both the hero of World War II and the head of the OAS (the Secret Army Organization that fought to maintain French Algeria). However, the reaction of some organizations, notably the Ligue des Droits de l'Homme, led to a compromise: the memory of the colonel, not that of the general, was honored.

The memory of the North African troops had more difficulty finding a place. In this respect the 2006 film by Rachid Bouchareb, *Indigènes* (Days of Glory), had a thoroughly cathartic and energizing effect. By presenting a version centered on the sacrificial heroism of colonial troops, he recalled a page of the history of World War II unknown to the general public and pointed to the ingratitude of the mother country toward those who had fought in its name. But the results were ambiguous.

On one hand, veterans were incorporated into the national saga and finally obtained equalization of their pensions with those of French veterans, solemnly announced by Jacques Chirac in his speech on July 14, 2006. The president's decision was the outcome of a long process. The veterans of the empire had filed claims in French jurisdictions for many years.

Tired of the battle, veterans from Senegal had appealed to the United Nations Human Rights Committee, which ruled in their favor in 1989. French administrative jurisdictions, however, persisted in their rejection until November 30, 2001, when a plenary session of the Conseil d'État acknowledged the rights of these veterans. The government abolished the discrepancy in pensions, but this decision was based on the principle of equity: empire veterans would receive a pension granting them a purchasing power equivalent to that guaranteed to French veterans. Coming into force in 2003, the measure cost 130 million euros in its first year (because of arrears), and 30 million euros in subsequent years. Hence, in 2006, Jacques Chirac simply abolished this equity provision that appeared to be unjust.

The film *Indigènes* thus had the result of fostering the integration—at least in memorial terms—of the populations of greater France, even though that integration had for years been the source of fantasies, demands, and controversies. At the same time it thwarted this ambition by recalling the egotism and cavalier attitude of metropolitan France, which, then as in the past, was doing little for those categorized as minorities. In any event the government of the Republic took the path of reparation, devoting large sums to increasing pensions beginning in April 2007. By September 1, 2007, Tunisian veterans had received 18.5 million euros and their Moroccan comrades 21.1 million. The material consequences were not negligible for the 27,000 veterans concerned (added to whom were nearly six thousand widows): before the change a Moroccan received an annual veteran's pension of 60 euros; afterward, he received 495 euros.[41]

These advances, however, did not pacify all resentments. Some veterans of the army of Africa were not pleased by the film *Indigènes*, not finding in it "the reality they had experienced. Extraordinary cohesion and fraternity were a matter of pride" for the French expeditionary force in Italy, they asserted.[42] Conversely, the combatants of the empire judged the belated gestures of the former colonial power to be limited: Senegal, for example, was left out of the change. Similarly, the Italians showed little inclination to hail the liberating role of the French armies. The intervention of forces under General Juin in Italy had been accompanied by violence against civilians, primarily theft and rape. Even today, in the mountains of Latium, the neologism *marocchinate* means "having been a victim of Moroccans," that is, raped.[43] The memory of the French Expeditionary Force (CEF) is thus a conflicted one. On the one hand, veterans and their spokesmen minimize the incidence of the crimes, emphasizing their low numbers (a hundred or so) and pointing to the harsh repression inflicted, in their view, by the military authorities. On the other hand, the Italians assert that the abuses can be counted in the thousands and suspect General Juin of having given his troops carte blanche, subjecting the civilian population to suffering and terror. And these opposing points of view remain unreconciled even today.

In the same way, the countries of North Africa are not disposed to share the view of World War II presented by the former colonial power. Created in Rabat in 1996 and inaugurated in 2000, the National Museum of the Resistance and the Army of Liberation presents the French authorities as the embodiment of colonial oppression. "The relationship between the Moroccan veterans of the French Army and the Royal Armed Forces is obscured and only two panels added subsequently recall the participation of Moroccan soldiers in the combats of World War II."[44] Of course, the cooperation developed between France and Morocco since 2004 has fostered the growth of a shared memory. But it is still heavily exploited by Rabat, which claims that the volunteers were responding to an appeal from Sultan Sidi Mohammed Ben Youssef, the future Mohammed V. By identifying the enlistment of the Moroccans as respecting instructions given by their political, religious, and spiritual leader, this view "glosses over the diversity of reasons for signing up (desire to rise in social status, financial considerations, taste for adventure, political fight against Nazism, or attachment to France). By so doing, it makes it possible to diminish the colonial aspect of the Moroccans' participation in the battles of World War II and to obliterate any memorial conflict with France."[45] Tunisia, for its part, seemed to lose interest in the question after having adopted an offensive attitude: in the 1970s the authorities presented the participation of Tunisian soldiers from the colonial angle, claiming that the French command had used these troops as cannon fodder. But the following decades were chiefly characterized by indifference, the Ben Ali regime showing little interest in the question.

This was not true for Algeria. Centering its legitimacy on the war of independence, the Algerian regime strove to present the participation of Algerian troops as the product of colonial domination. The old war memorial on the Forum of Algiers was encased in a concrete shell. On the new façade were carvings of fists breaking chains. And for obvious reasons May 8 commemorates the Sétif massacre and not the end of World War II.[46] Despite some gestures made by France—awarding the city of Algiers the Légion d'honneur in 2004 because of the role it played from November 1942 on—the Algerian government was not very inclined to worship at the altar of a shared memory, although Hamlaoui Mekachera, veterans affairs minister in the Villepin government, tried to give it some substance. The dispute resulting from World War II in fact masked many others, and it is hard to imagine Paris and Algiers establishing close ties in the memorial domain when so many disputes between the two coasts of the Mediterranean persist.

Shared Memories?

Aside from this particular case, during Jacques Chirac's presidency the memory of World War II had little influence on international relations, except in symbolic terms. At the dawn of the twenty-first century his regime did endeavor to develop the concept of "shared memory": "the intent expressed by the state to encourage, organize, and value its bilateral relations with the countries and peoples whose military history has crossed paths with that of France since the beginning of the twentieth century."[47] This relatively broad definition encompasses former allies and adversaries, decolonized nations, and states that France had supported when their freedom was threatened, such as South Korea. Agreements were signed with South Korea and Australia (2003); Morocco, Madagascar, the United Kingdom, and New Zealand (2004); Tunisia (2006); and Canada. The initiative is rather fragile, concerning only eight countries at the end of 2008.

Similarly, the government joined in a kind of internationalization of memory. Although it served—intentionally or not—to accentuate the cohesion of the national community, to reinvigorate patriotism, and to celebrate the nation, the politics of commemoration was increasingly tied to diplomatic considerations. Following in the footsteps of François

Mitterrand, who had grasped the hand of Helmut Kohl at Verdun, it served to anchor Franco-German reconciliation, not without some challenges. For example, in 1998 the authorities questioned the appropriateness of inviting a German delegation to commemorate November 11. The initiative provoked a debate. A government representative pointed out that for the Germans, November 11, 1918, corresponded to the beginning of Nazism. For that reason they would not want to commemorate that date. Chancellor of the Order of the Liberation General Jean Simon believed that if the Germans were invited to the Arc de Triomphe, they would come; "but that would be viewed badly by the veterans." President Chirac cautiously decided it was necessary to consult the associations: "If they are against, we cancel; if they are for, we consult the Germans."[48] On May 9, 2001, however, relighting the flame at the Arc de Triomphe with young Germans provoked no debate, and the initiative was hailed by all participants.[49] And, following a proposal made by a youth parliament that had met to celebrate the fortieth anniversary of the Élysée Treaty, preparation of a Franco-German textbook intended for secondary schools was begun in 2004. Hailed as a success, this book confirmed the convergence of French and German historiography, with tensions focused on two points: "the role of the United States in the development of Europe and the world after 1945 and the presentation and interpretation of Socialist experiences"[50]—still a sensitive subject in a recently reunified Germany. The discussion of World War II, however, caused no controversies.

Along the same lines, Jacques Chirac reinforced the internationalization of memory by placing it at the service of peace. This orientation was developed particularly at the eightieth anniversary of the victory of 1918, which praised "the international aspect of these commemorations. They should express how much the road traveled for eighty years, with its detours and backtracking, its moments of hope as well as its dark hours, requires that today, when perfect and lasting concord reigns among our once enemy peoples, we remain vigilant, in our country and around the world, in the face of the stirrings of discord or resentment that might arise again." Similarly, the junior minister of veterans affairs, the Socialist Jean-Pierre Masseret, suggested that the commemoration of 1918 be organized "around the idea of the shared history of combating nations."[51] This internationalization also marked, as we have seen, the sixtieth anniversary of the Normandy Landing.

Overall, Jacques Chirac strove, with some success, to settle the memorial disputes that opposed the state to a fringe of public opinion. Acknowledging the reality of the French State and the damage inflicted by its policies, emphasizing the importance and the uniqueness of the Shoah, he also actively supported a politics of memory that followed diverse channels—financial assistance, the creation of museums, the holding of ceremonies, and so on. Finally, he completed a generous policy of reparation, indemnifying the orphans of the Shoah and later the orphans of the Resistance. At a time when memory was managed primarily by the associations, the state was led to play an increasing role in the definition of memory, previously vivid enough to do without such oversight. But this involvement did not come without perverse consequences.

The president was inclined to give in to the memorial demands expressed by the most diverse groups. This abdication led to the proliferation of national days of homage. "Today they have reached the number of 12, twice as many as in 1999."[52] The government established days of tribute to the auxiliary or similar forces who served in Algeria (2001), to the victims of the racist and anti-Semitic crimes of the French State and to the Righteous French (2000), to the harkis (2003), to the veterans of the Algerian War and the combats in Morocco, and to the soldiers of the Indochina War; and June 18 also received recognition by the nation. This policy helped to render the meaning of national commemorations insipid and to prevent the development of a language with a wide scope by balkanizing the national memory. This produced an odd paradox: it was at the very moment that the state was taking on the question of memory that any shared vision disappeared.

Members of the National Assembly also intervened widely in the field of memory. For example the Gayssot law passed on July 13, 1990, punished any "racist, anti-Semitic, or xenophobic statement" and identified denial of the existence of crimes against humanity as an offense. Continuing along these lines, the legislature recognized the Armenian genocide (January 29, 2001), likened the slave trade to a crime against humanity (May 21, 2001), and asked that school curricula recognize "the positive role of the French presence overseas, particularly in North Africa" (February

25, 2005). And in October 2006 the National Assembly adopted the Masse proposal that applied to the 2001 law on Armenia the criminal penalties provided in the Gayssot law. This plethora of laws was no doubt motivated by specious reasons. What carried the day were above all

basically electoral considerations, which are certainly not contemptible, but have more to do with emotion than reason, have no scholarly legitimacy, and confuse memory with history. They all come out of the same aspiration of particular ethnic or religious communities to have their specific memory taken into consideration by the national community through the intermediary of history, which is taken hostage. It is against this exploitation that brings about a fragmentation of collective memory that historians have taken a position.[53]

It was indeed the mobilization of the historical community that brought the president of the republic to interrupt this inflation; in January 2006 Jacques Chirac declared that it was not up to parliament to write history.

These aberrations suggest above all the loss of influence suffered by history and historians. The parliament had effectively assumed the right to define, according to its standards, the true and the false, the licit and the illicit; and the force of scholarship seemed unable to impose its interpretation or interpretations of events, although the government, in the face of a mobilization of a portion of the historical profession, had stepped back.

It might also be pointed out that the effectiveness of the memorial policies carried out under the presidency of Jacques Chirac should not be overestimated, despite the emphasis placed on the "duty of memory." For example, in the final term of 1998 only 50 percent of the 110,000 young people who took the tests of the National Defense Information Day (Journée d'Appel de Préparation à la Défense, JAPD) were able to "state correctly the meaning of the four anniversary dates they were asked to identify (July 14, November 11, May 8, and June 6),"[54] a percentage that gives one pause.

A New Situation under Sarkozy?

Although it may seem premature at best to draw up a balance sheet, the memorial policy implemented by Nicolas Sarkozy appears to mark a turning point. He set out first to restore the prestige of the Resistance.

During his presidential campaign he visited the plateau of Glières (site of a celebrated Resistance battle) on May 4, 2007, and vowed to return every year. He kept the promise, returning on March 18, 2008, and April 29, 2009. On May 16, 2007, he announced that the letter from the young Guy Môquet, executed on October 22, 1941, would be read to French secondary school students every year. Unlike his predecessor, Sarkozy had thus set the memory of the Resistance at the heart of his memorial policy.

The president also intended to maintain a prominent place for the Shoah, following in the footsteps of his predecessors. On February 13, 2008, at a dinner of the Representative Council of French Jewish Institutions (Conseil Représentatif des Institutions Juives de France, CRIF), he suggested that every pupil in CM2 [i.e., fourth grade] be entrusted with the memory of a Jewish child deported during World War II. The initiative reflected the importance he attributed to the memory of the destruction of the French Jews; nonetheless, it touched off violent disputes. Serge Klarsfeld favored it, pointing out that "those who now disparage it will later claim to have inspired it." But his voice was isolated—Simone Veil challenged the notion that one could "ask a child to identify with a dead child. That memory is much too heavy to bear," she said. The proposal was not implemented.

There was a multiplicity of reasons behind these policies. The president obviously wanted to break from the policy of repentance that dominated the memory of the dark years, and he conspicuously distanced himself from it in a speech in Lyon on April 5, 2007:

I hate the fashion for repentance that expresses hatred of France and of its History.
 I hate the repentance that would forbid us from being proud of our country.
 I hate the repentance that is an open invitation to competition between memories.
 I hate the repentance that sets the French against one another according to their origins.
 I hate the repentance that is an obstacle to integration because one seldom wants to join what one has learned to hate, when one should love and respect it.
 That is my truth.

Indeed, the image of a France beating its breast hardly matched the image of the country he intended to forge—that of a nation sure of its past gallantly facing the future. From this perspective, the Resistance was an

ideal point of reference. A school of vitality, it had demonstrated that voluntarism had transcended the mask of appearances by overcoming the
falsely obvious German victory—a lesson no doubt valuable today for a
country confronting a serious economic crisis. During the war, the army
of shadows had also overcome divisions, uniting those who believed in
heaven and those who did not. This example could not fail to inspire a
man who, pursuing a politics of inclusiveness, claimed to be abolishing
the opposition between the party of order and the forces of progress.

The Nicolas Sarkozy, however, had always tied less lofty considerations
to the heights of the ideal. His way of dealing with the memory of the
war was no exception to that iron law: it seemed to be inspired by careful
political calculation.

The president was intent on modernizing the ideology of the French
right. From this point of view the glorification of the Resistance had nothing but advantages. It enabled him to break with a Vichyite past that a
fringe of the conservative camp had long struggled to shed, which facilitated support from a reactionary electorate now freed from that deadly
burden. Taking note of the waning of the Gaullist legend, Sarkozy replaced the epic saga of the general with a mythology that was particularly
effective because its ecumenical reach extended from the Communists to
the traditional right, thereby enabling him to avoid being locked into a
partisan view of the dark years. Displaying his resolve with respect to illegal immigrants as well as real or imagined troublemakers, Sarkozy could
finally counter the critics who challenged his security policy with his
profound attachment to the humanistic legacy of the Resistance. Indeed,
how could one suspect the pilgrim to Glières of conducting "roundups" of
undocumented immigrants?

The memorial policies pursued since 2007 also enabled the president
to embarrass a segment of the French left. By taking up Guy Môquet, he
annexed a hero of the Communist Pantheon, which reinforced his con-
ciliatory image while provoking the anger of some on the left. Speaking
of the figure of the young Communist at the congress of his conservative party, the UMP, on January 14, 2007, he drew a sharp reaction from
Marie-George Buffet. The national secretary of the French Communist
Party declared: "I forbid this cabinet minister, who hunts down children in
school, who wants to put minors in jail, to use the name of Guy Môquet."

In a totally different area the president's repeated visits to the plateau of Glières were designed to give him a symbolic site comparable to what were in their time Mont-Valérien and Colombey-les-deux-Églises for Charles de Gaulle or the Roche de Solutré for François Mitterrand. Glières had the advantage of having so far been exempt from any partisan appropriation, unlike the île de Sein or Mont-Valérien, which were immediately identified with wartime Gaullism.

But this ambitious policy soon began to mark time. The government, as we have seen, quickly gave up the notion of having elementary school students adopt a deported child. The reading of Guy Môquet's letter, required in 2008, was left to the teachers' discretion in 2009; generally, they had balked at this "subjection of memory: a letter read in every school, every year, on the same day, if not at the same time, practically standing at attention?" queried the historian Jean-Pierre Azéma.[55]

Nicolas Sarkozy's voluntarism thus soon came up against its limits, which is hardly surprising. For one thing, the government was counting on if not pathos, at least emotion, which invalidates any policy intended to last. In addition, seeking to multiply media events with no concern for the long term, he barely gave himself time to think, confusing speed with haste. Moreover, and perhaps most important, a memorial policy takes root only when it more or less responds to a social demand. And society was not asking that another gesture be made to commemorate the Shoah; it found it all the more difficult to accept the new image of the Resistance that Sarkozy wanted to present because his symbolic choice was surprising. Rather than a valiant Resistance fighter, Guy Môquet was a young Communist militant the Vichy government had arrested on October 13, 1940, and administratively interned in the camp at Choisel on May 16, 1941— well before the invasion of the Soviet Union. The adolescent executed at Châteaubriant was therefore anything but a Resistance fighter. "Arrested by French police for having violated the Daladier law of September 26, 1939, against Communist intrigues . . . Guy Môquet, who undertook no action against German interests, therefore never had anything to do with the occupying forces before his name turned up on a list of hostages on the morning of October 22, 1941."[56] So the hero presented as a model to French youth was a particularly bad choice, despite his tragic end. The example of Glières calls for an identical comment: the name probably has an echo only for the oldest generations and says nothing to their successors.

The memorial policy of the new president does not therefore seem to mark a radical break with the practice of his predecessors, despite the voluntarism it displays. It is, moreover, dominated by an equivocation. Indulging in media events, while simultaneously glorifying the values of the Resistance, will the policy be able to inscribe the legacy of the dark years in a formulation or reformulation of national identity? Only the future can answer that question, which public debate has made a matter of vital current interest.

Conclusion

Does the memory of World War II over the course of the second half of the twentieth century deserve that name? Unlike the Great War, the incidence of combat is minor, eroded by a memory focused primarily on the Occupation and the Vichy regime. But this does not mean that the memory of the soldiers of 1939 to 1940 and those of 1944 to 1945 has been eclipsed. On the contrary, the state has been careful to pay tribute to the combatants, granting them reparations and making sure that they have received decent burials. But a sign of relative lack of interest is the fact that military cemeteries have not always been meticulously cared for. For lack of appropriate maintenance, which would have required sizable budgets, some sites have deteriorated, providing a striking contrast to the care lavished on foreign military cemeteries. In 2006, for example, Senator Charles Guéné estimated that 15 percent of monuments and ossuaries required restoration; 15 percent of walls, entry points, paths, and stairways needed to be brought up to safety standards; and 20 percent of tombs in municipal cemeteries required renovation.[1] And France provided only eight euros annually for each soldier to maintain the tombs of its dead, whereas the Commonwealth had agreed to spend thirty-one euros.[2] Along the same lines, the authorities had commemorated the battles on the Italian front in 1943 and 1944 only in modest ways; and the fighting in Norway in 1940, the battle of the Vosges in 1944–1945, and the German campaign were practically forgotten. With the humiliating defeat of 1940, the soldiers, incapable of defending the nation, had been ejected from the memorial realm: how could one commemorate a rout? The fragment of the sword taken up by de Gaulle turned out to be too short to eradicate the indelible scar inflicted by that appalling defeat. Although it erected a few monuments, to honor the veterans of 1940, the government contented itself with relying on statistics that suggested the intensity of their sacrifice. In putting forward the figure of one hundred thousand dead, the government suggested that, contrary to a persistent legend, the soldiers had fought as well as their predecessors in the Great War, an idea repeated by the most competent historians. According to one of the best specialists of the period: "It should be said that, contrary to a legend that some have found convenient to encourage, 'on the whole the men did fight, and they fought well'; the 100,000 soldiers killed at the fronts in less than five weeks bear testimony to that."[3] But a recent study suggests these numbers should be revised, calculating the combat losses at a level "fairly close to 60,000," with a range between 50,000 and 90,000 men.[4] "It is therefore possible to state that in an equivalent period of time and in the context of a German offensive, the losses in the May-June 1940 campaign were not greater nor even equivalent to those of the Great War in the operations of August and September 1914."[5] Once exploited to defend the bravery of the troops, statistics are now unable to establish the cost of that bravery.

One can therefore understand why the governments of both Fourth and Fifth Republics chose to venture onto the safer terrain on the Resistance and the Free French Forces. In France, as in Belgium and Holland, this choice was adopted by the authorities for obvious reasons. "The risk of seeing the memory of the war crystallize, at best, on the powerlessness of the victim and, at worst, on complicity with the occupying forces, was avoided thanks to a patriotic Resistance memory."[6] This choice, it is true, came in response to the expectations of societies not very inclined to be reminded of their compromises or even complicity. The glorification of the army of shadows nonetheless had varying fortunes. Celebrated at the Liberation, the Resistance went through a relative eclipse in the middle of the Fourth Republic and then made a triumphant return under the Gaullist republic. Subsequently relegated to the background, it seemed to be experiencing renewed vitality at the beginning of Nicolas Sarkozy's presidency. But had it made its mark on the second half of the twentieth century in France? This is doubtful.

Consecrating "the spirit of the Resistance," after the war veterans frequently asserted that they were carrying the torch of a renewal of French political life, the foundation of which was the program of the Conseil national de la Résistance (CNR) adopted on March 15, 1944.[7] But the reforms carried out under the Fourth Republic, as important as they were, owed little to the legacy of the underground. Nationalization, planning, social protection, and the democratization of education all represented promises that had been formulated before the war by various sensibilities, ranging from heterodox circles (X-Crise) to some factions of the SFIO (Jules Moch, André Philip); even some men of the right accepted all or part of the program. Hence, the ideas of the Resistance were not strikingly original, particularly because the Resistance was cautious on certain points. When the movements called for a new deal in the empire, they were not thinking of decolonization, although its urgency was suggested by the Sétif insurrection in 1945 and the revolt of Madagascar in 1947; and votes for women seemed far from a burning obligation. The CNR program was moreover suspended in 1946 and abandoned in 1947. "At that point, the legacy of the Resistance was no longer the program of the CNR but the survival of courtesy between former Resistance fighters who had become fervent opponents,"[8] a sign that the ideas of the Resistance were only briefly the focal point of political debate.

Even though it did not propose novel programs, the Resistance might, however, have exercised a mentoring influence by imposing certain moral prohibitions on the polity—banning torture, for example. But this was merely a pious hope. Whatever its heralds may have later proclaimed, the Resistance, particularly that represented by the movements, had been a political enterprise from the outset: individuals had often joined to defend ideas rather than to pursue the war. The vigor of the debates conducted under the Occupation confirmed the pluralism of Resistance orientations and the contribution that made to democracy. Once peace had come, why would the survivors retreat to their tents and refrain from taking positions on the major questions of the day? This legitimate involvement, however, came at the cost of division. Unable to speak with one voice, the Resistance could not claim to be addressing a single message to the country. During major national crises—May 13, 1958; the Algerian War—its representatives adopted divergent positions, confirming the fragmentation of the political legacy that the Resistance veterans claimed they were bequeathing to posterity. Do we then have to admit that the memory of the Resistance has faded? Far from it. Its heroes are still very much alive, whether Jean Moulin, Pierre Brossolette, or Colonel Fabien. They provide to national consciousness models of commitment that civil society refers to and even adopts. So, the Resistance now survives through its men and women rather than its ideas, ideas whose originality remains to be demonstrated.

The primacy given to the army of shadows, however, ended up excluding some groups from that victorious memory, which sometimes conflicted with historical reality. The accepted image of a people unanimously standing up against the German occupying forces and even the Vichy regime did not, indeed, correspond to reality. A portion of the population had worshiped at the altar of Pétainism. And the Jewish victims, wounded to the quick, did not recognize themselves in a grandiloquent fable that had forgotten their suffering. A first awakening took place in the late 1970s, when the French discovered or rediscovered the reality of the French State. A second jolt, the seeds of which had been sown during the same period, shook the orthodox view in the 1980s and 1990s when Jewish groups demanded that the national memory include the memory of their suffering.

As these episodes suggest, over time the memory of the war fluctuated, obeying with regard to Vichy a chronology that has been outlined by Henry Rousso. France went through incomplete mourning (1944–1954), followed by a phase of repression (1954–1971), before the mirror broke (1971–1974), leading to a memory marked by the centrality of the Shoah and the Vichy regime.[9] Certain things persisted despite these changes. "Collaboration was not incorporated into the postwar national sagas and did not contribute to the construction of ideologies or identities after the Liberation. On the contrary, to a large extent those ideologies and identities were constructed in opposition to collaboration by adopting resistance and persecution as formative experiences for a new postwar order."[10] Along the same lines, neither the STO conscripts nor the prisoners of war really made their mark on the contours of memory. Even today they are oddly absent from national memory.

The influence of their associations can be measured by that yardstick. To be sure, they sometimes succeeded in improving the material conditions of their constituents by obtaining a favorable status for them. They strove to remind the nation of the sacrifice of their comrades by putting up plaques or erecting monuments. Sometimes with as many as hundreds of thousands of members—whether STO conscripts or prisoners of war—they were likely to secure favorable consideration from the state because they represented an imposing electoral clientele. The government was therefore often inclined to give in to their demands in view of the fact that some leaders had shared their misfortune, such as François Mitterrand's veterans affairs minister, lastingly affected by his captivity. But we should not exaggerate the influence of civil society and its galaxy of associations. For example, the prisoners of war were unable to influence public opinion: despite the efforts of the FNPG, the French did not really believe that the captives had been in the vanguard of the Resistance. The STO conscripts were no more successful in passing for "deportees," despite the efforts deployed to spread that image.

Similarly, the work of historians carried limited weight in memorial configurations. To be sure, Robert Paxton's book was well received, and books by Daniel Cordier made a substantial impression. But other books had preceded *Vichy France* that presented more or less comparable arguments. Eberhard Jäckel's *La France dans l'Europe de Hitler* had showed as early as 1968 that, far from responding to a German demand, collaboration had emanated from the French State. The book was greeted with polite indifference. Sometimes stubborn and solitary figures succeeded in shaping the contours of memory. Serge Klarsfeld managed to establish the statistical truth about the deportation of French Jews and in time to win over both government and public opinion. Similarly, despite daunting obstacles, Claude Lanzmann was able to complete *Shoah*, his masterwork, and impose it as a major point of reference. But some legends resisted. Historians repeat, for example, the figure of one hundred thousand dead during the French campaign, even though the government had refined its statistics by the 1970s. Whereas it counted 92,000 victims in 1957,[11] that number had declined to 72,079 in September 1975.[12] Similarly, journalists constantly repeat the assertion that it was the legislature of the Popular Front that voted to grant Marshal Pétain full powers on July 10, 1940, neglecting to mention that the Senate had brought about the fall of the government led by Léon Blum in 1937.[13]

At the risk of stating the obvious, associations, like historians, influenced memory only when public opinion was receptive. Having endured the harsh law of the Occupation, French society was not at all inclined at the Liberation to accept the argument that the captives of 1940 had resisted. During the same period, the sorrows of the Jewish deportees met indifference from the French who thought that they too had suffered. Conversely, the Resistance mythology collapsed when Gaullist magic stopped working in 1968, and the national identity crisis that began in 1973 made this heroic vision obsolete. Similarly, the denial of François Mitterrand's Vichy past lasted for many years until the disappointments of his second term and his ambivalent handling of the memory of the war made public opinion receptive to the arguments of the journalist Pierre Péan. With memory as with propaganda, far from being akin to a rape of the masses, it functions only when the arguments presented embody collective sentiments: the bottom-up wins out over the top-down.

That means that the authorities had only limited means to impose their views, assuming that was their intention. It is true that some leaders strove to conduct an active memorial policy, Charles de Gaulle first of all. By decreeing the status of Resistance figures, building museums, and revising school curricula, they exercised real influence, but this should not be overestimated. The laws were in fact the result of careful compromises negotiated by the executive, the legislature, and the associations. The government usually merely arbitrated among contradictory demands, sometimes acceding to corporatist demands rather than imposing its will. And when a president overestimated his strength and defied public opinion to impose a particularly solitary idea because it resonated with his personal history, he had to beat a retreat. Georges Pompidou pardoning Paul Touvier, Valéry Giscard d'Estaing abolishing the observance of May 8, and François Mitterrand laying a wreath at Pétain's tomb verified this iron law at their expense. When, conversely, the government was able to embody a social expectation, like de Gaulle at the Liberation or Jacques Chirac in 1995, no obstacle stood in its way. Voluntarism was seldom able to contradict collective belief, an obvious limit to government action.

Governments, however, did succeed in internationalizing the memory of the wars. For centuries, memories of combat had served to reinforce patriotism by recalling the past glory of the nation in arms. Since

Charles de Gaulle, the government had put those memories at the service of peace and of Europe. This view, of course, carried its share of illusions. It is at the least excessive to reduce the construction of European unity to the realization of the dreams harbored in the underground darkness. Nonetheless, powerful gestures fostered Franco-German reconciliation and strengthened understanding between peoples. Whereas the clichéd memories of contentious veterans exaggerated differences, for some years the memory of World War II has been mobilized in the service of international dialogue. One might scoff at this pacifism and feel skeptical about its impact. In contrast, by refusing to acknowledge by a powerful gesture the suffering it had inflicted on both civilians and soldiers between 1937 and 1945, Japan has confirmed the fact that the memory of war can disrupt international relations—as suggested by the way in which Beijing has frequently exploited the Nanjing massacre.

But the government has not succeeded—except for brief intervals—in forging a single shared interpretation of World War II. In fact, considering the variety of their experiences between 1939 and 1945, the French would have difficulty recognizing themselves in a single narrative. What is more, each group drew different if not antagonistic lessons from history, and they were mobilized at times of great national division—notably the Algerian War and May 1968. As demonstrators chanted thunderously, "CRS SS," making themselves out to be "new partisans," the Gaullists were outraged by the insult hurled at the first Resistance fighter in France. How could a government, however well intentioned, contain such contradictory interpretations within a consensus view—assuming it wanted to? For the government has always defended a certain idea of the war, a conception that led it to impose a partisan view that often distorted reality. Charles de Gaulle championed the view of a people that fundamentally supported the Resistance; Georges Pompidou proposed a rather odd national reconciliation; Valéry Giscard d'Estaing sacrificed the memory of May 8 on the altar of Franco-German reconciliation; and François Mitterrand held stubbornly to the illusions of his youth.

This stance led the state to use its powerful resources to prevent dissident voices from emerging. For many years historians had no access to the archives. The government also prevented *Le chagrin et la pitié* from being shown on television until the presidency of François Mitterrand.

In other words the authorities chose injustice over disorder, favoring the persistence of myth rather than exploration of the disturbing facts. This meant that memorial policy rested on fragile foundations: when the gulf between truth and legend grew, under pressure from associations or historians, the myth collapsed, leading by a classic swing of the pendulum to the birth of an opposite myth: once seen as Resistance fighters, in the 1970s the French were generally considered to have been collaborators. Memorial policies had contributed to that outrageous reversal. By falsifying the facts of the dark years or trying to conceal them, they had inaugurated the age of suspicion.

The radical character of the stakes involved in World War II explains why memory of it helped enflame passions. Whereas the memory of the Great War was centered on the figure of the combatant, that could not be the case for a conflict that had blurred the frontiers between civilians and soldiers. "Both because of the contingencies of total war and because of the ideological aims of the Nazi occupying forces, the Occupation affected the population very unevenly: deportation of workers, political and racial persecution, and repression of the Resistance each targeted specific social groups. The social consequences were therefore inevitably more diverse, particular, and discriminatory than those of earlier wars."[14] The demilitarization of memory consequently helped to politicize the terms of the memorial debate. Holding divergent views, associations, parties, and institutions confronted one another, as much to secure rights as to impose their views on French society.

Controversies did, of course, subside over time. Challenged even at the Liberation, at his death de Gaulle became a consensual figure, the figure of the General who belonged to everyone, in the words of Pierre Nora. But it had been a long road to travel. In 1959 the Communist Fernand Grenier stated that at Saint-Denis in 1940 "no comrade talked to me about the Appeal of June 18 or even about De Gaulle."[15] After the general's death, in contrast, Robert Levol, the Communist mayor of Le Plessis-Robinson, named a square after that illustrious figure:

For the unforgettable part he played in this epic struggle, General de Gaulle has marched into the history of the Nation. Citizens of all [political] opinions, Resistance fighters who are members of the ANACR each judges the later acts of the statesman according to his or her individual conscience. Their unanimous tribute today is of the greatest significance. It takes its source in their shared past, their shared love for France.[16]

It is hardly necessary to specify that these tributes honored the man of June 18 rather than the head of state. In 1995 a survey published by *Le Monde* revealed that two thirds of the French people identified de Gaulle as a Resistance figure, not as the founder of the Fifth Republic.[17]

The death of survivors partly explains this memorial pacification. Associations declined and the death of their members gradually sapped their strength. Similarly, the facts of the Vichy regime and the tragic fate of French Jews were now accepted, if not sanctioned by the authorities, under pressure from the converging forces of the memorial work carried out by some groups and the progress of historical research that at long last was finding public acceptance. At the same time, however, new demands arose, such as those made by the *Indigènes de la République*. These demands reflected the desire for recognition of groups who thought they had been excluded from the national memory. But they also consecrated the metaphorical value of World War II. Decontextualized, the fate suffered during the dark years was interpreted as a sign of the fate the French Republic had always reserved for the citizens of its former empire. This factor no doubt explains why the memory of the war was called on to lastingly impose its mark, especially because the cult of the victims had largely replaced the veneration of heroes. This meant that the project of a peaceful memory, bringing together all of the French people around a shared view of the dark years, was no doubt nothing but a pious hope.

Nor did the proliferation of museums help to forge a unifying view. Aiming to honor the "duty of memory," following a logic that mixed respect for the victims, pedagogical ambition, community development, the wish to attract visitors, and profit imperatives, this proliferation helped to balkanize memory, particularly because the results were uneven. Some museums obviously work, such as the Mémorial de Caen (which claims 400,000 visits annually) or the Museum at Arromanches (320,000). Others have only occasional visitors, like Fontaine-de-Vaucluse (10,000), Thouars (3,500) and Clerval (3,000).[18]

The memory of World War II, finally, is only a part of the national memory. Considering conflicts alone, it coexists with others, chiefly World War I and the Algerian War. Although the Great War used to excite less interest, the number of books published has grown considerably, and in recent years many films on the subject have been released (*Joyeux Noël, Un long dimanche de fiançailles* [A Very Long Engagement]). It also has in the Historial de Péronne a first class institution. But today it is especially the Algerian War that stirs passions, provokes controversies, divides French society, and fosters a significant dispute with the authorities of Algiers.

From this perspective World War II has entered into a new memorial system: not driven so much by veterans, whose ranks are thinning, provoking fewer debates, it is now taking its place in other areas. Beyond the tribute paid to the victims, it is considered an essential element in the civic education of the younger generations that it must arm against racism and fanaticism. But isn't this ambition a pious hope to the degree that the multiple meanings of the conflict have authorized and still authorize plural if not antagonistic interpretations? Memory, what is more, remains subject to the possible emergence of demands made by new actors, a corporatist aspect that undermines the disinterest with which the old veterans—or their spokesmen—like to clothe themselves. Unlike World War I, it thus risks dividing rather than uniting, so violent were the fratricidal rifts of the dark years. This means that this burning past can resurface at any moment, in likely but unpredictable guises.

Notes

INTRODUCTION

1. Clemenceau to parliament, 1918.

2. Following the Franco-Prussian War of 1870, Germany annexed Alsace and Lorraine.

3. Jacques Sémelin, *Sans armes face à Hitler: La résistance civile en Europe, 1939–1943* (Paris: Payot, 1989).

4. Gilles Vergnon, "Les associations de résistants sous le regard des historiens," in *Les associations d'anciens résistants et la fabrique de la mémoire de la SGM*, ed. Gilles Vergnon and Michèle Battesti (Paris: Cahiers du CEHD 28 [2006]), 12.

5. Claude Bourdet, "Votre Gestapo d'Algérie," *France-Observateur*, Jan. 13, 1955, quoted in Bourdet, *Mes batailles* (Ozoir-la-Ferrière, 1993), 87.

6. Pierre Nora and Françoise Chandernagor, *Liberté pour l'histoire* (Paris: CNRS, 2008), 16.

7. Ibid, 21–22.

CHAPTER I

1. I find the first occurrence in his speech of Sept. 18, 1941. See Charles de Gaulle, *Discours et messages* (hereafter *DM*) (Paris: Plon, 1970), 102–3.

2. Radio speech of April 25, 1945, *DM*, 544–45.

3. Claude Mauriac, *The Other de Gaulle: Diaries 1944–1954*, trans. Moura Budberg and Gordon Latta (New York: John Day, 1973), 49.

4. De Gaulle, speech of July 29, 1945, *DM*, 593.

5. De Gaulle, speech of Nov. 3, 1943, *DM*, 337–38.

6. Gérard Namer, *Batailles pour la mémoire: La commémoration en France de 1945 à nos jours* (Paris: Papyrus, 1983), 13.

7. Pieter Lagrou, *Mémoires patriotiques et Occupation nazie* (Brussels: Complexe, 2003), 45.

8. Jean Quellien, "La mémoire de la Résistance au travers des noms de rues," in *La France pendant la Seconde Guerre mondiale: Atlas historique*, ed. Jean-Luc Leleu et al. (Paris: Fayard, 2010), 282–83.

9. Philippe Oulmont, "L'hommage municipal: Continuité et fluctuations, 1940–2007," in "Les voies 'de Gaulle' en France: Le général dans l'espace et la mémoire des communes," special issue, *Cahiers de la Fondation Charles de Gaulle* 17 (2009): 22.

10. Ibid., 28.

11. Lagrou, *Mémoires patriotiques*, 46.

12. Namer, *Batailles pour la mémoire*, 27.

13. Michel Winock, "Jeanne d'Arc et les Juifs," in *Nationalisme, antisémitisme et fascisme en France* (Paris: Seuil, 1990), 145.

14. Namer, *Batailles pour la mémoire*, 77.

15. Henri Frenay, *La nuit finira*, vol. 2, *Mémoires de Résistance, 1943–1945* (1973; Paris: Livre de Poche, 1975), 346.

16. Namer, *Batailles pour la mémoire*, 141.

17. Nicole-Racine-Furlaud, "Mémoire du 18 juin 1940," in *De Gaulle en son siècle*, vol. 1, *Dans la mémoire des hommes et des peuples* (Paris: Plon-La Documentation française, 1991), 551.

18. Robert Belot, *Henri Frenay: De la Résistance à l'Europe* (Paris: Seuil, 2003), 445.

19. Ibid., 447.

20. Henri Frenay, circular to prefects, Nov. 1944, quoted in Lagrou, *Mémoires patriotiques*, 156–57.

21. Fabrice Virgili, "Les travailleuses françaises en Allemagne," in *Travailler dans les entreprises sous l'Occupation*, ed. Christian Chevandier and Jean-Claude Daumas (Besançon: Presses Universitaires de Franche-Comté, 2007), 376.

22. Report of the Commissaire de la République of Nancy, June 1945, quoted in ibid.

23. François Cochet, *Les exclus de la victoire: Histoire des prisonniers de guerre, déportés et STO (1945–1985)* (Paris: SPM, 1992), 170.

24. Charles Klein, *Le diocèse des barbelés, 1940–1944* (Paris: Fayard, 1973), quoted in Lagrou, *Mémoires patriotiques*, 145.

25. Jean d'Arcy, note, March 8, 1945, quoted in Cochet, *Les exclus de la victoire*, 198–99 (emphasis in the original).

26. Namer, *Batailles pour la mémoire*, 75.

27. Cochet, *Les exclus de la victoire*, 173.

28. Judith Keene, Elizabeth Rechniewski, and Matthew Graves, *La place de la mémoire combattante en Australie*, preliminary report to the DMPA, 2009.

29. Pierre Purseigle and Gary Sheffield, *Memory of the British Combatants of World Wars*, report to the DMPA, 2009.

30. Stéphane Courtois, *Le PCF dans la guerre: De Gaulle, la Résistance, Staline . . .* (Paris: Ramsay, 1980), 137.

31. Quoted in ibid., 272.

32. François Marcot, "Bilan de la répression," in *Dictionnaire historique de la Résistance*, ed. François Marcot (Paris: Robert Laffont, 2006), 774.

33. Philippe Buton, "Le PCF et la Résistance sous la IVe République," in *Résistance et politique sous la IVe République*, ed. Bernard Lachaise (Bordeaux: Presses Universitaires de Bordeaux, 2004), 101.

34. Namer, *Batailles pour la mémoire*, 13.

35. Serge Barcellini, "Les requis du STO devant la (les) mémoires," in *La main-d'œuvre française exploitée par le IIIe Reich*, ed. Bernard Garnier and Jean Quellien (Caen: Centre de recherche d'histoire quantitative, 2003), 589.

36. Namer, *Batailles pour la mémoire*, 106.

37. Ibid., 49.

38. Ibid., 68.

39. Ibid., 42.

40. Ibid.

41. Ibid., 35.

42. Lagrou, *Mémoires patriotiques*, 48.

43. Namer, *Batailles pour la mémoire*, 20–21.

44. See Pierre Nora, "Gaullists and Communists," in *Realms of Memory*, ed. Pierre Nora; English language edition ed. Lawrence Kritzman, trans. Arthur Goldhammer (New York: Columbia University Press, 1996–98), 1:205–40.

45. Annette Wieviorka, *Déportation et génocide: Entre la mémoire et l'oubli* (Paris: Plon, 1992), 141.

46. Cochet, *Les exclus de la victoire*, 102–3.

47. Antoine Prost, *Les Anciens Combattants* (Paris: Presses de Sciences-Po, 1977), 1:55–125.

48. Article 1 of the decree of March 3, 1945 (emphasis added).

49. The data are found on the website of the Ordre de la Libération, www.ordredelaliberation.fr.

50. P0 agents, who were occasional, supplied verbal intelligence; P1 agents acted more frequently but maintained their regular jobs; P2 agents were entirely at the disposal of the network and received regular pay.

51. Commandant Seailles, *Historique du réseau Sylvestre-Farmer*, undated, SHD/13 P148.

52. Anonymous, *Historique du réseau Adolphe*, June 11, 1946, SHD/13 P145.

53. Henry Rousso, "L'épuration en France; une histoire inachevée," in *Vichy, l'événement, la mémoire, l'histoire* (Paris: Gallimard, 2001), 515–25.

54. Anne Simonin, *Le déshonneur dans la République: Une histoire de l'indignité, 1791–1958* (Paris: Grasset, 2008).

55. Albert Camus, editorial, Sept. 27, 1944, quoted in ibid., 12.

56. Marc Bergère, *Une société en épuration: Épuration vécue et perçue en Maine-et-Loire de la Libération au début des années 50* (Rennes: Presses Universitaires de Rennes, 2004).

57. Ibid., 67–68.

58. Michel Debré, circular, Sept. 14, 1944, quoted in ibid., 68.

59. Jean-Marc Berlière and Laurent Chabrun, *Les policiers français sous l'Occupation* (Paris: Perrin, 2001), 321.

60. Ibid., 326.

61. Fabrice Virgili, *La France "virile": Des femmes tondues à la Libération* (Paris: Payot, 2000).

62. Pierre-Henri Teitgen, *Faites entrer le témoin suivant* (Rennes: Éditions Ouest-France, 1988), 208–9.

63. Claude d'Abzac-Épezy, "Épuration et rénovation de l'armée," in *Une poignée de misérables: L'épuration de la société française après la Seconde Guerre mondiale*, ed. Marc Olivier Baruch (Paris: Fayard, 2003), 460.

64. Anne Simonin, "1815 en 1945: Les formes littéraires de la défaite," *Vingtième Siècle: Revue d'Histoire* 59 (July–Sept. 1998): 49–50.

65. Olivier Wieviorka, *Orphans of the Republic: The Nation's Legislators in Vichy France*, trans. George Holoch (Cambridge, MA: Harvard University Press, 2009), 327.

66. Secretary General, Ministry of Population, order of Dec. 17, 1945, MAC/Caen 40 R3.

67. Julie Le Gac, *La mémoire combattante de la Seconde Guerre mondiale: De la Tunisie à l'Allemagne: Les campagnes victorieuses de l'armée française (1942–1945)*, report to the DMPA, 2009.

68. "L'exploitation de la main-d'œuvre française en Allemagne," 1948, quoted in Anne Simonin, "Pourquoi certains crimes doivent rester impunis: Les travailleurs volontaires français en Allemagne devant les chambres civiques de la Seine," in *La main-d'œuvre française exploitée par le IIIe Reich*, ed. Bernard Garnier and Jean Quellien (Caen: Centre de recherche d'histoire quantitative, 2003), 567.

69. Namer, *Batailles pour la mémoire*, 8.

70. Ibid., 158.

71. Sylvie Lindeperg, *Les écrans de l'ombre: La Seconde Guerre mondiale dans le cinéma français, 1944–1969* (Paris: CNRS Éditions, 1997), 83.

72. Ibid., 79.

73. Ibid., 158.

74. Ibid., 163.

75. Ibid., 222.

76. Namer, *Batailles pour la mémoire*, 162.

77. Ibid., 123.

CHAPTER 2

1. Pieter Lagrou, *Mémoires patriotiques et Occupation nazie* (Brussels: Complexe, 2003), 221.

2. Olivier Wieviorka, "Les avatars du statut de résistant," *Vingtième Siècle: Revue d'Histoire* 50 (April–June 1996).

3. Robert Bétolaud, statement, debate of Feb. 1, 1949, in the Conseil de la République, *JO CDR*, 1949, 92.

4. Junior Armed Forces Minister in the Ministry of Veterans Affairs (Ministère des Anciens Combattants, or MAC), Sept. 17, 1948, MAC/Caen, box 12.

5. Lagrou, *Mémoires patriotiques*, 55.

6. Quoted in ibid., 59–60.

7. Ibid., 61.

8. Michela Ponzani, *La mémoire de la guerre et de la Résistance dans l'Italie républicaine*, report submitted to the DMPA, 2009.

9. M. Kahn, Conclusions dans l'affaire Ainardi, *L'Actualité Juridique*, Feb. 20, 1957.

10. M. Beauchamps, Sous-Direction des statuts, to M. Mattéi, Direction des statuts, June 19, 1958, MAC/Caen 40 R4.

11. Annette Wieviorka, *Déportation et génocide: Entre la mémoire et l'oubli* (Paris: Plon, 1992), 157.

12. Lagrou, *Mémoires patriotiques*, 30–31.

13. ONAC, ministerial instruction, Dec. 22, 1977, MAC/Caen.

14. Direction du contentieux, de l'état civil et des recherches au secrétaire général, Sept. 3, 1948, MAC/Caen, subseries R40, box labeled "statistics 1939–1945." Added to this total were 9,643 civilians receiving pensions.

15. Statement of André Bord, Assembly session of May 10, 1973, *JO*, May 11, 1973.

16. Émile Fournier, statement in the debate of June 8, 1948, *JO CDR*, June 9, 1948, 1395.

17. Mattéi, Direction du contentieux, to cabinet secretary, March 13, 1948, MAC/Caen.

18. Édouard Depreux, circular to prefects, Jan. 4, 1947, quoted in François Cochet, *Les exclus de la victoire: Histoire des prisonniers de guerre, déportés et STO (1945–1985)* (Paris: SPM, 1992), 38.

19. Henri Frenay, statement to Jean-Marc Théolleyre, *Le Monde*, Nov. 11–12, 1945.

20. Sylvie Lindeperg, *Les écrans de l'ombre: La Seconde Guerre mondiale dans le cinéma français, 1944–1969* (Paris: CNRS Éditions, 1997), 184.

21. Gérard Namer, *Batailles pour la mémoire: La commémoration en France de 1945 à nos jours* (Paris: Papyrus, 1983), 167.

22. Lagrou, *Mémoires patriotiques*, 49.

23. Quoted in Wieviorka, *Déportation et génocide*, 146.

24. Christophe Lewin, *Le retour des prisonniers de guerre français: Naissance et développement de la FNPGD, 1944–1952* (Paris: Publications de la Sorbonne, 1986), 207.

25. Ibid., 95.

26. Yves Durand, "Les associations d'anciens prisonniers de guerre," in *Mémoire de la Seconde Guerre mondiale*, ed. Alfred Wahl (Metz: Centre de Recherche Histoire et Civilisation de l'Université de Metz, 1981), 41ff.

27. Georges Sentis, "Des amis des FTPF à l'ANACR," in ibid., 55ff.

28. Lagrou, *Mémoires patriotiques*, 51–52.

29. Remarks quoted in Olivier Wieviorka, *Une certaine idée de la Résistance: Défense de la France, 1940–1949* (Paris: Seuil, 1995), 407.

30. Quoted in Lagrou, *Mémoires patriotiques*, 48.

31. Roger Bourderon, "Principes fondateurs et mise en œuvre: L'activité de la Fédération nationale de déportés, internés, résistants et patriotes," in, *Mémoire de la Seconde Guerre mondiale*, 137ff.

32. Dominique Veillon, "L'Association national des anciennes déportées et internées de la Résistance," in ibid., 161ff.

33. Arnaud Schlipi, "La Fédération nationale des rescapés et victimes des camps nazis de travail forcé: Histoire et combats," in *La main-d'œuvre française exploitée par le IIIe Reich*, ed. Bernard Garnier and Jean Quellien (Caen: Centre de recherche d'histoire quantitative, 2003), 603ff.

34. Lagrou, *Mémoires patriotiques*, 174.

35. Lewin, *Le retour des prisonniers de guerre*, 160–61.

36. Ibid., 168.

37. Quoted in ibid., 183.

38. Ibid., 178.

39. Secrétariat d'État aux Forces armées, analysis, Nov. 2, 1949, SHD/3 R97.

40. Ibid.

41. Proposed law relating to the right to a combatant's card, July 27, 1949, SHD/3 R97.

42. History recalled by René Touzet (rapporteur of the social affairs committee), parliamentary debates, Senate, April 14, 1977, *JO*, April 15, 1977.

43. Lewin, *Le retour des prisonniers de guerre*, 187.

44. Ordinance of Nov. 2, 1945, SHD/7 T394.

45. Robert Schuman, Minister of Finance, to the Minister of the Interior, Nov. 14, 1946, SHD/7 T356.

46. Colonel Orliac, note for the Civilian Personnel Department, March 26, 1957, SHD/3 R97.

47. Decree of May 10, 1955.

48. All these texts are in the box relating to this question, SHD/19 T9.

49. Coudraux, note addressed to the Secrétaire d'État aux Forces Armées, March 27, 1950, SHD/7 T357.

50. Battalion chief Le Ray, bureau moral, Nov. 24, 1949, SHD/7 T357.

51. Jacques Gavini to the Minister of National Defense, August 22, 1951, SHD/7 T357.

52. Decree of March 11, 1952, *JO*, March 27, 1952, SHD/7 T356.

53. Lagrou, *Mémoires patriotiques*, 181ff.

54. Decree of August 13, 1953.

55. Annette Wieviorka, "La bataille du statut," in *La main-d'œuvre française exploitée par le IIIe Reich*, ed. Bernard Garnier and Jean Quellien (Caen: Centre de Recherche d'Histoire Quantitative, 2003), 623.

56. Serge Barcellini and Annette Wieviorka, *Passant, souviens-toi! Les lieux du souvenir de la Seconde Guerre mondiale en France* (Paris: Plon, 1995), 443.

57. See Stéphane Gacon, *L'Amnistie: De la Commune à la guerre d'Algérie* (Paris: Seuil, 2002), 161ff.

58. Vincent Auriol, *Journal du septennat*, quoted in Nicolas Picard, "La peine de mort en France (1906–2007): Pratiques, débats, représentations," mémoire de M2, Paris I, 2009, 124.

59. Ibid., 126.

60. Ibid.

61. Ibid.

62. Gacon, *L'Amnistie*, 227.

63. Ibid., 242.

64. Pierre Barral, "L'affaire d'Oradour: Affrontement de deux mémoires," in Wahl, *Mémoire de la Seconde Guerre mondiale*, 243ff.

65. Quoted in ibid., 248.

66. Ibid., 249.

67. Gacon, *L'Amnistie*, 244.

68. Henry Rousso, *The Vichy Syndrome: History and Memory in France Since 1944*, trans. Arthur Goldhammer (Cambridge, MA: Harvard University Press, 1991), 52.

69. Alain Bancaud and Marc Olivier Baruch, "Vers la désépuration? L'épuration devant la justice administrative, 1945–1970," in *Une poignée de misérables: L'épuration de la société française après la Seconde Guerre mondiale*, ed. Marc Olivier Baruch (Paris: Fayard, 2003), 486–87.

70. M. Lavaud, directeur de l'état civil, service note, August 27, 1946, MAC/Caen 40 R1.

71. *Le Parti* (Paris: PCF, 1949), quoted in Philippe Buton, "Le PCF et la Résistance sous la IVe République," in *Résistance et politique sous la IVe République*, ed. Bernard Lachaise (Bordeaux: Presses Universitaires de Bordeaux, 2004), 98.

72. Marie-Claire Lavabre, *Le fil rouge: Sociologie de la mémoire communiste* (Paris: Presses de Sciences-Po, 1994), 218.

73. Stéphane Courtois, "Luttes politiques et élaboration d'une histoire: Le PCF historien du PCF dans la Deuxième Guerre mondiale," *Communisme* 4 (1983): 8.

74. Ibid., 10.

75. Lavabre, *Le fil rouge*, 213–14.

76. Buton, "Le PCF et la Résistance," 103.

77. Ibid., 105.

78. Courtois, "Luttes politiques," 15.

79. Resolution adopted by the delegates of the sixth departmental congress of veterans of the FFI-FTPF of the Rhône, MAC/Caen, box 12.

80. Ministry of Veterans Affairs, note of Oct. 25, 1950, MAC/Caen, box 12.

81. Transcript of the meeting of Feb. 5, 1954, MAC/Caen, dossier 11.

82. Ibid.

83. Director of statues to the cabinet secretary, Feb. 4, 1956, MAC/Caen, dossier 11.

84. National Commission of Deportees and Internees of the Resistance, session of August 9, 1950, quoted in Ministry of Veterans Affairs, note of Oct. 25, 1950, MAC/Caen, Oct. 25, 1950.

85. C. Avignon, undated note (1955?), MAC/Caen 40 R9.

86. Jean-Marc Berlière and Franck Liaigre. *L'affaire Guy Môquet: Enquête sur une mystification officielle* (Paris: Larousse, 2009), 58.

87. Transcript of the meeting of the CNDIR, June 28, 1963, MAC/Caen, box 12.

88. Barcellini and Wieviorka, *Passant, souviens-toi!* 331–32.

89. Lagrou, *Mémoires patriotiques*, 222.

90. Hélène Camarade, "La réception de la résistance allemande en République fédérale d'Allemagne depuis 1945," in *La France, l'Allemagne et la Seconde Guerre mondiale: Quelles mémoires?* ed. Stephan Martens (Bordeaux: Presses Universitaires de Bordeaux, 2007), 102–3.

91. Berlière and Liaigre, *L'affaire Guy Môquet*, 58.

92. Of ninety-five cases decided between 1952 and 1955, fourteen decisions by the Conseil d'État invalidated the decisions of the government, undated note by C. Avignon (1955?), MAC/Caen 40 R11.

93. Transcript of CNDIR session, Feb. 1, 1957, MAC/Caen, box 12.

94. Barcellini and Wieviorka, *Passant, souviens-toi!* 42.

95. Luc Capdevilla and Danièle Voldman, *Nos morts: Les sociétés occidentales face aux tués de la guerre* (Paris: Payot, 2002), 53.

96. DMPA, *Le "Tata" des tirailleurs sénégalais*, Mémoire de pierre no. 11, undated.

97. Capdevilla and Voldman, *Nos morts,* 104.

98. Ibid.

99. André Le Trocquer, circular to prefects, April 12, 1946, MAC/Caen 40 R15.

100. Léon Blum, Prime Minister, decree of Jan. 16, 1947, MAC/Caen 40 R15.

101. Minister of the Interior, decree of Feb. 6, 1947, MAC/Caen 40 R15.

102. *Bulletin officiel de la Moselle,* quoted in William Kidd, *Les monuments aux morts mosellans* (Metz: Éditions Serpenoise, 1999), quoted in Julie Le Gac, *La mémoire combattante de la Seconde Guerre mondiale: De la Tunisie à l'Allemagne: Les campagnes victorieuses de l'armée française (1942–1945),* report to the DMPA, 2009.

103. Barcellini and Wieviorka, *Passant, souviens-toi!* 12.

104. Christian Delporte, "La Résistance dans la propagande gaulliste: Discours et images," in Lachaise, *Résistance et politique sous la IVe République,* 42–43.

105. Philippe Oulmont, "L'hommage municipal: Continuité et fluctuations, 1940–2007," in "Les voies 'de Gaulle' en France: Le général dans l'espace et la mémoire des communes," special issue, *Cahiers de la Fondation Charles de Gaulle* 17 (2009): 32.

106. Nicole Racine-Furlaud, "Mémoire du 18 juin 1940," in *De Gaulle en son siècle,* vol. 1, *Dans la mémoire des hommes et des peuples* (Paris: Plon-La Documentation française, 1991), 554.

107. François Audigier, "L'héritage de la Résistance pour les cadets gaullistes de la IVe République," in Lachaise, *Résistance et politique sous la IVe République,* 61.

108. Lagrou, *Mémoires patriotiques,* 76.

109. Ibid., 79.

110. Barcellini and Wieviorka, *Passant, souviens-toi!* 18.

111. Ibid., 15ff.

112. Annette Wieviorka, "La représentation de la Shoah en France: Mémoriaux et monuments," in *Musées de guerre et mémoriaux,* ed. Jean-Yves Boursier (Paris: Éditions de la Maison des Sciences de l'Homme, 2005), 54ff.

113. Barcellini and Wieviorka, *Passant, souviens-toi!* 45.

114. Ibid., 120.

115. Le Gac, *La mémoire combattante de la Seconde Guerre mondiale.*

116. Quoted in Lagrou, *Mémoires patriotiques,* 175.

117. Ibid., 179–80.

118. Ibid., 177.

119. Ibid., 177–78.

120. Ibid., 179.

121. Ibid.

122. Ibid.

123. Serge Barcellini, "Les requis du STO devant la (les) mémoires," in *La main-d'œuvre française exploitée par le IIIe Reich*, ed. Bernard Garnier and Jean Quellien (Caen: Centre de recherche d'histoire quantitative, 2003), 589ff.

124. Lagrou, *Mémoires patriotiques*, 182.

125. Schlipi, "La Fédération nationale des rescapés," 604.

126. Barcellini and Wieviorka, *Passant, souviens-toi!* 238.

127. Ibid., 243.

128. Stephan Martens, "La mémoire de la Seconde Guerre mondiale: Le débat allemand," in Martens, *La France, l'Allemagne et la Seconde Guerre mondiale*, ed. Stephan Martens (Bordeaux: Presses Universitaires de Bordeaux, 2007), 48.

129. Camarade, "La réception de la résistance allemande," 105.

130. Ibid., 97.

131. Steffen Prauser, *La mémoire combattante en Allemagne après la Seconde Guerre mondiale*, report to the DMPA, 2009.

132. Henry Rousso, "Le 'syndrome de Vichy': La justice, la mémoire et l'histoire," in *Les Juifs de France de la Révolution à nos jours*, ed. Jean-Jacques Becker and Annette Wieviorka (Paris: Liana Levi, 1998), 400.

133. Annette Wieviorka, "Shoah: Les étapes de la mémoire en France," in *Les guerres de mémoires: La France et son histoire*, ed. Pascal Blanchard and Isabelle Veyrat-Masson (Paris: La Découverte, 2008), 109.

134. Barcellini and Wieviorka, *Passant, souviens-toi!* 382.

135. Ibid., 457.

136. In 1974 it was renamed the Memorial to the Unknown Jewish Martyr.

137. Anne Grynberg, "Après la tourmente," in Becker and Wieviorka, *Les Juifs de France de la Révolution à nos jours*, 256.

138. Barcellini and Wieviorka, *Passant, souviens-toi!* 418.

139. Lagrou, *Mémoires patriotiques*, 75.

140. Ibid., 76.

141. Quoted in Sarah Farmer, *Martyred Village: Commemorating the 1944 Massacre at Oradour-sur-Glane* (Berkeley: University of California Press, 1999), 94.

142. Ibid., 73.

143. The affair is thoroughly analyzed in ibid.

144. Gilles Vergnon, "Les associations d'anciens combattants du maquis du Vercors, le souvenir et la mémoire," in *Les associations d'anciens résistants et la fabrique de la mémoire de la SGM*, ed. Gilles Vergnon and Michèle Battesti (Paris: Cahiers du CEHD 28 [2006]), 63.

145. Olivier Lalieu, "Les résistants et l'invention du 'devoir de mémoire,'" in ibid., 96.

146. Law of May 7, 1946, quoted in *Rassembler la nation autour d'une mémoire partagée*, information report no. 1262, Assemblée nationale, ed. Bernard Accoyer (2008), III.

147. Serge Barcellini, "Les journées commémoratives nationales en proie à l'inflation," in *Nos embarras de mémoire: La France en souffrance*, ed. Jean-Pierre Rioux (Limoges: Lavauzelle, 2008), 150.

148. Racine-Furlaud, "Mémoire du 18 juin 1940," 554.

149. Ibid., 558.

150. Transcript of the commission charged with determining the status of combatant of the 1939–1945 war, session of July 10, 1945, SHD/3 R97.

151. Lalieu, "Les résistants et l'invention du 'devoir de mémoire,'" 91.

152. Wieviorka, *Déportation et génocide*, 153ff.

153. Transcript of the commission charged with determining the status of combatant of the 1939–1945 war, session of July 10, 1945, SHD/3 R97.

154. Proposed law relating to the combatant's card of former prisoners of war, offered by Tinguy, Barrachin, Triboulet, Cogniot, Casanova, Teitgen, Senghor, Temple, Védrines, July 27, 1949, SHD/3 R97.

155. Lagrou, *Mémoires patriotiques*, 249.

156. Walter Liggins, "Le rôle des associations d'anciens combattants et victimes de la guerre dans le mouvement européen," in Wahl, *Mémoire de la Seconde Guerre mondiale*, 101.

157. Christian Pineau, speech to the National Assembly, August 30, 1954, quoted in Noëlline Castagnez, *Socialistes en république: Les parlementaires SFIO de la IVe République* (Rennes: Presses Universitaires de Rennes, 2004), 299.

158. Quotations in ibid.

159. Lagrou, *Mémoires patriotiques*, 273–74.

160. Lindeperg, *Les écrans de l'ombre*, 315.

161. Laurent Douzou, *La Résistance française: Une histoire périlleuse* (Paris: Seuil, 2005), 54ff.

162. Jean-Marie Guillon, "50 ans et 2000 titres après," in *Mémoire et histoire: La Résistance*, ed. Jean-Marie Guillon and Pierre Laborie (Toulouse: Privat, 1995), 31.

163. Serge Barcellini, "L'intervention de l'État dans les musées des guerres contemporaines," in Boursier, *Musées de guerre et mémoriaux*, 43ff.

164. Françoise Passera, "Les musées de la Seconde Guerre mondiale," in *La France pendant la Seconde Guerre mondiale: Atlas historique*, ed. Jean-Luc Leleu et al. (Paris: Fayard, 2010), 286–87.

165. 8 Mai, supplement to *Rhin et Danube* 21 (April 1953), quoted in Le Gac, *La mémoire combattante de la Seconde Guerre mondiale*.

166. Veillon, "L'Association nationale des anciens déportées et internées de la Résistance," 168.

167. Claude Lévy, "Une association de déportés en son temps: L'amicale des déportés d'Auschwitz et de Haute-Silésie," in Wahl, *Mémoire de la Seconde Guerre mondiale*, 159.

168. Lagrou, *Mémoires patriotiques*, 223.

169. Serge Wolikow and Jean Vigreux, *Les combats de la mémoire: La FNDIRP de 1945 à nos jours* (Paris: Le Cherche-Midi, 2006), 95–96.

170. Raymond Bossus, *Le Front des Barbelés 77* (Oct. 9, 1948), quoted in Lewin, *Le retour des prisonniers de guerre français*, 250–51.

171. Ibid., 270.

172. Remarks reported by Martin Evans, "La résistance française à la guerre d'Algérie," symposium *Pour une histoire critique et citoyenne: Le cas de l'histoire franco-algérienne*, Lyon-LSH (2006), proceedings available online at ens-web3. ens-lsh.fr.

173. Henri-Irénée Marrou, "Tribune," *Le Monde*, April 1956, quoted in Raphaëlle Branche, *La Guerre d'Algérie: Une histoire apaisée* (Paris: Seuil, 1995), 257.

174. Ibid., 97.

175. Jean-Paul Sartre, "Lettre au Tribunal," *Le Monde*, Sept. 22, 1960.

176. Guy Pervillé, "La génération de la Résistance face à la guerre d'Algérie," in *La Résistance et les Français: Lutte armée et maquis*, ed. François Marcot (Besançon: Annales Littéraires de l'Université de Franche-Comté, 1996), 445.

177. Quoted in ibid., 449.

178. Philippe Barrès, statement reported by *Combat*, Oct. 6, 1960.

179. Jacques Soustelle, "Lettre d'un intellectuel à quelques autres à propos de l'Algérie," *Combat*, Nov. 26–27, 1955, quoted in Pervillé, "La génération de la Résistance face à la guerre d'Algérie," 452.

180. A historiographical survey can be found in Branche, *La Guerre d'Algérie*.

181. Remarks quoted in Veillon, "L'Association nationale des anciennes déportées et internées de la Résistance," 169.

182. Jan Patocka, *Heretical Essays in the Philosophy of History*, trans. Ezrahim Kohák (Chicago: Open Court, 1996), 135.

CHAPTER 3

1. Serge Barcellini, "L'intervention de l'État dans les musées des guerres contemporaines," in *Musées de guerre et mémoriaux*, ed. Jean-Yves Boursier (Paris: Éditions de la Maison des Sciences de l'Homme, 2005), 45.

2. DPMAT, note for the minister's office, Dec. 29, 1961, SHD/19 T82.

3. Letter from Charles de Gaulle to Michel Debré, March 21, 1959, MAC/Caen 40 R15.

4. Minister of Veterans Affairs, order of June 24, 1960, MAC/Caen 40 R15.

5. Decree of the Prime Minister, Nov. 30, 1968, MAC/Caen 40 R15.

6. Minister of the Interior to the prefects, Dec. 10, 1968, MAC/Caen 40 R15.

7. *Rassembler la nation autour d'une mémoire partagée*, information report no. 1262, Assemblée nationale, ed. Bernard Accoyer (2008), 18.

8. Jean-Guy de Chalvron, Jacques Roudière, Georges Weill, and Nicolas Georges, summary report on memorial museums of the two world wars, Jan. 12, 1999, MAC/Paris.

9. Serge Barcellini, "L'État républicain, acteur de mémoire: Des morts pour la France aux morts à cause de la France," in *Les guerres de mémoires: La France et son histoire*, ed. Pascal Blanchard and Isabelle Veyrat-Masson (Paris: La Découverte, 2008), 213.

10. Interview of Michel Debré in Olivier Wieviorka, *Nous entrerons dans la carrière: De la Résistance à l'exercice du pouvoir* (Paris: Seuil, 1994), 134.

11. Marcel Paul, statement to the commission "De la situation des déportés politiques," Feb. 2, 1967, MAC/Caen, box 11.

12. FNDIRP, *L'égalité des droits à réparation entre les ressortissants des Statuts de la Déportation et de l'Internement*, Oct. 1966.

13. M. Piernet, statement to the commission "De la situation des déportés politiques," Feb. 2, 1967, MAC/Caen, box 11.

14. Note from M. Bailly to M. Silvy, directeur des Statuts, Nov. 15, 1966, MAC/Caen, box 11.

15. Raymond Triboulet to the prefects, Oct. 5, 1962, MAC/Caen, "documentation administrative," box 6.

16. Sylvie Lindeperg, *Les écrans de l'ombre: La Seconde Guerre mondiale dans le cinéma français, 1944–1969* (Paris: CNRS Éditions, 1997), 341.

17. Ibid, 350ff.

18. Quoted in Henry Rousso, *The Vichy Syndrome: History and Memory in France Since 1944*, trans. Arthur Goldhammer (Cambridge, MA: Harvard University Press, 1991), 92.

19. Ibid., 93–94.

20. Ibid., 92–93.

21. Lucien Febvre, "Avant-propos," in *Les idées politiques et sociales de la Résistance*, ed. Henri Michel and Boris Mirkine-Guetzévitch (Paris: PUF, 1954), xi.

22. Rousso, *The Vichy Syndrome*, 269.

23. Cécile Vast, "Concours de la Résistance," in *Dictionnaire historique de la Résistance*, ed. François Marcot (Paris: Robert Laffont, 2006), 1005.

24. Jean-Marie Guillon, "50 ans et 2000 titres après," in *Mémoire et histoire: La Résistance*, ed. Jean-Marie Guillon and Pierre Laborie (Toulouse: Privat, 1995), 32–33.

25. Analysis suggested by Marie-Claire Lavabre, *Le fil rouge: Sociologie de la mémoire communiste* (Paris: Presses de Sciences-Po, 1994), 215.

26. Pierre Juquin, *Cahiers du Communisme*, July-August 1961, quoted in ibid., 173.

27. Ibid., 175.

28. Ibid., 212.

29. Ibid., 219.

30. Stéphane Courtois, "Luttes politiques et élaboration d'une histoire: Le PCF historien du PCF dans la Deuxième Guerre mondiale," *Communisme* 4 (1983): 20.

31. Ibid.

32. Serge Barcellini and Annette Wieviorka, *Passant, souviens-toi! Les lieux du souvenir de la Seconde Guerre mondiale en France* (Paris: Plon, 1995), 413–14.

33. Ibid., 415–16.

34. Jean Quellien, "La mémoire de la Résistance au travers des noms de rues," in *La France pendant la Seconde Guerre mondiale: Atlas historique*, ed. Jean-Luc Leleu et al. (Paris: Fayard, 2010), 282–83.

35. Barcellini and Wieviorka, *Passant, souviens-toi!* 203.

36. Maréchale de Lattre de Tassigny to General de Gaulle, Dec. 7, 1959, MAC/Paris, unclassified archives quoted in Julie Le Gac, *La mémoire combattante de la Seconde Guerre mondiale: De la Tunisie à l'Allemagne: Les campagnes victorieuses de l'armée française (1942–1945)*, report to the DMPA, 2009.

37. Barcellini and Wieviorka, *Passant, souviens-toi!* 70.

38. Ibid., 71.

39. Stephan Martens, "La mémoire de la Seconde Guerre mondiale: Le débat allemand," in *La France, l'Allemagne et la Seconde Guerre mondiale*, ed. Stephan Martens (Bordeaux: Presses Universitaires de Bordeaux, 2007), 64.

40. Corinne Defrance, "Les jumelages franco-allemands," in *La France pendant la Seconde Guerre mondiale: Atlas historique*, 284–85.

41. Ahlrich Meyer, "L'occupation allemande en France," in Martens, *La France, l'Allemagne et la Seconde Guerre mondiale*, 171.

42. The Netherlands received 125 million marks, Italy 40, Luxembourg 16, Greece 115. See French embassy in London, information sheet, June 2, 1964, MAC/Caen, "Franco-German agreement" box.

43. Henry Petit, investigation report, April 9, 1965, MAC/Caen, "Franco-German agreement, continued" box.

44. Luc Capdevila and Danièle Voldman, *Nos morts: Les sociétés occidentales face aux tués de la guerre* (Paris: Payot, 2002), 124–25.

45. Henry Rousso, "Le 'syndrome de Vichy': La justice, la mémoire et l'histoire," in *Les Juifs de France de la Révolution à nos jours*, ed. Jean-Jacques Becker and Annette Wieviorka (Paris: Liana Levi, 1998), 401.

46. Julie Le Gac, *La mémoire combattante de la Seconde Guerre mondiale*.

47. General de Lesdin to the Minister of Veterans Affairs, Nov. 26, 1959, quoted in ibid.

48. The expression was used at the press conference of Nov. 27, 1967.

49. Annette Wieviorka, "Les Juifs en France depuis la guerre des Six-Jours," in Becker and Wieviorka, *Les Juifs de France de la Révolution à nos jours*, 367.

50. Pieter Lagrou, *Mémoires patriotiques et Occupation nazie* (Brussels: Complexe, 2003), 277.

CHAPTER 4

1. Statements quoted in Olivier Wieviorka, *Nous entrerons dans la carrière: De la Résistance à l'exercice du pouvoir* (Paris: Seuil, 1994), 127, 315, 403.

2. Quoted in Henry Rousso, *The Vichy Syndrome: History and Memory in France Since 1944*, trans. Arthur Goldhammer (Cambridge, MA: Harvard University Press, 1991), 110.

3. René Pleven to Hervé Villeré, Feb. 10, 1972, quoted in Hervé Villeré, *L'affaire de la section spéciale* (Paris: Fayard, 1973), 17.

4. On these points see Rousso, *The Vichy Syndrome*, 123ff.

5. Serge Barcellini, "L'intervention de l'État dans les musées des guerres contemporaines," in *Musées de guerre et mémoriaux*, ed. Jean-Yves Boursier (Paris: Éditions de la Maison des Sciences de l'Homme, 2005), 38, 45.

6. André Tourné, assembly session May 10, 1973, *JO*, May 11, 1973.

7. Gérard Namer, *Batailles pour la mémoire: La commémoration en France de 1945 à nos jours* (Paris: Papyrus, 1983), 187.

8. Jean-Guy de Chalvron, Jacques Roudière, Georges Weill, and Nicolas Georges, summary report on memorial museums of the two world wars, Jan. 12, 1999, MAC/Paris.

9. Claude Lévy, "Une association de déportés en son temps: L'amicale des déportés d'Auschwitz et de Haute-Silésie," in *Mémoire de la Seconde Guerre mondiale*, ed. Alfred Wahl (Metz: Centre de Recherche Histoire et Civilisation de l'Université de Metz, 1981), 154.

10. M. Plantier to B. Stasi, April 12, 1979, MAC/Caen, box 11.

11. MAC/Caen statistical file.

12. The number of political deportees increased from 26,570 in 1959 to 35,001 in 1985, the number of political internees from 12,676 to 22,001.

13. Jean-Pierre Azéma, "Vichy et la mémoire savante," in *Vichy et les Français*, ed. Jean-Pierre Azéma et François Bédarida (Paris: Fayard, 1992), 26ff.

14. Édouard Husson, "Syndrome de Vichy ou crise de la démocratie?" in *La France, l'Allemagne et la Seconde Guerre mondiale*, ed. Stephan Martens (Bordeaux: Presses Universitaires de Bordeaux, 2007), 37.

15. Rousso, *The Vichy Syndrome*, 277.

16. Ibid., 278.

17. *La valorisation patrimoniale de la ligne Maginot*, report to the Ministry of Veterans Affairs, undated (2000?), MAC/Paris.

18. Ernest Renan, *Qu'est-ce qu'une nation?*, quoted in Serge Barcellini "Les journées commémoratives nationales en proie à l'inflation," in *Nos embarras de*

mémoire: La France en souffrance, ed. Jean-Pierre Rioux (Limoges: Lavauzelle, 2008), 159.

19. Ibid., 150.

20. Survey by *L'Express,* 1975, cited in Rousso, *The Vichy Syndrome,* 293.

21. Jean-Paul Bourcheix, report to the minister, Jan. 9, 1980, MAC/Caen, box 11.

22. Direction du contentieux, report to the minister, Oct. 29, 1948, MAC/Caen, box 12.

23. André Bord, instruction of May 16, 1976, quoted in Bourcheix, report to the minister.

24. Statistics provided by MAC/Caen.

25. Jean-Jacques Beucler, ministerial instruction of Dec. 22, 1977, MAC/Caen 40 R16.

26. Director general of ONAC, instruction of Oct. 28, 1987, MAC/Caen.

27. Georges Nonnenmacher, "La constitution du dossier juridique de l'incorporation de force d'Alsaciens-Mosellans, de Luxembourgeois, de Belges dans les armées allemandes," in Wahl, *Mémoire de la Seconde Guerre mondiale,* 201–25.

28. Testimony of Serge Klarsfeld, May 13, 2008, in *Rassembler la nation autour d'une mémoire partagée,* information report no. 1262, Assemblée nationale, ed. Bernard Accoyer (2008), 226.

29. Quoted in Olivier Lalieu, "L'invention du 'devoir de mémoire,'" *Vingtième Siècle: Revue d'Histoire* 69 (Jan.–March 2001): 91.

30. Annette Wieviorka, "La bataille du statut," in *La main-d'œuvre française exploitée par le IIIe Reich,* ed. Bernard Garnier and Jean Quellien (Caen: Centre de recherche d'histoire quantitative, 2003), 624.

31. Ibid.

32. Paule René-Bazin, "La politique des Archives de France à l'égard de Vichy," *Vingtième Siècle: Revue d'Histoire* 102 (April–June 2009): 173.

33. Marie-Claire Lavabre, *Le fil rouge: Sociologie de la mémoire communiste* (Paris: Presses de Sciences-Po, 1994), 186.

34. Rousso, *The Vichy Syndrome,* 286.

CHAPTER 5

1. *Rassembler la nation autour d'une mémoire partagée,* information report no. 1262, Assemblée nationale, ed. Bernard Accoyer (2008), 145.

2. Hélène Camarade, "La réception de la résistance allemande en République fédérale d'Allemagne depuis 1945," in *La France, l'Allemagne et la Seconde Guerre mondiale: Quelles mémoires?* ed. Stephan Martens (Bordeaux: Presses Universitaires de Bordeaux, 2007), 107, 110.

3. Michela Ponzani, *La mémoire de la guerre et de la Résistance dans l'Italie républicaine,* report submitted to the DMPA, 2009.

4. Henry Rousso, "Le 'syndrome de Vichy': La justice, la mémoire et l'histoire," in *Les Juifs de France de la Révolution à nos jours*, ed. Jean-Jacques Becker and Annette Wieviorka (Paris: Liana Levi, 1998), 401–2.

5. Serge Barcellini, "Les requis du STO devant la (les) mémoires," in *La main-d'œuvre française exploitée par le IIIe Reich*, ed. Bernard Garnier and Jean Quellien (Caen: Centre de recherche d'histoire quantitative, 2003), 596.

6. Ibid., 597.

7. Ibid., 598.

8. Julie Le Gac, *La mémoire combattante de la Seconde Guerre mondiale: De la Tunisie à l'Allemagne: Les campagnes victorieuses de l'armée française (1942–1945)*, report to the DMPA, 2009.

9. Ibid.

10. Serge Barcellini and Annette Wieviorka, *Passant, souviens-toi! Les lieux du souvenir de la Seconde Guerre mondiale en France* (Paris: Plon, 1995), 322.

11. Ibid., 418.

12. Barcellini, "Les requis du STO devant la (les) mémoires."

13. Barcellini and Wieviorka, *Passant, souviens-toi!* 165.

14. Pierre Péan, *Une jeunesse française: François Mitterrand 1934–1947* (1994; Paris: Le Livre de Poche, 1995), 226.

15. Quoted in Olivier Wieviorka, *Nous entrerons dans la carrière: De la Résistance à l'exercice du pouvoir* (Paris: Seuil, 1994), 343–44.

16. On this affair, see Éric Conan and Henry Rousso, *Vichy: An Ever-Present Past*, trans. Nathan Bracher (Hanover, NH: University Press of New England, 1998), 126ff.

17. Patrick Gourlay, "Beg-an-Fry, un Solutré maritime? La construction d'un lieu de mémoire de la Mitterrandie en Bretagne," *Vingtième Siècle: Revue d'Histoire* 102 (April–June 2009): 145–57.

18. Noëlline Castagnez, "Résistance et socialisme: Brève rencontre," in *Résistance et politique sous la IVe République*, ed. Bernard Lachaise (Bordeaux: Presses Universitaires de Bordeaux, 2004), 129.

19. Alain Peyrefitte, *C'était de Gaulle*, vol. 2, *La France reprend sa place dans le monde* (Paris: de Fallois/Fayard, 1997), 601–2.

20. Annette Wieviorka, "Les Juifs en France depuis la guerre des Six-Jours," in Becker and Wieviorka, *Les Juifs de France de la Révolution à nos jours*, 403.

21. Leticia Rodriguez, "De la place accordée aux victimes civiles des bombardements et de la bataille de Normandie dans les commémorations officielles de 1945 à aujourd'hui," in *Les populations civiles face au débarquement et à la bataille de Normandie*, ed. Bernard Garnier et al. (Caen: CRHQ/Mémorial de Caen, 2005), 289–303.

22. Captain de Pury, reconnaissance report on Caen, July 12, 1944, quoted in Olivier Wieviorka, *Normandy: The Landings to the Liberation of Paris*, trans.

M. B. DeBevoise (Cambridge, MA: Belknap Press of Harvard University Press, 2008), 325.

23. Quoted in Eddy Florentin, *Quand les Alliés bombardaient la France* (Paris: Perrin, 1997), 430.

24. Quoted in Marc Pottier, *Classer les plages de la liberté au patrimoine mondial de l'Unesco*, report to the regional council of Basse-Normandie, 2009.

25. Ibid.

26. Quoted in Moïra Blandot, "Les cérémonies commémoratives du 6 juin 1944, de 1945 à 2002," DEA mémoire, Paris-X Nanterre, 2003, 40.

27. Stephan Martens, "La mémoire de la Seconde Guerre mondiale: Le débat allemand," in Martens, *La France, l'Allemagne et la Seconde Guerre mondiale*, 71.

28. Quoted in Blandot, "Les cérémonies commémoratives du 6 juin 1944," 80ff.

29. Stephan Martens, "Introduction," in Martens, *La France, l'Allemagne et la Seconde Guerre mondiale*, 10.

30. Martens, "La mémoire de la Seconde Guerre mondiale," 71–72.

31. Jean-Marie Guillon, "50 ans et 2000 titres après," in *Mémoire et histoire: La Résistance*, ed. Jean-Marie Guillon and Pierre Laborie (Toulouse: Privat, 1995), 40.

32. Gilles Vergnon, "Le mémorial de Vassieux, un mémorial hors-sol?" in *Musées de guerre et mémoriaux*, ed. Jean-Yves Boursier (Paris: Éditions de la Maison des Sciences de l'Homme, 2005), 160.

33. Sophie Wahnich, "Trois musées de guerre du XXe siècle: Imperial War Museum de Londres, Historial de Péronne, Mémorial de Caen," in ibid., 79–80.

34. Sophie Wahnich, "Les musées d'histoire du XXe siècle; les mémoriaux et les sites: comparaison internationale," in *Actes des premières rencontres internationales sur la mémoire partagée* (Paris: La Documentation française, 2007), 101.

35. Martens, "La mémoire de la Seconde Guerre mondiale," 58–59.

36. Jean-Jacques Fouché, "Le centre de la mémoire d'Oradour," *Vingtième Siècle: Revue d'Histoire* 73 (Jan.–March 2002): 125.

37. Ibid., 131.

38. Ibid., 136.

39. Jean-Guy de Chalvron, Jacques Roudière, Georges Weill, and Nicolas Georges, summary report on memorial museums of the two world wars, Jan. 12, 1999, MAC/Paris.

CHAPTER 6

1. Quoted in Éric Conan and Henry Rousso, *Vichy: An Ever-Present Past*, trans. Nathan Bracher (Hanover, NH: University Press of New England, 1998), 39ff.

2. Ibid., 18.

3. Ibid., 27.

4. Antoine Charbonnel, "Les ombres de la Révolution: Esquisse d'une analyse rhétorique révolutionnaire de la Résistance pendant la Deuxième Guerre mondiale," M1 mémoire, Paris I, 2009, 45.

5. Édouard Husson, "Syndrome de Vichy ou crise de la démocratie?" in *La France, l'Allemagne et la Seconde Guerre mondiale*, ed. Stephan Martens (Bordeaux: Presses Universitaires de Bordeaux, 2007), 40.

6. Stephan Martens, "La mémoire de la Seconde Guerre mondiale: Le débat allemand," in Martens, *La France, l'Allemagne et la Seconde Guerre mondiale*, 50.

7. Mission d'étude sur la spoliation des Juifs de France, *Rapport général* (Paris: La Documentation française, 2000), 14.

8. Ibid., 165–66.

9. Olivier Lalieu, "La mémoire de la Shoah aujourd'hui," in *Nos embarras de mémoire: La France en souffrance*, ed. Jean-Pierre Rioux (Limoges: Lavauzelle, 2008), 19.

10. Mission d'étude sur la spoliation des Juifs de France, *Rapport général*, 174.

11. Lalieu, "La mémoire de la Shoah aujourd'hui," 17.

12. Decree of July 13, 2000, *JO*, July 14, 2000. Those concerned were, however, not supposed to be receiving a life annuity paid by Germany or Austria.

13. Lalieu, "La mémoire de la Shoah aujourd'hui," 19.

14. General Secretariat for Administration (SGA) Christian Léourier to M. Hazel-Massieux, August 1, 2001, MAC/Paris.

15. Letter addressed to Jean-Pierre Masseret, May 31, 2001, MAC/Paris.

16. Letter addressed to Laurent Fabius, received on Dec. 19, 2001, MAC/Paris.

17. Letter addressed to Lionel Jospin, Sept. 14, 2001, MAC/Paris.

18. Decree of July 27, 2004, *JO*, July 29, 2004.

19. Conseil d'État, decision no. 315499, Feb. 16, 2009, available on the Conseil d'État website, www.conseil-etat.fr/cde/fr/.

20. Transcript of meeting of the Haut Conseil de la Mémoire Combattante, Nov. 10, 2004, MAC/Paris.

21. Louis Mexandeau, speech at the National Assembly, Dec. 9, 1992, *JO A[ssemblée] N[ationale] 1992*, 6830.

22. Gérard Chauvy, *Aubrac: Lyon 1943* (Paris: Albin Michel, 1997).

23. Jean-Pierre Azéma, "Il n'y a pas d'affaire Aubrac," *L'Histoire* 211 (June 1997): 82.

24. Chauvy, *Aubrac* (emphasis added).

25. Azéma, "Il n'y a pas d'affaire Aubrac," 85.

26. Jean-Pierre Rioux, "Mais qu'est-ce qu'on leur apprend à l'école?" in Rioux, *Nos embarras de mémoire*, 170.

27. Olivier Lalieu, "L'invention du 'devoir de mémoire,'" *Vingtième Siècle: Revue d'Histoire* 69 (Jan.–March 2001): 90.

28. Ibid.

29. Ibid.

30. Roger Perelman, *Une vie de juif sans importance* (Paris: Robert Laffont, 2008), 215.

31. Examples quoted in Conan and Rousso, *Vichy: An Ever-Present Past*, 178.

32. Lalieu, "L'invention du 'devoir de mémoire,'" 83.

33. Decrees of May 13, June 11, Nov. 10, and Dec. 28, 1998, and April 8 and Sept. 3, 1999, described in Paule René-Bazin, "La politique des Archives de France à l'égard de Vichy," *Vingtième Siècle: Revue d'Histoire* 102 (April–June 2009).

34. Rioux, "Mais qu'est-ce qu'on leur apprend à l'école?" 170.

35. Raphaëlle Branche, *La Guerre d'Algérie: Une histoire apaisée* (Paris: Seuil, 1995), 101.

36. Conan and Rousso, *Vichy: An Ever-Present Past*, 201–2.

37. Rioux, "Mais qu'est-ce qu'on leur apprend à l'école?" 167–68.

38. See, among others, Michel Boivin, *Les victimes civiles de la Manche dans la Bataille de Normandie: 1er avril–30 septembre 1944* (Caen: Éditions du Lys, 1994); Bernard Garnier and Jean Quellien, *Les victimes civiles du Calvados dans la Bataille de Normandie: 1er mars 1944–31 décembre 1945* (Caen: CRHQ/Éditions du Lys/Mémorial de Caen/Université inter-âges, 1995).

39. Leticia Rodriguez, "De la place accordée aux victimes civiles des bombardements et de la bataille de Normandie dans les commémorations officielles de 1945 à aujourd'hui," in *Les populations civiles face au débarquement et à la bataille de Normandie*, ed. Bernard Garnier et al. (Caen: CRHQ/Mémorial de Caen, 2005), 293.

40. Ibid.

41. Julie Le Gac, *La mémoire combattante de la Seconde Guerre mondiale: De la Tunisie à l'Allemagne: Les campagnes victorieuses de l'armée française (1942–1945)*, report to the DMPA, 2009.

42. *Bulletin des Anciens du corps expéditionnaire français en Italie* 200 (2007), quoted in ibid.

43. Ibid.

44. Ibid.

45. Ibid.

46. Ibid.

47. Internal note of the Ministry of Defense, undated, MAC/Paris.

48. Haut Conseil de la Mémoire Combattante, session of Jan. 13, 1998, MAC/Paris.

49. Haut Conseil de la Mémoire Combattante, session of Feb. 19, 2002, MAC/Paris.

50. Étienne François, "Le manuel franco-allemand d'histoire: Une entreprise inédite," *Vingtième Siècle: Revue d'Histoire* 94 (April–June 2007): 78.

51. Haut Conseil de la Mémoire Combattante, session of Jan. 13, 1998, MAC/Paris.

52. André Kaspi, *Rapport de la commission de réflexion sur la modernisation des commémorations publiques*, Nov. 2008, 12.

53. René Rémond, quoted in Pierre Nora and Françoise Chandernagor, *Liberté pour l'histoire* (Paris: CNRS, 2008), 9.

54. Jacques Chirac, statement to the Haut Conseil de la Mémoire Combattante, Jan. 28, 1999, MAC/Paris.

55. Jean-Pierre Azéma, "Guy Môquet, Sarkozy et le roman national," *L'Histoire* 223 (Sept. 2007): 11.

56. Jean-Marc Berlière and Franck Liaigre. *L'affaire Guy Môquet: Enquête sur une mystification officielle* (Paris: Larousse, 2009), 85.

CONCLUSION

1. Charles Guéné, *Lieux de mémoire: Comment ne pas les oublier?* Les Rapports du Sénat, 2008, 37. The numbers in this report refer to all war sepulchers, notably the cemeteries and necropolises of the Great War.

2. Ibid., 41.

3. Jean-Pierre Azéma, *From Munich to the Liberation, 1938–1944*, trans. Janet Lloyd (Cambridge: Cambridge University Press, 1984), 44.

4. Jean-Jacques Arzalier, "La campagne de mai-juin 1940: Les pertes?" in *La campagne de 1940*, ed. Christine Levisse-Touzé (Paris: Tallandier, 2001), 439.

5. Ibid., 442–43.

6. Pieter Lagrou, *Mémoires patriotiques et Occupation nazie* (Brussels: Complexe, 2003), 11.

7. This theme inspires, for example, Serge Ravanel, *L'esprit de Résistance* (Paris: Seuil, 1995).

8. Claire Andrieu, *Le programme commun de la Résistance: Des idées dans la guerre* (Paris: Éditions de l'Érudit, 1984), 131.

9. Henry Rousso, *The Vichy Syndrome: History and Memory in France Since 1944*, trans. Arthur Goldhammer (Cambridge, MA: Harvard University Press, 1991).

10. Lagrou, *Mémoires patriotiques*, 14.

11. Ministry of Veterans Affairs, response to an oral question from M. Louis Diefridt, May 21, 1947, SEAC/Caen, "general statistics" file.

12. Jacques le Meignen to General Fayard, president of Le Souvenir Français, Sept. 29, 1975, SEAC/Caen, "general statistics" file.

13. Olivier Wieviorka, *Orphans of the Republic: The Nation's Legislators in Vichy France*, trans. George Holoch (Cambridge, MA: Harvard University Press, 2009).

14. Lagrou, *Mémoires patriotiques*, 12.

15. Fernand Grenier, *C'était ainsi* (1959; Paris: Les Éditions sociales, 1978), 22.

16. Quoted in Danielle Tartakowsky, "Les voies de Gaulle en banlieue rouge," in "Les voies 'de Gaulle' en France: Le général dans l'espace et la mémoire des communes," special issue, *Cahiers de la Fondation Charles de Gaulle* 17 (2009): 114–15.

17. Philippe Oulmont, "L'hommage municipal: Continuité et fluctuations, 1940–2007," in ibid., 45.

18. Numbers given by *L'Annuaire professionnel des musées de la Résistance et de la déportation et de la 2e Guerre mondiale* (Paris: Fondation de la Résistance, 2007). These figures come from answers given by the museums to a questionnaire sent out in June 2006 and Jan. 2007.

Selected Bibliography

Citations to archives consulted at the Ministry of Defense, the rue de Bellechasse (MAC/Paris), the Caen branch (MAC/Caen), and the Defense Historical Service at Vincennes (SHD) are indicated in the notes. The same is true for preliminary reports submitted to the Direction de la Mémoire, du Patrimoine, et des Archives (DMPA) in the framework of the investigation: "the memory of battle: an international view." Only books and articles dealing with the memory of World War II are listed here.

Accoyer, Bernard, ed. *Rassembler la nation autour d'une mémoire partagée.* Information report no. 1262, Assemblée nationale, 2008.

Actes des premières rencontres internationales sur la mémoire partagée. Paris: La Documentation française, 2007.

Azéma, Jean-Pierre. "Vichy et la mémoire savante." In *Vichy et les Français.* Ed. Jean Pierre Azéma and François Bédarida. Paris: Fayard, 1992, 23–44.

Barcellini, Serge. "Les requis du STO devant la (les) mémoires." In *La main-d'œuvre française exploitée par le IIIe Reich.* Ed. Bernard Garnier and Jean Quellien. Caen: Centre de recherche d'histoire quantitative, 2003, 583–601.

Barcellini, Serge, and Annette Wieviorka. *Passant, souviens-toi! Les lieux du souvenir de la Seconde Guerre mondiale en France.* Paris: Plon, 1995.

Becker, Jean-Jacques, and Annette Wieviorka, eds. *Les Juifs de France de la Révolution à nos jours.* Paris: Liana Levi, 1998.

Berlière, Jean-Marc, and Franck Liaigre. *L'affaire Guy Môquet: Enquête sur une mystification officielle.* Paris: Larousse, 2009.

Blandot, Moïra. "Les cérémonies commémoratives du 6 juin 1944, de 1945 à 2002." DEA mémoire, Paris X Nanterre, 2003.

Boursier, Jean-Yves, ed. *Musées de guerre et mémoriaux.* Paris: Éditions de la Maison des sciences de l'homme, 2005.

Branche, Raphaëlle. *La Guerre d'Algérie, une histoire apaisée?* Paris: Seuil, 2005.

Burrin, Philippe. "Vichy." In *Realms of Memory.* Vol. 1, *Conflicts and Divisions.* Ed. Pierre Nora. Trans. Arthur Goldhammer. New York: Columbia University Press, 1996, 181–204.

Capdevilla, Luc, and Danièle Voldman. *Nos morts: Les sociétés occidentales face aux tués de la guerre.* Paris: Payot, 2002.

Cochet, François. *Les exclus de la victoire: Histoire des prisonniers de guerre, déportés et STO (1945–1985).* Paris: SPM, 1992.

Conan, Éric, and Henry Rousso. *Vichy: An Ever-Present Past.* Trans. Nathan Bracher. Hanover, NH: University Press of New England, 1998.

Courtois, Stéphane. "Luttes politiques et élaboration d'une histoire: Le PCF historien du PCF dans la Deuxième Guerre mondiale. *Communisme* 4 (1983): 5–26.

Douzou, Laurent. *La Résistance française: Une histoire périlleuse.* Paris: Seuil, 2005.

Farmer, Sarah. *Martyred Village: Commemorating the 1944 Massacre at Oradour-sur-Glane.* Berkeley: University of California Press, 1999.

Fouché, Jean-Jacques. "Le centre de la mémoire d'Oradour." *Vingtième Siècle: Revue d'Histoire* 73 (January–March 2002): 125–37.

François, Étienne. "Le manuel franco-allemand d'histoire: Une entreprise inédite." *Vingtième Siècle: Revue d'Histoire* 94 (April–June 2007): 73–86.

Gacon, Stéphane. *L'Amnistie: De la Commune à la guerre d'Algérie.* Paris: Seuil, 2002.

Gourlay, Patrick. "Beg-an-Fry, un Solutré maritime? La construction d'un lieu de mémoire de la Mitterrandie en Bretagne." *Vingtième Siècle: Revue d'Histoire* 102 (April–June 2009): 145–57.

Guéné, Charles. *Lieux de mémoire: Comment ne pas les oublier?* Les Rapports du Sénat, 2008.

Guillon, Jean-Marie. "50 ans et 2000 titres après." In *Mémoire et histoire: La Résistance.* Ed. Jean-Marie Guillon and Pierre Laborie. Toulouse: Privat, 1995, 27–43.

Kaspi, André. *Rapport de la commission de réflexion sur la modernisation des commémorations publiques.* Nov. 2008.

Lachaise, Bernard, ed. *Résistance et politique sous la IVe République.* Bordeaux: Presses Universitaires de Bordeaux, 2004.

Lagrou, Pieter. *Mémoires patriotiques et occupation nazie.* Brussels: Complexe, 2003.

Lalieu, Olivier. "L'invention du 'devoir de mémoire.'" *Vingtième Siècle: Revue d'Histoire* 69 (January–March 2001): 83–94.

Lavabre, Marie-Claire. *Le fil rouge: Sociologie de la mémoire communiste.* Paris: Presses de Sciences-Po, 1994.

"Les voies 'de Gaulle' en France: Le général dans l'espace et la mémoire des communes." Special issue, *Cahiers de la Fondation Charles de Gaulle* 17 (2009).

Lewin, Christophe. *Le retour des prisonniers de guerre français: Naissance et développement de la FNPGD, 1944–1952.* Paris: Publications de la Sorbonne, 1986.

Lindeperg, Sylvie. *Les écrans de l'ombre: La Seconde Guerre mondiale dans le cinéma français, 1944–1969*. Paris: CNRS Éditions, 1997.

Martens, Stephan, ed. *La France, l'Allemagne et la Seconde Guerre mondiale: Quelles mémoires?* Bordeaux: Presses Universitaires de Bordeaux, 2007.

Mission d'étude sur la spoliation des Juifs de France. *Rapport général*. Paris: La Documentation française, 2000.

Namer, Gérard. *Batailles pour la mémoire: La commémoration en France de 1945 à nos jours*. Paris: Papyrus, 1983.

Nora, Pierre. "Gaullists and Communists." In *Realms of Memory*. Vol. 1, *Conflicts and Divisions*. Ed. Pierre Nora. Trans. Arthur Goldhammer. New York: Columbia University Press, 1996, 205–40.

Nora, Pierre, and Françoise Chandernagor. *Liberté pour l'histoire*. Paris: CNRS Éditions, 2008.

Pervillé, Guy. "La génération de la Résistance face à la guerre d'Algérie." In *La Résistance et les Français: Lutte armée et maquis*. Ed. François Marcot. Besançon: Annales littéraires de l'Université de Franche-Comté, 1996, 445–57.

René-Bazin, Paule. "La politique des Archives de France à l'égard de Vichy." *Vingtième Siècle: Revue d'Histoire* 102 (April–June 2009): 171–80.

Rioux, Jean-Pierre, ed. *Nos embarras de mémoire: La France en souffrance*. Limoges: Lavauzelle, 2008.

Rousso, Henry. *The Vichy Syndrome: History and Memory in France since 1944*. Trans. Arthur Goldhammer." Cambridge, MA: Harvard University Press, 1991.

Schlipi, Arnaud. "La Fédération nationale des rescapés et victimes des camps nazis du travail forcé: Histoire et combats." In *La main-d'œuvre française exploitée par le IIIe Reich*. Ed. Bernard Garnier and Jean Quellien. Caen: Centre de recherche d'histoire quantitative, 2003, 603–16.

Simonin, Anne. *Le déshonneur dans la République: Une histoire de l'indignité, 1791–1958*. Paris: Grasset, 2008.

———. "1815 en 1945: Les formes littéraires de la défaite." *Vingtième Siècle: Revue d'Histoire* 59 (July–September 1998): 48–61.

Vergnon, Gilles, and Michèle Battesti, eds. *Les associations d'anciens résistants et la fabrique de la mémoire de la Seconde Guerre mondiale*. Paris: Cahiers du CEHD 28, 2006.

Wahl, Alfred, ed. *Mémoire de la Seconde Guerre mondiale*. Metz: Centre de Recherche Histoire et Civilisation de l'Université de Metz, 1984.

Wieviorka, Annette. *Déportation et génocide: Entre la mémoire et l'oubli*. Paris: Plon, 1992.

———. "La bataille du statut." In *La main-d'œuvre française exploitée par le IIIe Reich*. Ed. Bernard Garnier and Jean Quellien. Caen: Centre de recherche d'histoire quantitative, 2003, 617–24.

Wieviorka, Olivier. "Les avatars du statut de résistant." *Vingtième Siècle: Revue d'Histoire* 50 (April–June 1996): 55–66.

——. *Nous entrerons dans la carrière: De la Résistance à l'exercice du pouvoir*. Paris: Seuil, 1994.

Wolikow, Serge, and Jean Vigreux. *Les combats de la mémoire: La FNDIRP de 1945 à nos jours*. Paris: Le Cherche-Midi, 2006.

Lightning Source UK Ltd.
Milton Keynes UK
UKHW04083525O119
336179UK00007B/628/P